PRAISE FOR UCHIC

"This *UChic* guide is hands down the best resource available for girls heading off to college or already settling in to their college lives. It's filled with big sisterly advice that helps you make the right choices about everything from getting along with your roommate to picking a major. It helps make what can be an overwhelming experience more manageable, so you can create the college life you really want."

—*KIMBERLY PALMER, SENIOR EDITOR AT* U.S.NEWS & WORLD REPORT *AND AUTHOR OF* THE ECONOMY OF YOU

"This is the book that every college-aged girl needs on her bookshelf, nightstand, or desk. *UChic* is the ultimate 'how to' on collegiate survival, and reading it feels like a chat with your best friend! No matter what major you are studying, what university you are at, *UChic* is filled with inspirational takeaways fit for you!"

—*ELEANOR SMART, SOPHOMORE AND STUDENT-ATHLETE, UC–BERKELEY*

"*UChic* is an incredible resource written in an honest, inspirational, and informative way. It should be required reading for all college-bound girls the summer before their freshman year! Every girl will be able to relate to something in this book. I really like the personal stories. Reading it will no doubt equip and reassure girls as they venture into the 'unknown' with more knowledge and confidence.

I certainly wish I'd had this type of resource full of wisdom and practical advice when I went off to college!"

"*UChic*'s guidebook to college for girls is filled with valuable advice and is a must-read for any college-bound young woman. It's also the perfect graduation gift for the high school girls in your life!"

"Get ready to be empowered. This isn't just a manual to college, but to life!"

"*UChic* is an essential resource for anyone who is invested in preparing and supporting young women to succeed on campus. It provides current, relevant information in a no-nonsense, easy-to-use format. Women on campus and in the workplace still face roadblocks and barriers. Christie understands young women and the world in which they live. She provides guidance on ways to level the playing field and give women the tools they need to fully benefit from the college experience."

"Lots of clever strategies on how to have a fabulous time at college, combined with wise advice on how to avoid all-too-common mistakes. A great resource for anyone who wants to be a chic college coed."

—*KIM CLARK, SENIOR WRITER,* MONEY MAGAZINE

"Full of fun, sassy advice on how to make the most of a great time of life, *UChic* makes me yearn for my college days!"

—*MARCY MCGINNIS, SENIOR VICE PRESIDENT, NEWSGATHERING,* AL JAZEERA AMERICA

"From the sisterhood of girlfriends who've been there, *UChic* answers everything a college girl really wants to know."

—*TRACEY WONG BRIGGS, FORMER COORDINATOR OF* USA TODAY'S *ALL-USA ACADEMIC AND TEACHER TEAMS*

ALSO BY CHRISTIE GARTON

UCHIC'S GETTING A GRIP ON YOUR FRESHMAN YEAR:
THE COLLEGE GIRL'S FIRST YEAR ACTION PLAN

UCHIC'S DIPLOMA DIARIES: THE CHIC GRAD'S GUIDE
TO WORK, LOVE, AND EVERYTHING IN BETWEEN

U CHIC

THE

COLLEGE

GIRL'S GUIDE

TO EVERYTHING

Dealing with dorms, classes,
sororities, social media, dating, staying
safe, and making the most out of
the best four years of your life.

CHRISTIE GARTON

Published by Sourcebooks, Inc.
P.O. Box 4410, Naperville, Illinois 60567-4410
(630) 961-3900
Fax: (630) 961-2168
www.sourcebooks.com

Originally published as *U Chic: The College Girl's Guide to Everything* in 2009 by Sourcebooks, Inc. © 2009, 2011, 2013, 2015 by Christie Garton.

The Library of Congress has cataloged the fourth edition as follows:
Garton, Christie.
   Uchic college girls : real advice for your first year (and beyond) / Christie Garton. – Fourth edition.
      pages cm
   Includes index.
   1. College student orientation–United States. 2. Women college students–United States–Life skills guides. I. Title.
   LB2343.32.G39 2015
   378.1'98–dc23

                                        2015002231

                        Printed and bound in the United States of America.
                               VP 10 9 8 7 6 5 4 3 2 1

To the women of UChic.com and the 1,000 Dreams Fund,
the inspiration behind this book.

CONTENTS

MORE TIPS AND STORIES FROM GIRLS WHO'VE BEEN THERE

Don't have time to read a whole chapter? Here's a key to help you find quick tips and stories on the questions you need answered right now!

FOREWORD

From Christie Garton, founder and publisher, UChic.com

Without an older sister growing up, I occasionally had to learn things the hard way. There are advantages to not having to stand in anyone's shadow, but there were many times when a little tried-and-true advice could have helped, especially during my first few years in college. I definitely would not have registered for eighteen credit hours my first semester in school! After a few detours, roundabouts, and restarts, I eventually found my way through college and into the real world, but things would have been a whole lot easier with the right advice.

This was the inspiration behind this book and UChic.com. I wanted to create a place where college women could come together to find support and advice during one of the most important times of a girl's life. We worked tirelessly to recruit a group of contributors with a diverse range of experience for the book that you now hold in your hands. I want to thank all of the contributors for being completely open and honest in sharing their personal stories. It is my sincere hope that what you will discover in reading *UChic* is that we are all sisters in the end.

WELCOME TO *UCHIC: THE COLLEGE GIRL'S GUIDE TO EVERYTHING*

Whether you're headed to college or are already there, one thing is certain: college is the time to expand your horizons. You need to experience college in your own way, and our guide is here to help you discover it!

With the endless choices you'll face in college, you'll often have questions and find yourself in need of a little advice. Our hope is that you find your answers here. We asked college women across the country to dish about their collegiate experiences, challenges, and successes. The result? A guide that provides you with exclusive advice that could only come from those who have experienced it for themselves. From settling into your new life on campus, to dating, to balancing that all-important budget, to finding the right balance between academics and fun, you will find answers and insights to your important questions in these shared experiences from college women around the country. This is a book that you can turn to throughout your entire college career. But don't feel like you need to sit down and read the book cover-to-cover (though that certainly won't hurt anything!). Each of our contributors has answered specific questions, so you can turn right to the section you need, when you need it.

With *UChic,* the conversation doesn't stop at the last page. Let's say you have a specific question that is not directly addressed. You can head to UChic.com for even more great advice from our all-star college contributors. This guide is truly the start of a conversation that can last throughout your entire college career.

So what are you waiting for? Turn the page and be on your way to your <u>own</u> fabulous college experience!

xx,

Christie Garton
Founder
UChic.com
1,000 Dreams Fund

"Always remember who you are and where you come from. It's so easy when you're thrown into a new environment with thousands of strangers to stray away from your morals and lose yourself."

—KARA A., UNIVERSITY OF SOUTH CAROLINA IN COLUMBIA

1

GETTING STARTED

COLLEGE MAY SEEM FAR off (even for you recent high school graduates with a summer ahead of you), but it's closer than you think! No matter where you are in your preparations for the exciting transition to college, this chapter has you covered. You probably are already well aware that the transition to college is a major stress. Besides maybe summer camp, when else have you packed up your entire life's belongings into several boxes and suitcases to head off to an unknown place to live with some random stranger? To help you find your path, this chapter is filled with insider advice on making this transition with confidence and style...and even a little bit of chutzpah!

GETTING READY FOR THE COLLEGE EXPERIENCE

From the moment I got my acceptance letter to college, I couldn't stop thinking about my new life that was about to begin. The end of high school could not come fast enough. As excited as I was, I was also a bit anxious. This would be the first time in four years that boys would be in the same classroom with me. This would be my first time ever wearing normal clothes to class. And on top of that, thinking about the new experience of living with three girls I had never met before and being away from my family made me a bundle of nerves. I did my best to hide my anxiety behind my excitement to start a new chapter in my life.

I'm embarrassed to admit this, but I cried hysterically when my mom drove away from my dorm. It was then that I realized I wouldn't be seeing her the next day. I was being a bit dramatic, but I couldn't repress how I felt any longer. I had this fantasy that college was going to be a perfect place, and a chance for a new beginning. I think if I had spent more time appreciating my senior year of high school, instead of building up pretend scenarios about college in my mind, I would not have freaked out as much. I learned that the most important expectation you can have about college is that you have to be flexible.

WHEN YOU'RE NOT GOING TO YOUR FIRST-CHOICE SCHOOL

Allison Davis, Barnard College

I had known from the age of twelve that I was destined to attend Brown University. This had been decided before I had even visited the campus. I knew I was going to Brown to study theater and to be a free spirit under a requirement-free curriculum. And maybe join a naked protest or two.

Six years and a seventy-dollar application fee later, my hopes were dashed. *I didn't get in.*

Honestly, the rejection letter stung. A lot. You spend four-plus years slaving over SATs, GPAs, APs, extracurriculars, and enough community service to be on par with a Peace Corps member just to qualify for consideration at your dream school—the only university or college that you fervently believe matches who you are and, more importantly, who you want to become. It is disappointing to be so brusquely rejected by what was your collegiate soul mate. So even though I got accepted into and decided to attend Barnard College, which I knew was a great school, I was still feeling hung up on Brown. I wasn't convinced I was going to have the college experience I'd always wanted.

I had always considered myself the quirky, alternative-theater girl, and I had always intended to go to school for theater—something that I had done almost my entire life—so I thought Brown would be perfect for me. I thought I wanted to be in a small town where most of your life revolved around the campus. I also wanted a campus with a strong academic history and, yes, with ivy-covered buildings. At Barnard, I have my ivy-covered buildings. I'm involved on campus and have made great friends, but campus life is not the focal point of my social activities. I've always been an active writer, so I decided to check out Barnard's strong writing program. It turns out I love writing even more than I love theater. Truly, Barnard helped me discover my real passion and develop into a person I didn't even know I could be.

If you are in this situation, don't expect the worst or assume that you're not going to enjoy college just because you aren't going to your dream school. You have to keep an open mind. Take a *tabula rasa* approach. In high school, it is so easy to be pushed into a neat little box with a concise label. I'm sure you can hear it now: you are "the really athletic girl" or "the really brainy girl." But maybe there is another girl inside you that you need to explore. College gives you that opportunity, no matter where you go. There will be so many new possibilities open to you to explore.

After three years at Barnard, I knew that I loved where I was, but I always wondered, "What if I had gone to Brown?" Well, I went to visit a friend of mine who attends Brown last year. The campus was as beautiful as I had remembered. Providence is a great town, and I really liked the people. But there was something missing for me this time. If I had gone to Brown, I never would have been able to take a writing class where Rachel Weiss made an appearance so we could learn the art of interviewing. I would never have been able to spend my semesters interning at the *New York Times*, and I would not have been able to hop on a subway and see a Tony-winning play and then come back to campus and hang out at a dorm party later in the evening. I would have missed out on so many different and wonderful opportunities.

And the funny part of this story is that my friend who goes to Brown chose it because she hadn't gotten into Columbia University in New York City. After I had been going on and on about how much I loved going to school in the city and how much I love Barnard, she said, "If I had gone to Columbia, I would have been lost. Brown was such a better fit."

I know it's cheesy to remind you of the old saying that you'll end up where you were meant to be, but it's kind of true. Somehow, even if the school you end up going to isn't the one you thought you wanted, it may end up being the best fit.

WHEN THINGS DON'T GO AS PLANNED

My freshman year I had a set schedule. I was a cheerleader and worked part time on top of taking a full courseload. It was perfect for my type-A personality. Even to this day, I thrive on routines. This routine turned out to be critical in helping me get used to my new life in college.

However, even with a set schedule and routine, you can't plan for everything. Life happens and you can either go with it or fight against it. I started at Manhattan College as a business management major. I never would have expected this to happen, but the spring semester of my freshman year, I failed a math class that I needed for my major! I was devastated. I had never gotten a grade lower than a B+, let alone failed a class. I called my mom and she told me I'd have to pay my own way in order to retake the class. So I got a job on campus that summer. I worked full time and saved enough to retake the class. But guess what happened. Even though I had enough money to retake the class, my gut was telling me not to register for it. Was I scared I would fail again? Or was there an even bigger issue? Was this major not right for me?

BEING FLEXIBLE WITH EXPECTATIONS

I spent that fall semester miserable with my classes, but comfortable with my routine. I still had that uneasy feeling in my gut that I may have picked the wrong major.

A friend told me how he was minoring in communications, and that he was loving it; I was instantly intrigued. I made an appointment with the School of Arts advisor and brought up the question of switching majors. I would still have to make up the credit, but it would be a science class. And I was more interested in science than math. Even after talking with the advisor I was hesitant to change the "plan" I had made for myself during my senior year of high school. It took some time, but I realized I was a different person than I had been two years ago. In a matter of months, I had changed. A few signatures later, I was in the School of Arts, majoring in communications with a public relations concentration.

WHY I CHOSE A HISTORICALLY BLACK COLLEGE OR UNIVERSITY (HBCU)

Briana Peppers, Spelman College

My school, Spelman College, is an HBCU and a women's college in Atlanta, right next door to Morehouse College, an HBCU for men. What I love most about attending a black college is that I can be whoever I desire to be. I can embrace any style or social outlet wholeheartedly and be welcomed. In fact, when it comes to personal style, the more different, the better. I exit my residence hall to regularly see hairstyles from the '80s paired with classic pearls and '70s dress. On other days, I exit my residence hall to see suits and laptops. For the males, it's not uncommon to see the bow tie, and I absolutely love it! It is, indeed, a Southern gentleman's necessity. What I'm referring to here is more than just fashion. The style reflects a deeper truth in that the students are always so poised and well versed. They are genuine "Renaissance" women and men. I knew that I wanted to earn the same title. I wanted to be refined and perfected. This is what compelled me most to attend Spelman College.

WHAT TO EXPECT

Overall, life at a black college can be described as peaceful hysteria. It is full of constant excitement and passion but also comfort and support. To make things even more exciting, a social or academic event is always going on at a black college. Every Friday, Spelman hosts an outdoor celebration complete with music and food and vendors. We call it Market Friday.

Other great aspects of HBCUs are the experiences and traditions that are specific to black colleges. For example, every year during freshman orientation each member of the freshman class must experience an "initiation" into the Spelman sisterhood. I am not referring to anything danger-ous or illegal. I am only referring to a memory that links every Spelman student and every Spelman woman together!

There really is genuine sisterhood. The bond is somewhat like being in a sorority without the pledging and initiation process. No matter what stage you are at in life, there will always be a group of people everywhere—ranging in all ages and social hierarchies—who are willing to give their last to you just because you, too, are a student or alumna of their alma mater. What I'm referring to is being a family. Just saying the name of the school can immediately turn a stranger into a family member. For example, a Spelman alumna once told me how she actually chased a vehicle with a Spelman College sticker just so she could say hello. Once she got close, filled with excitement, she jumped out of her own car to shout, "My Sister!"

BE PREPARED FOR A CHALLENGE

Students in a black college must be ready to combat the belief that our education is not as challenging as other col-lege academic programs. It most definitely is. Our academ-ics are equally as challenging and serve as an equivalent preparation for life.

What is different are the unique academic offerings

that you'll find at an HBCU. A black college is one of the few places where books such as *Gender as Analytical Category* by Beverly Guy-Sheftall or Aimé Césaire's *Discourse on Colonialism* can truly educate and empower you. This knowledge is a rarity and a treasure. We are so fortunate at HBCUs for this kind of enlightenment to be our foundation. When I was a senior in high school, a recruiter from Tuskegee University shared this fact with me. At the time, I understood the message, but now, attending Spelman, I understand its truth.

There is something really unique and special about students at an HBCU that no one adjective can pinpoint. The one thing that binds us together the most is not race but our potential and vision. Some may argue that all college students are bound for something great in their future. This is probably true, but the future for students in HBCUs is more than a future. It is a destiny. Everything we do is powerful. Your time in an HBCU will be incredible!

There is a persona and a mystique that will be with you forever, and it cannot be found anywhere else. So welcome. We are waiting.

WHY I CHOSE A WOMEN'S COLLEGE

Rebecca E. Mill, Sweet Briar College

I went to an all-girls' high school, and when I first shared with my friends and family the news of my decision to attend a women's college, I heard the various comments ranging from "Are you a lesbian?" to "Another all-girls' school?"

Sure, the comments were harsh, but picking the "perfect" college is a very personal decision. After stepping on campus for the first time, I instantly knew that the school I had chosen—Sweet Briar College—was the right choice for me.

At single-sex institutions, female students are shown from day one that they can do anything. Women serve as presidents, chairwomen, captains, interns, researchers, performers, and most of all—intellects. We see that we can do anything.

In the year that I have been at Sweet Briar, I've been pushed in every direction. I've taken advantage of probably more opportunities than I should have. I don't regret any of my choices, and I certainly wouldn't change anything.

Choosing an all-women's college meant more than a community of learners with at least one thing in common—our gender, of course. To me, a women's college is a family—a sisterhood. I'm sure you could find a great group of friends at any college, but how often is it that you can say you found your sisters?

In addition to academics, you may be wondering about what the social scene is like at a women's college. Most of you are probably used to sitting in a classroom full of boys, if you attended a coed high school. Although that is not exactly the case at a women's college, I don't want you to think that you're never going to see guys. Most, if not all, women's colleges have ties with area coed colleges. It's also easy to find and hang out with guys. It's entirely up to you!

Women's colleges certainly aren't for everyone, but it was the best choice for me.

LOOKING BACK

Fast-forward to the present, I am a proud college alumna working for a nonprofit and volunteering in my hometown. Looking back on my "failure" I actually see it as a success because it was through my communication courses that I found my strength as a writer. Trust me, life in college didn't instantly become a breeze after I changed my major. There were a few more hurdles along the way, but it was worth it. Those experiences made me who I am today.

My advice is to savor every moment of the journey of college. Embrace setbacks you may face along the way. Find a support system of friends, professors, mentors, and, of course, your family members to pick you back up. Be willing to do the work, but also be open to changing course when needed. Don't worry if your plans change, because they will. After all, that is why you are in college—to figure your dreams out and then make a plan to go for them. Sometimes life isn't what we expect it to be; sometimes it is so much more.

Insights provided by Susan Fiorentino, Manhattan College

WHAT TO DO THE SUMMER BEFORE COLLEGE

Preparing for college is sort of like getting ready for a big trip. There are things to pack, good-byes to say, and plans to coordinate before taking off. While most people (myself included) picture the summer before college as one big graduation party/bonfire/sleepover before parting ways, the reality is that there are several tedious preparations you need to undertake before heading to campus.

Here are some tips that can help you along the way.

MEET THE FUTURE ROOMMATE

I didn't get to meet my roommates until orientation. But thanks to technology we began chatting, brainstorming, and organizing our dorm before we met in person. (Thanks, social media!) We made a group Pinterest board with room ideas for our suite. We made a Google Doc with major dorm items that each person was bringing, and we had a group chat running to make it easier for all four of us to stay in touch. I had friends who met their new roommates for lunch or coffee one afternoon. This was doable because they both lived close to campus. This provided them with just a little more confidence heading into move-in weekend and orientation.

WELLNESS PREP

I had my mind set on avoiding the infamous "Freshman 15," but I soon realized that staying healthy at school was so much more than worrying about gaining weight. I had to make sure I had all of the shots and tests required by my school, in addition to medications I needed to have with me in my dorm. I also made a little "pharmacy basket," with Tylenol, allergy medicine, a thermometer, Tums, extra contacts, and Band-Aids to have with me, as I wouldn't have a car on campus. It's also a good idea to have a physical before you leave, just to make sure that you're caught up with your doctor and health plan—surprises once getting to school are not fun!

LIFE SKILLS TO DEVELOP

Unless you like learning the hard way, you should learn how to do laundry before you go off to college. (Yes, there are a few among us that still don't know how to do laundry.) I can be a little messy, so my mom taught me how to get tough stains out and gave me a little guide with home remedies for different spills. These tips helped. I didn't shrink any jeans or turn white clothes pink. Thanks to tapping mom's expertise on these matters, I was confident going into school. Also, watch for notes from housing or your RA addressing details about laundry. During the semester I had to switch from laundry pods to regular detergent because of the type of washing machine in my dorm. Those notes can make all the difference.

A FASHIONISTA'S TIPS ON FITTING IT ALL IN

Alyssa Vande Leest, University of Wisconsin

How do you fit a roomful of clothing, shoes, and accessories into a tiny four-by-three-foot cube? No, it isn't a riddle or a math problem; it's the dilemma faced by every fashion-loving college-bound student. Read on for easy tips to ensure your wardrobe is ready to fit in that tiny dorm-room space when you arrive on campus in the fall.

TIP 1: RECOGNIZE THAT YOU CAN'T TAKE IT ALL

I know, it's tough, but some things are going to have to stay behind. Follow this general rule of thumb: if it's too much to fit in the trunk of a normal-sized car (not a station wagon or SUV), it's probably too much.

TIP 2: LIST YOUR FAVORITES

Make a short list of the items in your closet that you turn to again and again, the ones you love to wear. Make sure you include items that work together in different combinations to make a wide array of outfits.

TIP 3: LIST YOUR NECESSITIES

These are the things you wear because you have to: plain camis, workout clothes, the obvious socks, underwear, and bras, and so on.

TIP 4: EVALUATE YOUR STYLE

Women in their late teens and early twenties often do not have a single, developed style and instead toy with various trends and looks, but identifying patterns in the way you dress will make it easier to choose other items to complement your favorites and necessities. Try writing a short explanation of your style or creating a Pinterest board. This may also spark new ideas.

TIP 5: GO SHOPPING!

It may seem counterintuitive, but shopping smart will actually allow you to bring less, buy less later, and look better more often.

Look for gaps in your lists and fill them with versatile items that fit into the style you're going for. Also look for items that will complement the things you're already sure to bring and wear—things like neutral-colored cardigans, simple jewelry, and leather belts that will keep the same outfits looking new and fresh, even if you have to repeat them twice in one week. To save money, check out stores like T.J.Maxx, Filene's Basement, or Saks OFF 5th, where you can always find great deals and unique pieces.

TIP 6: PLAN FOR THE SEASONS

If you're attending a school in a climate where you'll see all four seasons, you'll need to plan accordingly. If possible, consider swapping out warm- and cold-weather wardrobes during trips home or by coordinating FedEx or UPS shipments with your parents.

TIP 7: GET THE GEAR

Maximizing your closet space is essential. Organizational accessories like a second rod for your closet (it hangs from the built-in rod and doubles your hanging space), a belt hanger (doubles as a purse hanger), quality plastic-tube hangers, and a hanging shoe rack can help you get the most out of your closet space. Space Bags (www.spacebag.com) can be a good alternative for storing bulky things like coats and sweaters until they are needed.

TIP 8: LEARN BY TRIAL AND ERROR

Many girls change their style a bit after spending a few weeks or months on campus, and some (like myself) simply realize that those cute leather flats aren't friendly to their feet during their daily treks to class. You'll learn what works and what doesn't as the year goes on.

With a little planning and creativity, you'll be able to create a college wardrobe that meets your lifestyle needs and keeps you looking stylish, even when space is limited.

Another thing that I found helpful was acquiring car knowledge before heading to college. I was riding home once with a friend who got a flat tire. Thankfully, my dad had taught me how to change a tire before I left. Just the basic oil-checking and tire-changing knowledge made a big difference when friends were in a pinch. And while it may sound strange, I was also given a toolbox before moving in, and I used it all the time. And bonus! It doubled as an icebreaker and networking opportunity when my roommates and girls down the hall needed it from time-to-time.

ADVENTURE PREP

I quickly realized that leaving for school meant taking on a whole new set of adventures. There were weekend retreats, outdoor trips, and opportunities to get involved in the local, national, and international communities. Make sure you have an up-to-date passport before leaving for school. There are so many alternative spring breaks, interim session trips, and study abroad opportunities. Don't procrastinate. Get your passport! Not having it in time can prevent you from going on the trip of a lifetime. Plus, it's always good to have another form of ID for future employers and internship opportunities.

IT'S JUST: "SEE YOU LATER..."

The worst part of preparing for college is saying good-bye to people who have been your lifelines, sidekicks, brunch bunch, and your biggest cheerleaders. It's hard to imagine starting over without them by your side. A lot of my best friends from high school have been close friends since preschool—how was I supposed to say good-bye to them? My solution: "See you soon." Maybe it's cheesy, but it's oh-so-true. The people closest to your heart will still be there despite the miles between you. There are group messages, email chains, tweets, Snapchats, and Google+ Hangouts to keep you close.

When it comes to how to actually say good-bye, I found that dinners at home with close friends were the best way to chat and get the hugs (and tears) out of the way. I tried to squeeze too many people into my last week at home, though, and ended up feeling overwhelmed. To avoid that, plan a little gathering that feels best for you, and know that it isn't forever.

As for saying good-bye to your parents? Know that they have prepared you for this very moment. I was so nervous when my parents dropped me off, but I realized that they are just a call or text away. They'll always be your biggest fans and support team, no matter what. This life change is a new adventure for them too.

It's a crazy whirlwind getting ready to go off on your own to college, but there are ways to make the process easier. Make checklists and schedule errand runs ahead of time. The last summer goes by quickly. With some time management and preparation, you'll still find time to enjoy it!

Insights provided by Sarah Dougherty, University of Alabama–Tuscaloosa

GETTING TO KNOW YOUR ROOMMATE BEFORE YOU ARRIVE ON CAMPUS

Once I received that fateful acceptance letter detailing my dorm information the summer before my freshman year, I immediately assigned all my new roommates code names. I knew very little about them at this point, just their first and last names, hometowns, and pretty much all the information I could gather from their Facebook profiles.

For the three weeks leading up to freshman move-in day, my future roomies and I spent a lot of time messaging each other back and forth about who would bring stuff like the fridge, TV, etc. I told all of my friends back home how I would be living with "Nineties Girl" (who flashed a peace sign and

U CHIC Tip!

Many colleges will allow you to choose your roommate ahead of time—like your best friend from high school who's attending the same college. This may seem like a no-brainer. But a word of advice here: while choosing to live with a current friend can be a good choice because she's someone you already know and love (it's comfortable!), *living with someone that you've never met can be a great way to become exposed to an entirely new set of friends.*

wore ripped, faded jeans and a black crop top in her profile picture), "The Party Nerd" (who had a profile picture of her aiming for a beer pong cup preceded by a profile picture of her wearing a Science Olympiad tee), and the "Tomboy" (the tough-looking lacrosse and hockey pics said it all).

Sure, me and my friends from high school found the whole thing amusing, but imagine my shock when I met them in the flesh and all my expectations and prejudgments flew right out the window. One of my most important tips for preparing for college is not to make *any* judgments about anyone or anything before you get there. When it comes to roommates especially, you could be setting yourself up for disappointment if you expect your roommate to be your best friend, or you could be missing out on a potentially great relationship because you've already decided that your roommate is too different from you and you're not going to get along.

To avoid falling into either of those traps, here are some tips for how to get to know your roommate before you leave for college—and how to arrive on campus with an open mind.

ICEBREAKERS THAT WON'T LEAVE YOU OUT IN THE COLD

The key to getting to know your new roommate is to be proactive. Don't wait until a few weeks before school starts to drop her a line— do it as soon as you have her information sitting right in front of you. Introduce yourself via email/Facebook, chat up your background a bit (keep it brief), and start facilitating a conversation about the logistics of living together. Something as simple as offering to bring your DVD player can spark a dialogue about which movies you both like (just one surefire way to get a sense of who and *what* your new roomie is all about).

Tip 1: Break the Ice

While it's fine to talk a bit about yourself, do make sure to ask *her* questions and genuinely think about the responses you get before you make any judgments. If she's your total carbon copy, great. But if not, that doesn't mean the two of you won't get along. Keep in mind, this is just as weird and awkward for her, so it might take a little while before she warms up and starts sharing more personal things.

Tip 2: Dip Your Toes in

Once you've established an email relationship, take the next step and suggest a weekly phone call. This is your chance to talk about more in-depth topics like class schedules, room decor options, likes, dislikes, and personal pet peeves. Be honest—not brutal. If she's obsessed with Hello Kitty and has her heart set on an all-pink bedroom, this is the time to gently let her know that's not your thing, but you're open to compromise. The same thing goes for any obvious personality quirks that may derail your relationship down the road. If she's the ultimate social butterfly and you're a total bookworm, don't be afraid to speak up and let her know you prefer not to have any guests over while you're trying to study.

A FEW THINGS TO CONSIDER ASKING YOUR ROOMIE-TO-BE

Madeline Greene, Minnesota State University and Anna Prestek, University of Washington–Seattle

- **What is she planning to bring?** Deciding who is bringing what makes life easier once you get to campus. Items that are usually split between roommates include futons, TVs, mini refrigerators, microwaves, rugs, etc. Splitting the costs of these items can also help alleviate the financial strain as you begin the new school year.

- **When is she planning to move in?** It might be a good idea to coordinate your move on the same day, as this provides the opportunity for the two of you to configure the furniture and decorate the room in a way that is mutually acceptable.

- **Is she a morning person or a night owl?** Differences in sleeping schedules can pose a problem when on the first night you find out that she keeps the lights blazing 'til 1 a.m. and you're in bed by 9 p.m. sharp. Knowing her personal schedule beforehand can prevent an unexpected surprise when it's time to get some shut-eye. Consider buying a sleep mask and some high-quality earplugs. These can block the light of your roomie's desk lamp and the "ping" of her instant messaging when you're trying to catch some much-needed Zs.

- **Would she like to grab coffee or lunch the first day you meet?** If you can't move in on the same day, no worries. As soon as the dust settles, invite your roommate to go

> to coffee, have lunch, or just take a walk through campus. By making an effort to get to know her, you show that you care about being a good roommate and possibly even friends.

Tip 3: Dive In Headfirst

Meeting your new roommate is like going on a date—first impressions are everything. Before you even hit the dorms, turn off your cell phone, slip on a smile, and vow to give her your full attention. Still nervous? Why not bring something special like a batch of your mom's cookies to share, or a movie or book she's been meaning to buy. In each instance, a simple gift shows you're not only excited about living with her, but also invested in the idea of making it a positive experience.

Insights provided by Kylie Thompson, Harvard University

HOW TO GET THE MOST OUT OF FRESHMAN ORIENTATION

It's a sunny end-of-summer day on campus. There are students everywhere you look, wearing matching T-shirts in a rainbow of colors and more face paint than circus clowns. Your school mascot is doing cartwheels and giving out free hugs. The cheering is as loud as a rock concert and your feet are sore from jumping and fist pumping. Welcome to freshman orientation.

Freshman orientation takes place just before classes start and usually lasts about a week. Packed full of fun activities, games, and events, it serves as an introduction to campus and university life. But what's all the fuss about? Why is it considered such a vital part of the university experience?

WHAT TO EXPECT

Freshman orientation is a great way to get acclimated to university life, the campus, and your new city. Attending events across campus is a quick way to learn how to find your way around. It can provide you with important information about your school and where life's necessities are located, such as health services or the nearest grocery store. At my freshman orientation, we had an event called "Halifax Explore," an *Amazing Race*–style scavenger hunt where we had to find clues across the city, getting to know our new surroundings and the public transit system.

With everyone looking to make friends after arriving at school, there is no better time to meet new people than freshman orientation. It's hard not to meet new people when you have to be three-legged-race partners with a total stranger. I met many of my close friends at freshman orientation.

Freshman orientation can help you battle homesickness. Being constantly busy and out of your dorm forces you not to dwell on missing home. It helps you focus on becoming comfortable in your new surroundings.

Typically during freshman orientation, there is an academically focused event. This gives you an opportunity to meet professors and other students in your area of interest. When classes start, you may recognize someone from the event and have a familiar face to sit next to. This also makes you more visible to your future professor or advisor.

JUST SHOW UP

Make an effort to attend as many events as possible, even if organized games aren't your style. Every event is a chance to possibly make new friends.

Don't be afraid to put yourself out there and introduce yourself. Chances are that that nice-looking person standing next to you is nervous too. The first event of my freshman orientation was a field carnival on the quad. The orientation leaders said we could go introduce ourselves to the group if we wanted. I was never one for classroom icebreakers, but I knew I would make friends faster if I took the first step. So I stood up and said my name and some of my interests. On the way back from the field party, a girl walked up to me and said, "You're the one who likes rowing, right?" Now we're roommates *and* best friends.

Smile and be enthusiastic. People tend to gravitate toward those who look friendly. By looking more relaxed and open, others are more likely to approach you.

GET TO KNOW THE EXPERTS

No one knows campus like your orientation leaders. Get advice from these experts around you. Ask them about their university experiences. You might gain a study buddy or some insider tips on the best places to get late-night takeout.

While orientation may seem crazy and overwhelming, it's an integral part of the first-year experience. By getting everyone excited for the upcoming year, it serves as the perfect kickoff to university life.

Insights provided by Anna Jonas, Dalhousie University

HOW TO SURVIVE
AND THRIVE WHEN
IN THE MINORITY

Growing up in a small town where every fourth name in the school directory was Feldman or Cohen, it is easy to assume that being Jewish is just as common as having brown hair. But you know what they say about assuming things: it's bad. So when you finally hit college—an overwhelming occasion in itself—what do you do when you find out how very much in the minority you may be?

DON'T PANIC
First of all, don't panic. Check out opportunities on campus. Attend new student fairs and collect pamphlets, or go to the student life office on campus where you'll find lists of clubs and organizations. And let us not forget, the mother of all information sources—Facebook. From the local Temple to Hillel (the largest Jewish student organization in the world), there were plenty of Judaism-affiliated opportunities for me to choose from at UC–Davis. Bottom line: all I had to do was look around.

SHOW UP
As lame as it sounds to be the new kid in five different clubs, sometimes just showing up will demonstrate that you are really

serious about making connections. Go somewhere and join something that is related to your religion or ethnic heritage. When I went to my first sorority recruitment event, I had no clue that sorority membership would help me connect to the Jewish community at my school. Nevertheless, I wound up attending Friday night services once a month (which I had never done before), hosted my own Shabbat dinners, and did much more for the Jewish community than I'd ever done before in my life. And now, I'm the president of a Jewish-interest sorority. Go figure.

REMEMBER, MINORITY DOESN'T MEAN LONELY

It can be hard being in the minority for any reason—politics, ethnicity, sexual orientation, or religion. But remember that even though you're not the majority, that does not mean you are alone. Think about it this way: if all the minorities got together, we would likely rival the majority. Take solace in that fact, and remember that if you're feeling alone, someone else is probably feeling the same. Perhaps you can help each other out so that neither of you have to be sad in your perceived solitude.

STAYING TRUE TO YOUR ROOTS

Raneisha Williams, Ripon College

The instant I set foot on campus my first day in college, I could hardly believe what I had gotten myself into. I was truly in the minority—an African American female on a predominantly white campus. I knew that this would be outside my comfort zone. But my desire to learn encouraged me to conquer any fears that I had about going. I simply wanted a good education. Certainly, I have come across racial stereotypes along the way. However, what I've found is that those generalizations are based on ignorance rather than hate. Instead of getting upset when people have questioned my abilities or counted me out, I have worked harder to prove myself. This means that I always have to be on my toes, but the funny thing is, I have been doing that my whole life.

So here I am, and I'm not backing down. Instead of accepting how things currently are, I am constantly searching for ways to alleviate racial tension and discrepancies. And, because of this, I feel powerful. If you're in a similar situation, it's completely normal to feel that people may not quite understand where you're coming from at times. But if you stay true to yourself, work hard, and make an effort to educate others about where you come from and how you see things, you are taking the best steps forward in getting a great education while helping educate the world.

HAVE FAITH

When it comes to surviving and thriving, being yourself is the only thing to hold on to. If your beliefs come under siege, having faith is mandatory. People can try to threaten your beliefs through hurtful words, vandalism, or just general meanness. I wish I could say that never happens, but it does. However, no one can take away your beliefs or your sense of self-worth. End of story.

AND JUST REMEMBER...

If it's important to you, don't lose sight of your identity. Hang on to
your values, your traditions, and the connections that you have to
your religion and heritage. Create your own community, whether that
means joining an existing one or starting from scratch.

Insights provided by Emily Kaplan, University of California–Davis

UCHIC ESSENTIALS—
GETTING STARTED

PLAN AHEAD
Reach out to your roommate, pack smart, and brush up on life skills during the summer for a smooth transition to college in the fall.

ARRIVE WITH AN OPEN MIND
If you arrive on campus with too many preconceived ideas, you might miss out on experiences or friendships you never would've expected. Stay open-minded and be ready for anything!

GET TO KNOW YOUR NEW HOME
Take advantage of freshman orientation to get to know the campus resources and people who are there to support you in your exciting journey ahead.

Looking for more great advice? Head to UChic.com for even more resources and information—they come highly recommended from our contributors and editors. Be sure to leave your suggestions as well!

"Whoever you were in high school, it doesn't matter anymore. Never stop finding ways to challenge yourself and expand your horizons."

–LAUREN T., SYRACUSE UNIVERSITY

2

SHARING SPACE
AND CAMPUS LIVING

THE PREVIOUS CHAPTER WAS all about the critical pre-college stuff. In this chapter, we are focused on the next critical set of issues—those early-stage college experiences from sharing space with a roommate to making new friends to dealing with homesickness. Sharing a room in the dorms—especially when the room is an itty-bitty hole in the wall—is no easy feat. Before you even arrive, common questions you may face include: Should I room with my BFF from high school? What if my roommate is a freak? Where do I find extra-long bed sheets? Are coed dorms the way to go? Is the scholarship hall or sorority house for me? It's normal to have all of these concerns and questions when it comes to sharing space. We tackle these questions, one by one, so you've got all the info for a great start to your new life in college.

So here's the lowdown on how to "live it up" in college no matter what your living situation may be.

BRINGING SOME SANITY TO DORM-ROOM CHAOS

When you're entering college as a freshman, it can seem that the classes and the countless hours studying, preparing presentations, and writing papers are the defining focal points of your new life. But an equally important part of the college experience involves your living situation. Here's some tried-and-true advice on how to manage dorm-room chaos while making the best out of your living situation.

MOVE-IN DAY

Moving is stressful for anyone, but the move from home to college can be particularly stressful. Not only are you worried about physically moving your things from home to your dorm room, but you also are nervous about meeting new people, especially your roommate. Add in the emotion that goes along with leaving your family, and it just might put you over the edge. Remembering to keep calm and maintain a good attitude while moving may be your saving grace. Don't let your emotions get the best of you! If you're really anxious, get in touch with an older family member or a friend who has just been through the process. Share how you're feeling, and ask for their advice. Simply getting these feelings off your chest with someone will go miles in helping you de-stress about the big day.

Your university or college might have strict requirements about the layout of furniture or assign you to a specific side of the room; or it might give you freedom to decide these things. You might be able to find detailed information about your dorm on your school's website to help you plan in advance, or you might be walking into your dorm room on move-in day with no idea what to expect. Whatever the case, try to communicate with your roommate ahead of time about options for room arrangements to help move-in day go smoothly. When you move in, be sure that you're splitting the space as evenly as possible. And try to unpack your things in a timely manner, making the space feel like home as soon as possible. Not having all those distracting boxes sitting around will help the transition to college feel more real. Not to mention that once classes begin, you won't have much time to take care of this important chore.

MESS = STRESS

Katie Reynolds, Central Connecticut State University

When I was in high school and couldn't find my notebooks, books, pens, and paper, I could enlist my mom's help. She stayed on my back about being organized, and if I didn't do it, she usually did. Probably not a good thing because once I arrived at college, I realized that I completely lacked organizational skills. My first semester was rough. From the new dorm to new friends to new classes, I was a mess. Literally. The piles of clothes, dirty dishes, and clutter in my dorm room made it hard for me to focus and study. And that meant I was seriously stressed during exam time.

The stress of all the change finally made me realize that I needed to change too. With my roommate's help, the two of us became more organized together. Simple things like designating a spot for common items made a world of difference. Assigning a spot for my books, jacket, keys, and bag helped me start organizing the rest of my life, and things got a lot better from there.

COME PREPARED

Since you're sharing a room, each inhabitant is entitled to equal space in said room. However, dorm rooms, being as small as they are, become even smaller once you move in TVs, microwaves, stereo systems, and minifridges. Be considerate of your roommate by not taking up too much of the communal floor space. If you have a bike, store it in a bike room to keep your bedroom clear and prevent dirt from tracking in. Put your laundry basket on top of your closet if there's space, or under your bed.

If you opt for a shared fridge, make sure you don't take up more than your half. Free up even more space by foregoing items like microwaves and mini-ironing boards. Many dorms have kitchenettes on each floor that contain essentials such as microwaves, sinks, ovens, and ironing boards. You can also make an impromptu ironing board by putting a towel on your bed. Basically, it all boils down to coming prepared and being resourceful. Only bring items into the dorm room that you know you will use, and if you're in doubt, leave it at home. It can always be shipped to you later or you can get it during a visit home over the holidays. Space is at a premium, so pack light and enjoy your clutter-free environs.

UCHIC TIPS FOR DORM-ROOM BLISS!

TIP 1: MUST-HAVE FURNISHINGS

There are just some things you do not want to neglect bringing, including a file cabinet or several storage bins to keep your papers organized; a rug for those cold dorm-room floors; and tall shelves so you can store a lot without taking up space.

TIP 2: A COMFORTABLE BED MAKES FOR A COMFORTABLE ROOM

You must get extra-long twin sheets. That's the number-one rule for dorm-room bedding because dorm-room beds are notorious for being extra-long. Also, bring several sets of sheets. There will be times when you want clean sheets at 2 a.m. but are obviously not in the mood to do the laundry. Finally, a mattress pad will ensure your much-needed beauty rest.

TIP 3: UTILIZE EVERY INCH OF SPACE

Consider lofting your bed. You can usually get lofting kits from maintenance or the front desk of your residence hall. When finished, the area under your bed can become a great place for a comfy chair and a reading lamp, creating another sitting area besides your bed and desk. To additionally free up some space, add hooks to the backs of doors. You'll be surprised how an extra towel or two on the ground can really detract from the room's overall good vibe.

TIP 4: GO GREEN!

If protecting the environment is of concern to you (of course it is!), you can introduce eco-friendliness to your dorm room through green furniture, a recycling bin, and energy-saving items like compact fluorescent lightbulbs.

I also recommend making your toiletries as easy to carry as possible by investing in a good shower caddy with holes for water to drain. I made the mistake of buying one that didn't have holes in the bottom, causing water to puddle in the bottom and mold until I had to stab a hole in it myself with a pair of scissors. Also, consider decanting your shampoo, conditioner, body wash, and the like into travel-size bottles. This will lighten your load considerably when you're making morning and nightly treks to the bathroom.

KNOW AND MAKE KNOWN YOUR BOUNDARIES

So you've moved in your stuff and shared some pizza slices and a chat. But what happens when you discover some red flags about your roommate? Maybe you find out that she has a long-term boyfriend who's big on PDA and wants to hang in your room on a nightly basis. Or does she listen to Evergreen Terrace and Avenged Sevenfold while you're an Alicia Keys and Sara Bareilles fan? Worst-case scenario: she's allowing drugs or alcohol in the room and, through guilt by association, you could potentially get in trouble.

Though you generally can't control what other people do, being clear about what is or isn't acceptable will make it easier for you to voice your opinions without having to second-guess yourself.

TAKE IT FROM A GIRL
WHO'S BEEN THERE

I didn't have many high school friends who were going to the same college, so I opted to allow the university to choose a roommate for me. My new roommate, Grace, was completely different from me in family background, music tastes, clothing, and pretty much everything else under the sun. At first, I was worried that we wouldn't get along, considering my abiding love of Britney Spears and celebrity gossip websites and her complete distaste for these "frivolous" things. But for the most part, it was a great experience. Yes, she liked to listen to the Aquabats and hang slides from her presentation on leprosy in our window, but these initial annoyances taught me to be tolerant of others and be open to someone else's tastes. Because I kept an open mind, I was exposed to films, music, and people I would probably never have encountered if left to my own devices. Since she was a junior—a couple years older than me—Grace was also a good source of information on important things, from where to grab a bite on campus to negotiating the vast library system. She was virtually a stranger to me when we met, but over time and with an open mind, we came to enjoy each other's company.

A FEW BIG THINGS TO REMEMBER
Do Not Borrow Your Roommate's Things without Asking

I know it is tempting when you don't have any clean clothes (or even when you do have clean clothes) to hop over to your roommate's closet and borrow her favorite sweater because luckily it looks great on you too! But unless you've asked, I urge you to stay away.

If, by chance, you do borrow your roommate's things without asking, make sure to return the item(s) in their original condition, washed (if worn), and in a timely manner. If she asks about it, apologize and tell her it won't happen again…then don't let it happen again. Remembering how you would feel in that situation is important because you should treat others as you would like to be treated.

Do Your Part around Your Dorm Room

Splitting the chores, such as dusting, sweeping, and taking out the trash, is a crucial part of living on campus and with a roommate. Make sure once you've decided who is doing what, you really stick to that deal. If your roommate is constantly the one cleaning up the mess, she may start to resent you and that is the last thing you want while living together. Just do your part and chip in to buy cleaning supplies when needed.

COED DORMS ON THE RISE: WHAT YOU NEED TO KNOW

Despite what your parents may say, campus life has changed quite a bit since their college days. The traditional view of dorms is same-sex floors or same-sex buildings, but many colleges offer alternatives. My college, for example, offers housing where members of the opposite sex can live on the same floor.

Some colleges even have "gender neutral" dorms where members of the opposite sex can share dorm rooms and suites. Though this sounds like an intriguing idea, there are definitely pros and cons to the situation.

PROS:

- **Hang with the boys:** Want someone to watch the game or play soccer with? You might not have to look any further than your roommate.
- **Meet new people:** Since you'd be living with a guy, that definitely means there will be more opportunities to meet new boys through his group of friends.
- **A guy's perspective:** Some guys can shed light on our problems in a sincere way and give really good advice.

CONS:

- **Awkward moments:** Since you'd be living in the same room as a guy, you are going to run into some awkward encounters. You'll have to think more about changing in the room or what to do after you hop out of the shower.
- **Possible mess alert:** If you are a perfectionist about your room staying neat and tidy, make sure the guy you room with is the same way.
- **Lack of sensitivity:** While some guys can be really

> sensitive, many are not. If you're not going to miss the dramatic elements of living on a female floor, then this could be for you. However, you're not going to get a lot of sympathy from your boy roomie when you cry for hours and hours over the jerk who dumped you.

UTILIZE OTHER AREAS

So you've talked to your roommate and have made sure that everything fits in your tiny living space. But what to do when she has unexpected guests over? That's one of the great and, at times, most irritating things about the dorms: you're constantly surrounded by people. Certainly, there will be times when you or your roommate will want to invite others to your room to watch movies, eat, or just hang out. This is fine until the day comes when you have to study for an exam and your roommate and her four closest friends want to play *Mario Kart*. This is a perfect time to check out the other amenities your dorm has to offer. Some dorms have study rooms, usually a windowless room set up with a table and a chair where you can take your laptop and books to read or write in solitude. Maybe there's a lounge on your floor with couches and tables where you can study in relative peace and quiet. Keep in mind, though, since it's a shared space, you may have to vacate if a group decides they want to watch TV.

Don't forget that you can always leave the dorm and check out a library on campus. Many schools have at least one library that's open late or even twenty-four hours. Another reason to get out of the dorm: sometimes all you need is a break from your roommate and from your regular surroundings to reset your outlook. We all have to take a break from others at times, even the people we love the most.

When all is said and done, there are going to be moments of great fun and frivolity in dorm life and also some frenzy and frustration, too. Knowing and accepting this ahead of time will make the transition to dorm living a whole lot easier than coming unprepared.

Insights provided by Madeline Greene, Minnesota State University and Anna Prestek, University of Washington–Seattle

ROOMMATE DRAMA: RESOLVING TENSION AND CONFLICT

People do not always get along. Even if you initially hit it off with your roommate, it does not mean that later down the road, after spending so much time together, you may not get into an argument or two. There are many reasons why arguments begin but if you handle them correctly, you may be able to avoid some major blowouts.

If there are situations with your roommate that are bugging you, talk to her about it. Don't let the little things build up. Your roommate may not have any idea that what she's doing is bothering you. Some people simply have a higher threshold as to what is acceptable behavior around others. For instance, she might not think that having her friend lean his greasy bike against your bed frame is offensive, while you may be deeply disturbed.

If you feel uncomfortable with something that's happening, let your roommate know. Don't be afraid that you're being inconsiderate by voicing your concerns. It's like that famous line in a wedding ceremony: "Speak now or forever hold your peace." Think about it: there's never a "right" time to bring up a topic that's bothering you. But trust me. It'll go better if you speak your mind early on rather than suffering in silence and having that influence your attitude toward her.

TAKE IT FROM A GIRL WHO'S BEEN THERE

When I was a freshman in college, my boyfriend went to another school, so when he came to visit, he was always in my room. Not only was it cramped and crowded for the two of us, but also for my poor roommate. She didn't exactly want a sleep-in guest all weekend long. It's a huge adjustment, and it's really important to be aware of not only your own needs and your guy's, but also how your roommate feels about having your guy around all the time. And if your roommate is unhappy with the situation, you need to ask your boy to leave soon.

Also, if you are having problems with your roommate, talk to her instead of talking about her behind her back. If your roommate hears that you've been talking about her instead of to her, it may cause more trouble than you had before. Everyone needs to vent, but venting to your mom or to your pillow—rather than to fellow classmates—will be less harmful in the long run.

Same goes for the online world. Many people resort to social media as a way to vent. But posting pictures of your roommate's messy side of the room or tweeting about how annoying she is may get you into trouble. After all, you may be potentially violating her privacy to do this, which can get you into a lot of trouble down the road. Talking to your roommate about the problem, instead of venting on Facebook, will allow you to work things out before they blow up. Something is bothering you, but where to begin? Start by speaking up.

HOW I WORKED THROUGH MY ROOMMATE ISSUES

Emma Ehlers, University of Arkansas

Freshman year was a whirlwind full of positive and negative moments, and many of them were associated with learning to live with someone new. Due to my perseverance, I was able to learn so much about myself and the world I live in.

When I was assigned a random roommate, I was anxious it was going to be difficult to get along with another person in such close living quarters, especially because I struggled with anxiety during my freshman year. Before I really got to know my roommate, I was nervous that I was doing things that would make her mad, and I didn't know if I could speak up. I even feared that I was annoying her if I stayed up late studying. My anxiety continued to heighten, and I ended up going to the doctor to get a prescription for my general anxiety disorder. However, I was extremely lucky to have a roommate that I could trust and confide in.

Following winter break, I discovered that we were both struggling with anxiety. We both acknowledged the issue and started taking anxiety medication. Because of this, we were able to talk each other through tough times. We became each other's therapists during this difficult time, because we knew that in the end we were going to be there for one another.

I also think what helped us keep on track was the agreement we created *together* at the beginning of the year regarding potential troublesome situations and pet peeves.

When issues came up, we were then able to vocalize our feelings and resolve the problem maturely—resulting in some of my most positive memories and a lifelong friend in my roommate from freshman year.

WORKING THROUGH ROOMMATE ISSUES WITH MEETINGS

Learning to cope with other people's lifestyles is one of the major stresses you'll face during your transition to college. Start out the year by agreeing on some rules. My senior year, I lived in a suite with one bathroom, a living room, and three very tiny bedrooms for six girls, and we had major messiness issues.

The first weekend, we each had our own idea of "fun" in the suite. Before heading out to the bar, a couple of us decided to have our friends over for a party. One of our other roommates wasn't so enthusiastic about our fun, and I guess I can't blame her. The littered floor and the loud music coming from our bedroom probably did not make for a welcoming first weekend for her. Needless to say, she called a suite meeting soon after to go over some "ground rules." The meeting caught me off guard, because the last thing I wanted was someone telling me how to live. But once it started, I realized it was a positive thing for all of us.

First, each person got a chance to share her pet peeves no matter how silly they sounded to say out loud, and then we discussed ways to avoid each other's pet peeves. One girl had a real pet peeve about the trash not being emptied in a timely manner. Another roommate—I never did find out who—had a terrible habit of leaving her birth-control

UCHIC Tip!

If drugs are involved, go speak with your Resident Assistant immediately. *Drugs are illegal*, and you should not have to put up with them.

patch stuck to the shower wall. No one ever admitted to the deed, but addressing it in the meetings actually made the mystery stop. Apparently the embarrassment of an open discussion was enough to make the patch bandit rethink the error of her ways.

Sometimes, just addressing common issues can help put an end to them. The meeting was such a success that we held similar ones on a regular basis all year to keep us all on track. I'd highly suggest that you follow a similar strategy with your roommates.

That's not to say that every roommate experience will work itself out. Friends of mine have had roommates who did drugs in the room, and some even stole from them. These things are not acceptable. It's up to you to know when you've reached your limit. There is always a solution, and if need be, don't be afraid to ask for a new roomie.

WHEN ROOMMATES BREAK UP

Solange Gorleku, University of South Florida St. Petersburg

During my sophomore year, I lived in a suite with three other girls. For Thanksgiving, we decided to celebrate with a "Friendsgiving" dinner in our common room. Sounds like a fun idea, right? Unfortunately, one of my roommates wasn't on board. This led to a big argument that required our RA to get involved. While the situation finally got resolved, none of us expected what she did next—moved out.

When you or a roommate chooses to move out, it can be pretty upsetting. The last thing anyone wants is an argument that causes someone to completely leave the situation. I kept asking, "What else could we have done to avoid this from happening?" Unfortunately, this particular roommate did not tell the rest of us that she was leaving until the day she moved out. It was a complete shock to the remaining roommates, and it showed just what can happen if roommates don't address problems well. I tried to remain positive about the whole situation, because ultimately it was her decision and she needed to do what made her most comfortable. Some people might have even followed her lead, but I chose not to. I never considered moving out because the situation seemed manageable. In my eyes, the problem has to be so extreme for me to even think about packing up my bags and leaving. But everyone deals with conflicts differently, and that's okay. It's important not to shame someone if they don't handle problems in the same way you might.

If you're in a similar situation where things get really serious and it's you who is thinking about moving out, it's important to remember that you are paying for the space and deserve to change any situation that is making you unhappy. Try talking to your RA first to see if a resolution can be found without having to move. In the worst-case scenario, moving out is always an option. If you live in a residence hall like I did, residents are under contract to stay in their specific room until the end of the academic school year. Any room change is typically only approved for an unsolvable circumstance. This can be even more difficult if you live off-campus and are under an even more strict contractual agreement. Always look into all options and possible outcomes (good and bad) before making the difficult decision to move out.

If it's your roommate who is thinking about leaving, stay optimistic and put yourself in her shoes. Try to remember that you're not only their roommate, but also their friend. No one ever wants any bad blood—especially if you're living in the same space. It's definitely worth talking through any issues you may be having to see if you can't find some common ground. And that is definitely something you can build on.

RAs are used to these kinds of issues, and most are happy to help you find a roommate who better suits you.

WHAT TO EXPECT FROM YOUR RESIDENT ASSISTANT

Alisa Sutton, Temple University

THE REAL ROLE OF THE RA

There are many misconceptions about the role of a Resident Assistant (a.k.a., "RA"). For starters, they are not your babysitter, and they are not your parent. An RA is there to look out for you, provide guidance, and help make your transition to college as smooth as possible! He or she has been in your shoes and knows what you are going through. So don't be afraid to knock on their door if you need something. For example, I had problems with my first roommate, but by going to my RA, I was able to get a room change, and ended up meeting some of my best friends in my new room. RAs are there to talk you through any problems you may have, whether with your roommate, new friends, or classes, and help you find solutions.

GET OUT OF YOUR COMFORT ZONE

RAs are usually required to host social events for their residents a few times a month. This is the perfect opportunity to get closer with your RA and meet your hall-mates. Sometimes these events can be awkward, but remember that everyone is in the same boat. The boy down the hall looks just as silly playing icebreaker games as you do.

TRUE LOVE WAITS 'TIL MAY

Everyone has heard the cliché story of a resident falling for his or her RA. While this is highly forbidden, you cannot control who you like. If you find yourself in this situation, it is important to remember that your RA is technically your superior, and a relationship between the two of you could get him or her in serious trouble. If the feelings are mutual, talk about where the relationship will go and keep in mind that it would be best to wait until the end of the year to be together.

THINKING OF BECOMING AN RA?

RAs have a tough job, but their role is crucial to the running of a residence hall. Most schools require RAs to be "on duty" three days a month, which means once the front desk or office closes, they are required to assist any resident that may need help until it reopens in the morning. This means dealing with any type of incident that may occur throughout the night, like lockouts, guest policy violations, or alcohol-related incidents. The requirements can seem daunting. But because RAs are so important, there are also great perks to the job. Housing and meal plans are often included for RAs, as compensation for their work. With the cost of education rising, this is a huge bonus. Overall, the job is very rewarding. If you think you have what it takes to be an RA, don't be afraid to put yourself out there, even if you're only a sophomore!

MAKING IT WORK

When a bunch of different personalities are thrown into one small living space, friends or not, people are bound to butt heads. Take responsibility for your own actions and belongings. If something's bothering you, talk about it. It's important to remember that you're living in a shared space, and rules that existed at home don't always follow you to college. But if you respect one another, your roommate situation will be a success.

Insights provided by Madeline Greene, Minnesota State University, Anna Prestek, University of Washington–Seattle, and Katie Reynolds, Central Connecticut State University

AFTER THE FIRST WEEK: SETTLING INTO YOUR NEW LIFE ON CAMPUS

I fear change—and college is a big change. So it was no surprise that I spent the majority of my summer before college *freaking out* about the thought of being in a new place without my friends, without my boyfriend, without my family. As if preparing for a coming storm, I went around buying everything that I could think of to start a "home" emergency kit—a stash of items that would remind me of home when I was stuck in a tiny dorm room. Why wouldn't I? In my mind, the dorm was that weird place that conjured up images of Girls Gone Wild meets summer camp. I even went so far as to ask my mother to get custom-made bedding inspired by my bedding at home. Sadly, she declined, so to cope I instead bought dorm accessories with the same purple and gold color scheme as my childhood bedroom.

Well, despite all of my numerous breakdowns in the Target store, my first week of college was fine. I think I even had fun during the first week's orientation! The wonderful thing about orientation is that they keep you busy with so many activities that you forget to be homesick. And most of these activities are the special kind of lame that have you instantly bonding with members of your orientation group just to survive. Voila! Instant friendships.

AFTER THE FIRST WEEK

The real challenge during your transition to college is after orientation—your first unstructured weekend. I almost couldn't handle it. Who was I supposed to hang out with? These people weren't really my friends; I'd known them for only five days! And communal bathrooms? I was so over it after the first time some random guy caught me shaving my legs in the sink.

I just wanted to go home and see my best friend, watch a movie with my boyfriend, and pee in the privacy of my own bathroom. Between you and me, I almost did. I was about five minutes away from booking a train ticket home for the first weekend when I made myself pause. I realized that if I went running for the comforts of suburbia every time things became uncomfortable, I'd spend my college experience in a friendless black hole with nothing but my books to keep me company. So, against my instincts to cut and run, I decided to stay. Looking back, that decision was the best one I have made over the course of my four years at school. In fact, I met some of the girls who would become my best friends at school that weekend.

Renee and I were both terminally bored at a tropically themed Alpha Epsilon Pi frat party (read: warm jungle juice and underdeveloped shirtless frat boys). We both decided to leave the party in exchange for a band's live show elsewhere on campus.

That was one of the best nights of my college career. After that, Renee and I started going out to events that interested us rather than the ones that felt "college-y," and eventually found a lot of people were interested in doing the same. Once I started finding things I liked to do and inviting people, I made friends.

Once I started making more friends and building a life by taking risks and going out with new people, the homesickness went away. If you're concerned that you too may experience a difficult transition, there are several things you can do to make the transition a little bit easier and get yourself out of the funk a little bit faster.

TRY SOME PREEMPTIVE PEP TALK

Just take a deep breath and accept it: you are probably going to get homesick. It may vary in degrees of awfulness, but at some point, you are going to miss the people and places that you encountered every day for the past eighteen years. Don't suppress these feelings: it's completely natural and pretty common. If you go into college thinking you are never going to miss anyone or anything, you are setting yourself up for a fall and may be caught off guard, unable to deal with the unexpected sad feelings. By taking the time to accept the fact that you may get lonely or begin to miss home a time or two, you can prepare yourself rather than being surprised by these feelings of homesickness. It may be hard to deal with these emotions, but it isn't impossible. This preemptive pep talk goes a long way.

IT'S OK TO BRING THINGS THAT REMIND YOU OF HOME, BUT DON'T BRING HOME

Sure, bring a few pictures of your friends and family, your favorite stuffed animal, and maybe even a special tchotchke. (The ceramic pony my dad gave me when I was seven will always be on my desk regardless of what anyone says.) They are even good conversation starters. It makes complete sense that you want to surround yourself with familiar things, but there is a limit to how much. Filling up your new space with remnants of the past makes it really difficult to enjoy the present. (Plus your roommate may not appreciate all your trinkets from home.) It is probably not a good idea to bring all of your yearbooks from high school, your collection of sweatshirts from old boyfriends, or that sweater you haven't worn since you were seven but swear you can still smell your first grade teacher's perfume on.

You're in college to make new memories and develop into a well-rounded person. How to do this? Make sure your eight-by-ten-foot cell of a dorm room has space for your new life. It will fill up before you know it.

GET YOURSELF OUT THERE

It may be easier to go to bed early or spend hours in the library in order to get ahead in your classes, and these are good habits in most cases, but taking it to the extreme can lead to a dangerous pattern. Even worse, you could have done the very same thing at home! You're ignoring the perks and pleasures of college life, and that's not healthy.

Take advantage of being in college by seizing those opportunities to socialize and meet people you would not have met otherwise. It might feel like you're putting yourself out on the line by trying to hang out with new people, so to make it easier, simply join a new club, write for the student newspaper, or strike up a conversation with someone in your freshman seminar course. What do you have to lose? For the first few weeks, everyone is looking to make friends, so people will be receptive. After you introduce yourself, it's only awkward for the first few minutes of conversation, or until you find out that Sarah in your Intro to Poli-sci course also shares your love of obscure Austrian electro hip-hop.

Once you start talking, you'll be amazed at how much you have in common with and have to learn from the new people around you.

KEEP IN TOUCH WITH FRIENDS AND FAMILY, BUT TO A REASONABLE DEGREE

Thanks to the communication age we live in, you can call, text, email, instant message, Skype, or Facebook all the people you left behind for hours on end. But try not to. It's hard at first, but spending hours talking to people via whatever your preferred communication method might mean that you are losing precious hours of face-to-face conversation with people at your college. A good rule of thumb: until you have started building a niche for yourself at school, avoid spending more time talking to people from home than you do talking to your classmates.

TAKE IT FROM A GIRL WHO'S BEEN THERE

My freshman-year roommate talked to her boyfriend for about eight hours a day. I really wasn't surprised when she transferred to her boyfriend's college after the first semester because she felt so alone.

It makes it harder to create a home at school when you're constantly talking to people from home. Plus your best friend is trying to make friends at her own school, so give her—and yourself—a chance to create a new life for yourselves at college.

TIPS FOR COMMUNICATING WITH PARENTS

Alisa Sutton, Temple University

ESTABLISH SOME GROUND RULES

Saying good-bye when your parents drop you off at college is often very emotional, especially when you realize you may not see each other for a while. Make the drop-off easier by establishing how often you'll be communicating. Talk with them and decide in advance how catching up will best fit into your schedule. Remember, do what works for you. It is perfectly normal to be homesick. At the start of college, you may speak with your parents more frequently. It is also okay if you are busy or don't feel like talking. Don't forget, your parents miss you and just want to know how you are doing. So be sure to check in with a text from time to time!

EVERYTHING'S CHANGING—AND THAT'S NORMAL!

Being away gets easier as time passes. Time away also changes your relationship with your parents. While they are still your parents and you will always be their "little" girl, their role is to sit on the sidelines more as you acquire the experiences and know-how to lead your own life as an adult. That can be a tough transition for your parents at first; they aren't going to be constantly aware of what you're doing anymore. But with time, when you talk to them, it will be more like they are one of your friends who want to catch up, and you will begin to see them as "real people." And guess what: it's a good thing!

IT'S TIME TO GO HOME

School is out, and you're headed home for a break. Rather than spending your entire fall, spring, or summer break out with friends, make some time to hang with your parents. You often don't realize how much you miss your family until you come home. Something as simple as taking the time to watch a movie together or even being home for dinner is a great way to spend some time together. Let Mom or Dad cook you dinners and bake you cookies again! You'll feel rejuvinated by letting them take care of you for a bit again. And your parents probably won't mind either.

REALIZE THAT MOST STUDENTS ARE GOING THROUGH THE SAME THING

It may seem like everyone is having an easier time making friends and having a life than you—but they aren't. Most of the time, people like to act like they're partying every night and have thousands of friends. This is actually a fact you may learn in your first psychology course—if you act popular, people are more likely to perceive you as popular. But deep down, everyone feels a little lost and alone at the start of school. It's just that people show it in different ways. If you are feeling really alone, reach out to someone—your roommate or a hall-mate—and say, "I'm feeling a little alone. How are you coping with all of this?" If you think that is lame, just take solace in the fact that everybody is feeling a little disoriented and may appreciate the opportunity to share their feelings. I guarantee that you will quickly discover that you are not the only one feeling alone. Think of it this way: if someone confided their feelings, you would hear them out without hesitation.

GET SOME STRUCTURE

The first week of college feels like a scene out of *Camp Nowhere* where everyone can run around and do whatever they want, whenever they want. That's kind of cool after having your life scheduled down to the minute in high school. But trust me: it takes almost a week, but this kind of freedom does lose its novelty. Don't forget that your goal is to build a life at school, not to become a professional spring-breaker. Once you start classes, join clubs, become active, and find people to join you at the dining hall, you'll find that all these things require a schedule, and a structured schedule is your best friend. You'll waste hours wondering what you are going to do and who you are going to do it with if you're not careful, so embrace your fabulously busy life with a fabulous schedule.

STAY TRUE TO YOURSELF

There are some tempting shortcuts to getting over homesickness, including things like drinking a lot, sleeping with random boys, or joining the chess club even though it bores you to tears. In short, it is easy to silence who you really are for the sake of having companions. But remember, if you build false relationships now, they won't last, and you'll find yourself lonely again. It may suck to feel alone during the early stages, but it's going to suck more when you find yourself friend-less at the end of the second semester because you feigned an interest in being in a sorority. Or conversely, you shunned sororities because a friend told you to, even though you knew it was right for you. Take the time to build true friendships that are based on your real interests at the very beginning of school. I promise it will pay off later.

TRY NOT TO GO OVERBOARD

For every girl who thinks staying in her room doing nothing is the best way to cure homesickness, there will be another that has to join every club, get every person's number, and knock on everyone's door. Don't be that girl either. She generally ends up burned-out and friendless because she annoys people. It is great to put yourself out there to make a big network of friends and activities, but don't force it to happen right away. Bottom line: it's about the quality, not quantity, of friendships. So what if you only play one sport or only have one or two really good friends at first? If these friends are fun and worth your time, you only need a few. And definitely don't worry about winning any popularity contest. By the end of college you will have tons of friends and way too many activities; just give it time.

> **U**CHIC Tip!
>
> My mom sends me care packages for everything; it has been the one saving grace of my college experience. I went to London to study abroad for a semester and she sent me packages filled with Oreos and American peanut butter. I was the most popular Yank in my flat! *If you are feeling sad, ask your parents for a care package*—it's a nice way to be reminded that people out there love you. And offers of your mom's chocolate chunk cookies are great icebreakers for making new friends.

IF IT DOESN'T GET BETTER, TALK TO A COUNSELOR

There is a difference between being a little (or even a lot) sad about missing home and being depressed. If months go by and you still really hate school, your grades suffer, you can't stop crying, and you sleep too much or not enough, go talk to someone. There are counseling centers on every college campus that are there to help students cope with homesickness or any other issues on your mind. Going to college means a lot of new and wonderful opportunities, but it also means a lot of changes that we aren't always equipped to handle.

If you are lucky enough to never be homesick, I certainly envy you. But if you are, these tips are a surefire way to beat homesickness. Once you do that, you're ready for four unforgettable years.

Insights provided by Allison Davis, Barnard College

MAKING FRIENDS

I am a natural introvert. The thought of putting myself out there petrifies me. So naturally, meeting people for the first time and making good first impressions are not my forte. Growing up, I only had a small handful of girlfriends at any one time. And I was never really close to any of them. For some reason, I always imagined that college would be the time to finally find a big group of close girlfriends, and I headed off for my first year fully expecting that to happen.

I had met my roommate in a Facebook group for my school's incoming honors class before leaving for campus, and we hit it off immediately. The first few weeks of freshman year were wonderful. My roommate and I were close, and we became good friends with the girls in my dorm. We spent the first few weekends getting ready together to go out, scheduled dining hall dates, and constantly talked via group chat. I thought I was getting what I had always dreamed of from my college experience. As the semester continued, however, my homesickness and need to stay within my comfort zone got in the way of maintaining my new friendships.

My first semester of college was unpleasant to say the least. It wasn't until my second semester that I decided to make a change and finally started making the friends I envisioned for myself in college. Here's how I did it.

DO NOT LET YOUR HOMESICKNESS CONTROL YOU

The number one tip I could give you is to limit the amount of times you go home, and if you go to a school far from home, don't spend your free time sulking.

My biggest problem my first semester of freshman year was the amount of time I went home. I live twenty-five minutes away from my school and as a homebody, going home every weekend seemed like an easy way to cure my homesickness.

However, all those weekends that I was home, my roommate and friends from the dorm were hanging out and getting closer. I began to feel left out and disconnected. The invites began to decrease until eventually I would spend a weekend at school and watch my roommate get ready to go out, without inviting me. I was fortunate enough to go to school with my high school boyfriend. But I would spend all of my free time with him rather than trying to make friends, because it was the comfortable thing to do. On the weekends when I did decide to stay at school, I would stay with my boyfriend and neglect my new friends. I felt that I had to choose between making friends and being with my boyfriend. I think the same thing tends to happen if you go to school with your best friend. Try to spend most of your time at school, with new friends. Set aside separate, specific time for hanging out with your friends or significant other from home, calling your parents, and going home to visit. Balancing it all may seem impossible at the time, but it is the key to having a great year and making new friends.

RELYING ON OLD AND NEW FRIENDS

Melanie Harris, Virginia Tech

Let's say that you're having a difficult time and need to chat with your old friends for some support. Go for it. Don't hesitate to call your besties from high school, but do so only when you need to or have something particularly great to share— definitely not every day. I can't emphasize enough how important it is to work on building a new life, and you can't move on when you're too much in touch with your old pals. And really, it's not fair to be calling or texting them all the time.

As an alternative to calling old friends all the time, reach out to your new friends. The National Mental Health Association encourages students to seek support from a roommate or a friend from class. Friendships can help make a strange place feel more friendly and comfortable. Sharing your emotions reduces isolation and helps you realize that you are not alone. This way, you're working on making a new life for yourself and moving on in a healthy way. Before you know it, these new bonds and connections will change your whole outlook on the college experience for the better, and your old friends might happily end up wondering why you're not calling as often as you used to.

Don't limit yourself. Don't stay within your comfort zone. One of the best parts about school is experiencing new things. Don't miss out on things like eating new foods (pho, anyone?), listening to new music, or karaoke!

KEEP YOUR DOOR OPEN

One of the best aspects of my freshman year was how friendly and open everyone was. Everyone kept their doors open and would walk around to introduce him- or herself.

My first week, my roommate forced me to walk around our dorm building, see ourselves into open rooms, and introduce ourselves to fellow students. At the time, I was so embarrassed and absolutely hated my roommate for making me do that. But looking back, it was one of the best ways to meet people in the building. So keep your doors open when you're just hanging out in your room, say "hi" when you walk by your dormmates, and don't be afraid to approach people. Everyone is a bit uncomfortable. So smile, there is nothing more comforting than a friendly face.

GET INVOLVED

As cheesy as this sounds, this is the absolute best way to meet people in college. This is where you will find your niche. If something even remotely interests you, do it! During my freshman year, the resident hall association planned different events to get freshmen involved. Events included a

UCHIC Tip!

Meeting people who share your interests is a great way to make friends in college. But you should also *try spending time with people who you normally wouldn't.* Take a random elective outside of your major and get to know the people in your class. If you are going to school for math, spend some time with your dormmate who is a painter. People go to school for a degree, but they also go to expand their perspectives. Getting to know people who aren't like you can lead to unexpected friendships.

field day, barbeque in the quad, a night where all freshmen went to Target, etc.

After the first semester of my freshman year, I decided to get involved with Greek life and go through spring recruitment. Joining a sorority was the best decision I have made in college so far. I learned so much about myself, realized what I wanted to major in, what I was good at, and what career path I wanted to follow. My sisters became my best friends. The time commitment helped me learn how to prioritize and balance my social, school, and extracurricular life. Joining a sorority also helped me get over my homesickness. I was always so busy and always looking forward to hanging out with my sisters. I didn't have time to sulk!

Take advantage of what your school has to offer, and you will find people who share the same interests, passions, beliefs, and hobbies as you. Whether you decide to join a sorority or any other organization, just put yourself out there. Homesickness will pass. But your friendships are forever.

Insights provided by Victoria Mazzella, Rutgers University

MAKING THE MOVE OFF CAMPUS

You may reach a point in your college career where you want to explore ditching the dorms and moving off campus. Many students do this as a way to solve the problem of warring roommates, being stuck with a party animal, or just wanting more personal space.

Considering an off-campus move but can't decide? Try making a list of the pros and cons to moving off campus to help guide the decision. Here is a list that I came up with to help get you started.

PROS

- You have complete control over your own space to arrange and decorate as you see fit. And it's always nice to have your own personal space, so you don't have to hide behind a closet door so your dormmate doesn't see you change.
- You have the opportunity to establish a rental history—valuable when you apply for other apartments down the road.
- It's not the most responsible reason, but once you're off campus you can throw parties without worrying about RAs breaking them up.
- Because you're the one cooking the food, it's likely a million times better than what's being served in the dining hall.

- There's something to be said for a bathroom where you don't have to wait in line for the shower and the outlets don't short out because 16 girls are trying to blow-dry their hair at the same time.

- Student apartments are usually pretty reasonable price-wise. I paid a mere $550 per month for a decent-sized room (it's probably a bit more expensive these days) that had its own bathroom, a covered parking space, and all utilities included. Yes, the apartment had lime green shag carpeting that was probably originally installed when Nixon was in office, but it was so worth it to have my own space when it came to studying and sleeping.

CONS

- Unlike in the dorm, you no longer have a built-in network of friends. You're lucky if you even see your neighbors, let alone meet them. This was something I had to deal with as an apartment-dweller; it seemed lonely without the constant flow of people coming in and out.

- You now have to deal with apartment management. Mine was a strange, senile man who would come into our apartment with no advance notice and ask, "Do you live here?" as if he had forgotten we had ever moved in. Some apartment managers seem to go out of their way to take advantage of inexperienced college student renters. Take what happened to us: our manager "lost" the list where we noted all the preexisting damages upon moving in, and my roommates and I had to pay for things that were broken long before we got there. Word to the wise: always, always make a copy of any document between you and the management and always send correspondence regarding legal matters, such as giving notice of moving out, via certified mail. Having a documented paper trail will save you from a lot of potential headaches in case something gets "lost."

- Those meals you cook? You also have to clean them up. Including the kitchen. And the bathroom. And the living room. Tasks that were once performed by a janitorial service, such as taking out the trash, are now yours. Although to a lesser degree, you still have to deal with roommates and their annoying quirks. Maybe someone doesn't take their turn doing the dishes or shortchanges you on a utility payment; whatever it is, there may still be problems with your roommate, they'll just be different problems.

- If you throw parties, the dorm staff won't break them up—but the police will.

SO YOU'VE DECIDED TO MAKE THE MOVE

If you've already decided to head off campus, now it's time to get serious about looking for your new home. The best places to look for an apartment are classifieds in student newspapers, Craigslist (www .craigslist.org), and word of mouth. Walk around the neighborhood you want to live in and look for vacancy signs. Check out a few places with your potential apartment-mates and make sure everyone agrees on a place before signing anything. Take pictures of each potential unit to compare later; after looking at, say, five units, it will be difficult to distinguish one from another. Talk to parents who have been down this road and friends who are already renting to make sure you know what to look for before you sign on the dotted line. Is it a year's lease or month-to-month? Is the damage deposit refundable? When is the rent due and where is it due? Just make sure you read everything before signing the lease, and if you're unsure, ask if you can read it over and then fax or mail it back after signing.

Whether you decide to stay in the dorms until graduation or leave after your first cafeteria meal, you will encounter situations there that will make you wheeze with laughter, roll your eyes in frustration, or thank the Almighty that it didn't happen in your room. If you move off campus, you do have to take on more responsibility, but you also gain a better understanding of what it takes to make it in the post-collegiate world. And no matter where you live in college, you're in for a once-in-a-lifetime experience!

Insights provided by Anna Prestek, University of Washington–Seattle

UCHIC ESSENTIALS— SHARING SPACE AND CAMPUS LIVING

WHEN IT COMES TO THE DORM, MAKE IT YOUR OWN!
We all know how that right accessory can make an outfit perfect. The same goes for your dorm room. It's the special touches like a bright-colored window treatment or a vintage lampshade that can really make a space your own.

COMMUNICATION IS KEY
Good relationships with your roommates can go a long way in making dorm living enjoyable. If things aren't going well, don't be afraid to speak up. And just as important, listen to any grievances that a roommate may have. Most

problems can be resolved if both parties are willing to listen and work together.

STAY TRUE TO YOURSELF

It's tempting to silence who you really are for the sake of having companions, especially in your first few months of college. But remember if you build false relationships now, they won't last, and you'll find yourself lonely again.

Looking for more great advice? Head to UChic.com for even more resources and information—they come highly recommended from our contributors and editors. Be sure to leave your suggestions as well!

"It's really, really, really easy to fall behind during your first semester. Have fun, but remember that you're there for an education. Get your work done before you go out at night."

—LAUREN T., SYRACUSE UNIVERSITY

3

HEAD OF THE CLASS

VALEDICTORIAN IN HIGH SCHOOL? Honor roll every semester? Maybe neither of these things were you. But guess what: even if you weren't at the head of your class in high school, you can still be a star in college. As any academic advisor will tell you, your high school performance does not determine your potential success in college because college is the time to pursue the things that you are good at. Bottom line: getting to the head of the class is something that everyone can do in college. The secret is that you just have to want it bad enough.

Now, before we dive into the secrets of success in school, we need to set the record straight: getting an A is not everything. It doesn't hurt, of course, but sometimes what you do outside of class matters just as much as what you do in it. Striving to do your best in school while maintaining balance with an active social and extracurricular life will help you succeed in both college and in life. So where to start in the quest to be at the head of the class? Start by reading this chapter!

TIPS AND TRICKS FOR MAKING THE PERFECT CLASS SCHEDULE

Scheduling your classes is the hardest and most important thing you will probably do all semester. Scheduling bad or great courses can really affect you academically and can impact other things like whether or not you will keep a scholarship or make the Dean's List.

The classes you take will also help you develop your world view, so it is important that you choose wisely and take the classes you need to graduate as well as classes that interest you.

A typical college schedule for a full-time student is anywhere between twelve to sixteen credit hours, but that is just the tip of the iceberg. College students are usually involved in so much more than just class. They have club activities, sports, part-time jobs, and friends to keep them busy, so it is crucial that a great schedule reflects not only time spent in class but time spent outside of class as well.

Once you've evaluated what extracurriculars you're likely to be involved in outside of class, you should then make a draft list of the classes you want to take. To make this list, you have to evaluate yourself on a few essential questions:

1. **What time of day do I achieve my best work?**

   Do you get more done before 8 a.m. than most people get done all day, or are you a night owl who loves to stay up all night and work on projects while the rest of the world is sleeping? Take this into consideration when you are figuring out your schedule. It is also good to note that night classes in college usually only meet once a week. So be careful if you decide to choose mostly night classes, as you could end up in one class three hours in one night, which can be long and tiring at that time of day.

2. **How many hours am I willing to go to class?**
   Whether you take twelve hours or turn up the heat and do eighteen just depends on how much time you are willing to devote to going to class. Sometimes, you can balance it out so that you take more courses in one semester than another and will still be able to graduate on time.

3. **How difficult do I want my classes to be?**
   You should never make a schedule too hard or too easy, because you don't want a particular semester to be so hard that it ends up being a GPA buster or too easy so that your next semester is harder. Balance is key.

4. **How spaced out are my classes from one another?**
   Each school allots a different amount of time in between classes, depending on the size of the campus. Somewhere between ten to fifteen minutes is typical. It's important to block out which class is where to make sure you can get to your next class on time. Try to avoid running across campus, if possible!

Now that you have a good feel for what works best for you in terms of timing for classes, it is time to start making a schedule.

WHAT DO YOU WANT TO TAKE?

First things first, gather all of your necessary materials. This includes general education checklists, major and minor checklists, and any other necessary sheets that tell you more about class listings. Find the classes you want to take that semester, as well as some backup classes that you would be willing to take in case your first choices don't go through.

Be sure to schedule an appointment with your advisor at this point. Usually you need to see your advisor before you can register for classes, so while you are there, you can review the classes you plan to take or ask for their advice. Even if your school doesn't require a meeting with an advisor, still seek out his or her input, as advisors are great for alerting you to any potential pitfalls, like classes you may want to avoid taking at a certain time in your college career.

> ## UCHIC Tip!
>
> Don't forget to **consult your course guide every semester.** It is easier than you think to forget to take that one random class required for graduation.

SCHEDULING IN THE DIGITAL AGE

Log on to your school's website to find information about the classes you want to take. The website can tell you when they are offered, who teaches them, where they are located, and how many spots are available. Jot down as much of this information as possible. If one class has so many teachers and time slots available it makes your head spin, consider narrowing that specific class down to a specific timeslot or two. This way you won't have as many classes to evaluate or look at.

There are also several different websites out there that can be used to help planning make more sense. To learn more about your potential professors, check out RateMyProfessors.com. It's a website where other students rate the teachers they had and can write reviews on them. It is extremely helpful because you can get so much more feedback about a professor than you could ever get from just asking everyone in your group of friends. As with any online review site, take these reviews with a grain of salt. Even though a few students may have had a bad experience with a professor, most students may have had a good one but just didn't write reviews. If you are looking for a device to plan your schedule for you, a site like MyEdu .com can take information from your school and turn the mass amounts of schedules available into a schedule that is tailored to your needs.

UCHIC Tip!

More and more college students today are adding online classes to their course schedules. And why not? The length of the course is usually shorter, and it's generally cheaper than regular courses. But online classes can also be more hectic to keep up with. In my experience, *the most important thing to do with online courses is to plan ahead of time*—use your calendar and plan out the hours you will spend on classes and homework each week. If you schedule the course time into your life like a regular class, you will be able to stay organized and on track.

DON'T PUT ALL YOUR EGGS IN ONE BASKET

If you think a class that focuses on a cool topic or has a well-respected professor is the one to take, chances are others will too. Always have backup courses ready in case you don't get your first picks, especially if you go to a large school, if you know a class is really popular, or if you are one of the last people to register.

REGISTRATION DAY HAS ARRIVED

If you are an incoming freshman, you will usually register during your freshman orientation. At most schools, you'll sign up for classes online after your first semester.

Here are some tips to make your registration day run more smoothly:

1. Wake up early. Give yourself plenty of time to get together any needed materials, wake up, get your computer up and running, etc.

2. Have your course registration numbers on hand. You can usually write them all down on a sticky note and attach it to your computer the night before. Or, to make things quicker, you can save it all in a Word document on your laptop so you can copy and paste. It is just important to do this so you can register as quickly as possible.

3. Stay calm and don't freak out. Sometimes the system will crash or not work because of an overload of people getting on to register— be patient. If you really need a class and couldn't get it, consider directly petitioning the professor or dean, depending on how your school operates, to see if you can get a seat.

SAVING MONEY ON TEXTBOOKS

Amanda Cross, University of Central Arkansas and Victoria Reitano, Quinnipiac University

Once your class schedule is finalized, it's time to buy your textbooks for the semester, and you'll soon find out that they cost a lot more than you bargained for. Textbooks are expensive, heavy, and not very useful (or worth much) after the semester is over. If you want to avoid trips to the crowded bookstore for overpriced textbooks, consider these alternatives to lighten your load and save money.

One option is to rent all the textbooks you need online for much less than the cost of buying them. Online rental companies, like Chegg.com and CampusBookRentals.com, provide a variety of rental options and prices. Renting textbooks is a great way to save money. In fact, during my last semester of college, I saved $300 on textbooks alone by renting them online. I was able to return them quickly and efficiently with a prepaid label and box.

Another option is e-book readers (e-readers) or tablets. Ebook editions of textbooks usually cost less, and they are yours to keep forever and alter in any way you like. You can highlight, add a note, get a definition, or bookmark a page. Kindle, Nook, or the iPad—which one is right for you? It's a question of personal preference, but my favorite is the iPad— it has every single e-reader feature built into it, but it's a tablet that you can use in a lot of other ways too. And you can use Barnes & Noble books, Amazon books, and, of course, download books from the Apple Store.

The only downside to ebooks is that the page numbers usually don't correspond with the exact pages of the print version. A way around this? If you're going to use an e-reader for all your books this year, be sure to ask your professor for a chapter-by-chapter breakdown of assignments.

CRISIS! ALL OF THE CLASSES YOU NEED ARE FULL!

The big problem here that you absolutely want to avoid is not having enough credit hours to be considered a full-time student. Why? If you're not a full-time student, it may jeopardize the scholarship or loan money you were relying on to pay your tuition. Take a deep breath. There is a solution.

The first step to preventing this potential disaster is signing up for your backups or getting into any classes that are still open as soon as possible. That way you'll make sure you're at least registered for the minimum number of credits required to be full time. Many students make the mistake of solely relying on the petitioning process, which is not a smart decision because teachers are not required to let you into a full class. Any class is better than no class. Keep in mind that you can always rearrange your schedule after teachers add you to their roster.

PARTING ADVICE

Making a schedule can be a stressful process. The key is to take it one step at a time, plan far in advance, and register as soon as possible. Don't sit around working on your schedule for longer than you should. And it doesn't have to be done in one night! Remember that you can always go back in and move things around later, if needed.

Insights provided by Amanda Cross, University of Central Arkansas, and Kelly Leslie, San Francisco State University

HOW TO GET TO
THE TOP

There are many different ways to get top grades. For one, you could literally sit at the head of the class—in the front of the classroom. This actually works for many reasons. You're forced to pay more attention to the professor, you'll always have an unobstructed view, and there is no one to hide behind during class discussions.

But sitting in the front row will not guarantee you top grades: there's no way to avoid the work and responsibility that comes along with being a top student these days. Hard work is the only way to get ahead. Lucky for me, my high school prepared me well. I was ready to buckle down as a college student after facing the challenges of high school and going through the college application process. But it was not just my high school preparation that put me at the top. I also had a strategy to be successful from the start. Want to get to the head of the class? Read on to find out how.

THE STRATEGY

When you're going for top honors, let's be honest—it's competitive. Would you head into a sporting competition without a success strategy? That is why I highly recommend devoting some time to developing a plan for your study and achievement. With a little effort, this strategy will help you, at a minimum, keep up with the competition. At its best, you'll be at the top.

WHAT YOU CAN DO INSIDE THE CLASSROOM
Find Out What You're Dealing With

After you've attended all your courses the first week of the semester, take a couple of hours over the weekend to devise your "strategy" for the semester. Try to determine which courses seem like they'll be fairly easy for you or won't require too much work and which ones could end up being a nightmare. Some things to look out for in separating the tough from the easy courses: the existence or frequency of quizzes, number of required papers, midterms, term papers, and yes, the final. If a particular course has many of these items, you're most likely dealing with a class that's going to keep you really busy.

Once you've categorized your classes, figure out a schedule that will have you spending the right amount of time on each course in order to keep up with all the readings and assignments without completely stressing yourself out. Also, be ready to revise this strategy along the way if necessary. With a good schedule, you will not be surprised by any pop quizzes, you will stay on track for any midterm or term papers, and finals preparation will be a whole lot easier than if you waited until the last minute to catch up.

If Nothing Else, Just Go

Attendance is a major factor in being successful in school. Students who attend class often are far more likely to succeed than students who do not attend class. Any professor whom you speak with will back this up. At some point you'll probably hear something along these lines: "Ninety percent of success is showing up," because for a lot of students the hard part is getting to class. If you have to be absent from a class, pair up with someone who is also in it. This way, you have someone to contact about what was assigned and discussed that day and even to get notes from. Also, make up any missed work as soon as possible. Being absent is an easy way to fall behind and lose a spot at the head of the class. From my own experience, showing up on time and being ready to learn is the only real way to get ahead.

WHEN TO DROP A CLASS

Madeline Greene, Minnesota State University

While there are a lot of great aspects to college, the academic side (after all, we are here to get a degree and graduate!) is not always easy. I know what it feels like to be overwhelmed with my schoolwork. So how do you know when dropping a class is the right decision?

There is likely one course that is causing all the trouble, so take time to identify it. Then talk to your academic advisor to ensure that dropping it would not mess up important things like financial aid or your graduation plan.

Before pulling the trigger, be honest with yourself. Are you being lazy or do you really have too much on your plate? If you're up until all hours of the night finishing homework and you're exhausted all the time, you should consider dropping the class. However, if the class is just a hassle to take because it's really hard, don't give up on it yet. College is meant to challenge you, and if you're being challenged (in a good way), take a deep breath and stick with it—as long as it's not taking too much away from your other studies.

One last piece of advice: you don't always have to drop a class to lighten the load. You could consider taking the class "pass/ fail," where instead of getting a letter grade, you either pass or fail the class. You still receive credit for the course, but it isn't counted in your GPA. You should use this option sparingly, however, as pass/fails on your transcript do not always look good to future employers.

Just remember that college is the time to challenge and push yourself. You just don't want to push yourself too far.

Pay Attention to Your Communication Style

While your communication style is hugely important in your social life, it also plays a specific role in getting good grades. Take a look at your syllabi for the breakdown of the grading scale in your classes and you'll often find that a percentage of your grade is tied to that elusive "classroom participation" factor.

So what does this mean for your strategy? First, you have to understand your communication preferences. Ask yourself, "Am I a good listener who is somewhat shy in a public setting, or am I someone who enjoys speaking up and debating from time to time on subjects that interest me?" Understanding your personal preferences for classroom involvement is key to figuring out how to stand out in the classroom. If you're shy, make an effort to speak at least once a week on a subject that you either know a lot about or are somewhat passionate about. The knowledge or passion will help carry you through your shyness. Also, take time to go visit your professor during office hours so that he or she can get to know who you are and come to appreciate your efforts even if you're not speaking up on a daily basis. And if you're the gregarious type, by all means, speak up! However, you need to be careful that you're not speaking simply in order to hear your own voice. Your classmates and professor will know the distinction. Make sure that your comments are thoughtful and either advance the discussion or introduce a new idea. By planning your strategy for communication inside the classroom, you're guaranteeing that you're meeting your professor's expectations for A-worthy classroom participation.

Volunteer

We all know that community service is an important component of being a college student. Guess what? Volunteering in class can also help you get ahead. When the professor asks for someone to volunteer for *anything*, be the first to take the assignment. Taking the initiative is a great tool for success. I had a professor in college who gave extra credit to anyone who volunteered to do something for the class.

ON-CAMPUS RESOURCES FOR STUDENTS DEALING WITH A LEARNING DISABILITY

Alisa Sutton, Temple University

DISABILITY RESOURCE SERVICES

Universities are knowledge hubs that exist to help students reach their highest educational dreams. If you have a learning disability, don't let that stop you. There are many programs and resources available to help you succeed. One of the most important is your campus's Disability Resource Services (DRS) office, which can help coordinate whatever type of personalized assistance you may need.

Make sure to notify your DRS office of your documented learning disability as soon as possible, so they can coordinate accommodations for you before the semester starts. Depending on your needs—however extensive or small they may be—you may qualify for such accommodations as a personal aide, a peer note-taker, or materials in alternative formats that are more conducive to your learning. Testing accommodations, such as extra time or limited distraction locations, are also usually available. The most important thing to remember is not to be afraid to speak up and take advantage of your on-campus resources!

TECHNOLOGY

Today, technology is changing how all of us interact with the world, especially those with disabilities. Ray Kurzweil recently invented an app for the blind called the KNFB Reader, which can read almost all types of printed text back to you, from your mail to a restaurant menu, or even text projected from a PowerPoint. Apps to aid with learning disabilities are popping up everywhere, and some, like Lumosity Brain Trainer, can help people without disabilities too.

Being in a university setting gives you the major advantage of access to assistive technology. There are plenty of unique software and hardware adaptations available to students with disabilities. No matter what your needs are, the technology coordinators at your school will do their best to find you a solution.

SCHOLARSHIPS

Many people with learning disabilities are not aware of the amount of scholarship opportunities available to them. Visit your school's DRS website to see if any specific scholarships are available or if there are local organizations willing to help offset the costs of tuition or other disability-related expenses that you may have.

WHAT YOU CAN DO OUTSIDE OF CLASS

Now that you've got a strategy for success, it's time to focus on how you'll conduct yourself outside of the classroom in order to ensure your success. In some cases, you may need a little extra help, and by all means seek out that support!

DON'T BE ASHAMED: SEEK OUT TUTORING AND HOMEWORK SUPPORT!

Susan Fiorentino, Manhattan College and Emma Ehlers, University of Arkansas

As a straight A student in high school, I didn't think I would need any extra help in college from my professors or other students. Just a few weeks into my first semester, I realized how wrong I was! Studying for college is definitely different from high school, and I quickly realized that my old studying habits would result in disappointing grades.

Fortunately, my professors had office hours and I made a point to visit them to go over material when I was struggling. I also reinforced the material I learned by forming study groups in my classes.

Need a little extra support in addition to office hours? Many universities have math centers where professors and math majors work to help students who are struggling. For athletes, my campus, among others, offers an academic resource center where tutors and professors make themselves available for athletes who need extra attention. Writing centers on campus offer free help with essay writing and research paper critiquing. Many students utilize these resources so they stay on top of their grades.

A tutor is just one of the many resources that are available to students. I enjoy being a tutor through my sorority. I am assigned girls who are having trouble with classes I have already taken. The way the system is set up makes the process of getting help very easy. Members email the scholarship chair what courses they want a tutor for and the scholarship chair keeps records of older members who volunteer to tutor in certain classes.

When I am assigned a member to tutor, I try and make our sessions as fun and relaxing as possible. I make sure the student knows it is not bad that they need help; it is actually expected in college for students to struggle until they figure out how to manage their time and classes.

Extra help isn't exclusive to freshman; resources are available for students in any year. If regular tutoring or study groups haven't been useful, there are other ways to get assistance. Chegg.com, for example, has an online tutoring section. You simply type in the subject you need help with along with the specific issue you have, and you will be connected with a tutor who has experience in this area. Otherwise, use professors, alumni, and upperclassmen as resources. Their previous experiences may provide insight into different study methods that may work for you.

Make a Study Schedule—and Stick to It

Besides attending class, a few hours per week must be dedicated to homework and studying. There is just no way around it. Most likely, quizzes and exams will make up the majority of a class grade, so good study skills are crucial to graduating at the top of the class. A few nights before the test or quiz, reread any notes and material that will be covered. It may also be a good idea to write a summary of the notes that were taken in class. From my experience, it takes an average of one to two hours of studying per week for each class to get a good grade (although this varies with different majors), and even more during midterms and finals.

You also need to figure out how you study best—alone or in a group? In a quiet area, or a busier place with people around? See the article later in this chapter on final exams to learn more about finding the study style that works best for you.

Treat Yourself Right

Good preparation for class involves allowing yourself a good night's sleep, getting regular exercise, and making an effort to eat healthy. These activities are proven to help classroom performance. Exercise is also of great importance. There are tons of scientific studies showing how good exercise is for your brain. I suggest reading some of them if you ever need some motivation to go to the gym! While weightlifting and walking are good, it is generally thought that vigorous cardiovascular exercise (thirty minutes or more of running or biking, for example) is the best workout for your mind.

DID YOU KNOW?

A general rule of thumb is that for each credit hour you're enrolled in, you should spend two to three hours studying per week. If you're taking 15 credits in a semester, that adds up to 30 to 45 hours of study time every week. But according to the National Survey of Student Engagement's 2014 study, *the average college student only spends about 17 hours per week preparing for classes.* The result? Less than a third of students ended up earning the good grades they expected to get when they first entered college, and 19 percent of students significantly underperformed.

Eating healthy is also important. Breakfast is the most important meal of the day! It sets your mood and energy level every morning for the whole day. Start the day with anything that has a decent amount of protein in it, because protein decreases your hunger better than carbs and provides a steady energy source all morning. Eggs, nuts, health bars, and many other foods are perfect for this. Just find what you like and make sure it has some protein.

Fat also provides a steady energy source and decreases your appetite more than carbs do; just don't overdo the trans fats and saturated fats that are in donuts, creams, and the like. Also remember that with too many carbs, you will get an energy high and crash a couple hours later, which is no good for learning. If you still need your bread or bagel, try to make it wheat or whole grain, which will help keep your energy level more even over a longer period of time.

Caffeine is always a tempting way to stay awake and study, but too much caffeine can actually make you less productive. For more advice on how to handle those tempting caffeinated beverages, check out the article later in this chapter on final exams.

After-Hours

No, I'm not talking about partying here (but of course you should have fun too!). A student does not need to be failing to want to improve a grade. Extra help is available for anyone who simply wants to do better. There are usually tutors or study sessions on campus. This could add an hour or two on top of what you're already doing outside of class, but it will be well spent.

Also, make an effort to get to know your professors. They like to see that their students are interested in their class. Make time to talk to professors about their material. Discuss anything of interest and ask them any questions about the subject. If your effort was sincere, they will most likely take this into consideration when it comes time to give you a final grade.

EMAIL ETIQUETTE

Amanda Cross, University of Central Arkansas and Victoria Reitano,
Quinnipiac University

When using email to communicate with your professors and classmates, it is super important to keep the tone professional. First things first, make sure your email has all the necessary information and that it is written concisely, as professors and classmates alike already get a ton of emails every day.

Do your best to use correct grammar and avoid slang. It's never appropriate to curse. Run spell check before you send and make sure any necessary documents are attached. After all, nobody's going to take you seriously if you spell the course name wrong in the subject of your email. It's smart to practice good email etiquette for when you want to start emailing potential employers about those dream internships or jobs!

If you don't get a response right away, don't bombard people with additional emails. Professors, especially, will try to respond as quickly as possible to your inquiries, but you have to give them time. If they don't respond in a timely fashion, consider stopping by their office or leaving a voice mail on their campus phone. If after several days of patiently waiting you still get no response, follow up with a short and sweet note, asking if they received your first note and that you look forward to their response. And those tardy responses from your student peers? They probably either didn't want to answer you or they couldn't help you. So you may just want to consider moving on to someone else who can help.

STAYING AHEAD OF THE GAME
Stay Organized

Every semester you receive so many handouts and take so many notes for each class that it can be hard to keep track of all of them. Many of my teachers recommended a three-ring binder that is categorized by date and subject. This way, notes can be easily located when it comes to preparing for a test or quiz. Students who are disorganized waste time looking for notes instead of preparing for the exam itself. I also use highlighters to keep track of any important information. Note cards and Post-its can also be useful.

Another way to keep organized is to keep an assignment book. List each assignment's due date and make sure to refer to it every day. Then, check off each assignment as it is completed; it's a great way to make sure everything gets done on time. Make sure to prioritize since the workload can get heavy at times.

Actually Do the Reading

Reading is another way to get ahead and be more knowledgeable about a subject. By actually reading your textbooks and other materials, you'll gain a deeper understanding of the subject. Many students do not want to dedicate the time to read or even purchase their college textbooks, but it's foolish to try to rely solely on a professor's notes and lectures. Reading books is the only way to be fully prepared for class, since the professor assigns those books for specific reasons. And it is impossible for the professor to discuss everything that will be covered on the tests or quizzes. Therefore it is your responsibility to read everything you are assigned when it's assigned and be ready to discuss it or take a quiz on it.

Work Ahead

Completing assignments a few days before they are due is a good idea. It allows you extra time to make any last-minute changes or revisions in the work before it's graded. In general, make sure you are consistently knowledgeable about the coursework as the semester progresses rather than cramming the day before a test, midterm, or final. By staying on top of things, you will save time (and your sanity!) when it comes to studying for a difficult exam, midterm, or final since there won't be as much to review.

STAYING AHEAD DOES NOT INCLUDE CHEATING

Jennifer Rubino, Kean University

Cheating is becoming a widespread epidemic in American high schools and colleges, at almost every level. The statistics are overwhelming: 75 to 98 percent of college students admit to having cheated. Blame it on extreme pressure to succeed from parents, or even a heightened fear of failure from the students themselves. Whatever the case, schools are taking drastic action to ensure that cheating becomes a thing of the past.

For example, at the University of Central Florida, testing is now computerized and computers are recessed into desks so students can't photograph other students' work with their smartphones. Scratch paper is provided, but it must be dated and handed in to the professor at the end of the test or exam. If a student is suspected of cheating, a professor can even direct an outside security team to video record the student while taking a test to determine if the person has in fact been cheating.

Plagiarism has become a serious issue as well. Just Google the phrase "term paper help" and see how many links come up for companies that provide term papers and essays in exchange for money. Schools like Duke and Bowdoin have implemented plagiarism surveys and testing materials for this year's crop of incoming freshmen, to reinforce the difference between stealing and creating original work.

Other schools are taking an extremely hard-line approach and are using plagiarism software like that provided by Turnitin.com. The software measures word algorithms and phrases to determine if content was lifted from material published on Wikipedia or other websites. To date, 9,500 colleges and high schools around the country are now employing Turnitin, even as students try new and complicated ways to beat Turnitin's system. (The irony here is obvious—for all the time and initiative students take to try to find cracks in Turnitin's software, they could just as easily be channeling their energy into researching, studying, and creating their own unique work.)

The bottom line? Cheating is becoming harder to do, so you might want to try another approach...like actually doing the work. After all, the only person you're really cheating is yourself.

MIDTERMS AND FINALS

Midterms and finals can seem overwhelming, especially since they usually cover a lot of information. Don't try to study the material for each course all at once. Start early and study a little bit at a time. Take it chapter by chapter and slowly begin to become familiar with the information. Only at the very end will everything be integrated. Also, one strategy that worked for me was to focus on one test at a time. If I had two tests in one week, I would study nothing else except the material for these courses. This kept my stress level down to a minimum, and I was able to go into each exam feeling very confidently prepared. You can find more advice on acing final exams later in this chapter.

U CHIC Tip!

Many students hand things in late or ask for an extension. If you want to get ahead, don't do this. If you really are spending too much time on an assignment, *it is time to ask for help.* Work hard to stay on top, but if for some reason your efforts aren't paying off, talk with your professor to make sure that you understand the material. This will prevent you from falling behind and possibly even failing a course.

FINALLY, REPUTATION MATTERS

Work on building a reputation for being one of the most dedicated and responsible students in your class. Your professor will greatly appreciate it, and this can also serve as a deciding factor when it comes to grades.

No one said that it's easy to be on top. As you'll find, it can take a lot of time to get ahead. But, if you follow some of the advice provided here, this is definitely an achievable goal. Graduating with high honors and an impressive grade point average is something you can be proud of after graduation, as well as something that will help you get ahead in the future. The hard work and determination you will need are worth it.

Insights provided by Jennifer Rubino, Kean University

WHICH MAJOR IS FOR ME?

Do you remember those multiple-choice tests that were supposed to tell you what you should be when you grew up? I wish that choosing a major in college was as simple as filling in a few circles and waiting for a machine to do the deciding for you.

The first thing to understand and accept about choosing a major is that your first choice may backfire on you and, more important, not to be discouraged if it does. Sometimes, you find that a certain major is too hard, or too easy, or just isn't what you want to do anymore. And that's OK: it's better that you switch than study (and get an expensive degree in!) something that makes you miserable. Finding the right major is a very personal process that is different for every student, including you!

HOW DO YOU FIND A MAJOR?

The answer to this question depends entirely on your situation.

For freshmen, I can share some general advice based on my own experiences as a student. Most college students will have general education requirements. It may seem like an unimaginative and controlled system, but there are great benefits: you'll get a taste of everything, allowing you to discover a subject and potential career you might never have considered. So, for those of you who don't know what major to pursue, go for a well-rounded educational experience the first semester of your freshman year while simultaneously getting some of these requirements out of the way. Try taking intriguing classes in each area you're interested in—and some you're not!—and you may end up finding your true passion just by chance.

For nonfreshmen, start by printing out a list of all the classes that you have taken thus far. Go through the list and cross off the names of classes that made you want to scream. Next, look to see if you can spot any trends in your course selection. If you find that you mostly enjoyed your English classes, maybe you should consider a major in English. What about science? This is a pretty broad category, so you'll have to narrow the choices down. So take some more science classes! Another approach to picking a major for nonfreshmen is to peruse the entire list of degrees that your school offers. There may be a major that is perfect for you that you didn't know existed. For example, I had a friend who loved her English classes and her foreign language class. And voila! After doing a little research, she discovered that she could use both of these skills if she majored in Comparative Literature.

If you come into college with a specific career in mind but you are unsure what to major in, talk to people who are working in that particular field. See what they studied in college and get advice on how they landed your future dream job. Most people are more than happy to answer questions about "how they got there," especially when you tell them that you hope to pursue a similar career path. Some schools have online databases of alumni networks that are available for student use. Don't be shy. Get in touch with these alums to find out how they did it, and stay in touch with them throughout school and even after your college years. These individuals can become mentors who will help guide you along your career path.

MAJOR ADVISORS

Once you've found a major you're interested in, you should immediately meet with an advisor or counselor. They will help you figure out what classes you have to take and plan out a general course timeline. It is good to continually check on your progress with an advisor before signing up for classes each semester, to make sure you're on track to graduate on time. Some schools may assign specific advisors to you while others may have certain advisors for specific majors. And don't be afraid to pick your own advisor. You may have really clicked with one professor who may end up being the best advisor you could have ever asked for, regardless of their specialty. The better the advisor knows you, the better they can assist you with making the right academic decisions and even help guide you toward scholarships, fellowships, and training that can enhance your overall education.

WHEN TO DECIDE

If you're on a strict four-year college timeline, you should not wait longer than spring semester of sophomore year to decide on your major. That's when most schools have their deadlines for declaring majors, and you'll likely need as much time as possible to take all the required classes for the major. This will also give you more time to meet with your advisor to discuss classes and careers.

If you waited until your junior year, it will require more effort, but you still can complete your major in four years. You will need to sit down as soon as possible with your advisor to find out whether you can finish the major in the next two school years. If you can't, you should look into taking summer classes, which may end up being cheaper than an extra semester or two of school. And be sure to look for other ways to complete your major on time. Some colleges have a "speedy" summer session after your fourth year. At my school, UNC–Chapel Hill, this summer session is affectionately known as "Maymester." You can still walk at graduation, but you have to finish the summer classes in order to get your official diploma.

WARNING! YOU MAY HAVE PICKED THE WRONG MAJOR

If you are getting bad grades in classes and you are not feeling motivated to do the work, you may be going down the wrong path. If your GPA is below 2.0 for a semester and you put in an honest effort, it could be an indication that you're pursuing the wrong major. (If it's something else, like too much drinking and partying, be honest with yourself about it.) You should not have to struggle just to get through the major that is right for you. I am not saying that every class is going to be wonderful and completely stress-free, but you should feel like it is worth the effort that you're putting into it.

CHANGING YOUR MAJOR

If you discover halfway through college that you were not meant to be a chemical engineering major, for example, get out fast. But be sure to call your parents or whoever is helping fund your education to loop them in on the decision and to logically explain why you have to switch majors. Explain that it would be a total waste of your abilities to stick with a course of studies that is making you cry every night and that you're likely to fail. Your parents will (probably) understand, because in the end, they want you to be happy.

Once you have decided to change your major and have made the necessary phone calls, you need to make an appointment with an advisor. Some of you may even have to go to the advisor within your current major to get their approval to change. Get started as soon as possible. You are initially going to have to do a lot of paperwork to change your major, but just remember why it's so important to you and that you'll soon be studying a subject you love.

GOING FOR A MINOR

If there is an additional area of study that you find yourself interested in but don't have the time to pursue as a major, why not go for a minor? I'm studying graphic design, but I also enjoy writing, so I've decided to minor in creative writing. I was writing so much in my free time that I thought, "Why not get credit for it?"

It is also possible that if you've taken lots of classes in a specific area (i.e., if you changed majors halfway through), you may end up with enough credits or close to enough credits to minor in that topic. My older brother was surprised to find out his senior year that he had enough credits to minor in history if he took one more class. No surprise, he decided to go for it. Having a minor shows ambition and well-roundedness to future employers or grad schools, and it can add fun and variety to your education.

THE END GOAL

Would you rather have a career that you love or finish school on time? Yes, doing both would be ideal, but sometimes that's just not realistic.

The real reason you go to college is to discover your life's path—but this doesn't happen overnight. In fact, on average, it usually takes a college student more than four years to graduate. So don't be afraid if you are going to have to stay a little bit longer to pursue a course of study that you are totally passionate about. Choosing a major is not easy, but once you have figured it out, you've already made a "major" accomplishment in discovering your path to success in college and in life.

Insights provided by Kathryn Lewis, University of North Carolina–Chapel Hill

F.I.N.A.L.S.: FUDGE, I NEVER ACTUALLY LEARNED SQUAT!

Make a list. Check it twice. Maybe three times. Maybe even four. Where did the semester go? Where did those simple days of just worrying about homework go? Times have changed, and all of a sudden you find yourself faced with those dreaded final exams.

HOW PREPARED ARE YOU?

One of the first things to take into consideration when studying for finals is what level of preparation you're starting from—how good of a note-taker you've been all semester and if you've been following the reading.

For the "I Love to Take Obsessive Notes/ I've Done All My Reading" Student

For those good note-takers out there, the obsessive-compulsive ones who write down everything the professors say, the challenge is narrowing things down. Grab that nice, big highlighter and your note-filled notebook and find a comfortable chair to curl up in. *It's time to power through it*. In getting started, first ask yourself, "What's on the exam?" If there's a list of terms or ideas or even chapters, make sure that, as you go through your notes, you're collating your lists and highlighting only the most important stuff. The next step depends on what you like to do. If you're one of those people who loves index cards with a passion—you know, one of those people who buys index cards in different colors, shapes, sizes, and maybe even with a spiral going through them—grab that stack of blank note cards and write out all the highlighted terms from your notebook.

Writing things down and rereading them again and again, at least three times, will immerse your

> **U CHIC Tip!**
>
> If your laptop is with you wherever you go, like mine is, open a Word document and *get cracking on retyping out the important sections of your notes*—a condensed crib sheet.

mind in the key terms and ideas you need to know. And before you know it, the knowledge you will need to ace the test will just be there.

For the "I Fell Asleep during Lecture/I Prefer Doodling to Notes" Student

For those of you who fell asleep on that severely uncomfortable wooden lecture desk or daydreamed about the boy sitting in the front row, or just forgot to write things down because you needed to finish that elaborate design on the corner of your spiral notebook, it might be a bit harder to catch up. But don't give up; it can be done.

Here's what you need to do to quickly get on track. Take whatever is left of your doodled notebook (or just get a new one), head to the library, and find the books you were supposed to read for class. Since you are short on time, there is no way you can read through all the required material in time for the exam. Not to worry. Actually, the worst thing you can do right now is to freak out.

Now that you know what might be on the exam (especially if your professor told you during a review session or handed you some sort of study guide), your catch-up reading can be *very* focused. Go through and skim the chapters that are relevant. Make sure to make good use of the table of contents and the index to focus your reading. Once you've read what you needed to and have taken some quality notes, start making a study guide.

Since you still might not be sure that you have all the notes you need, your best option is probably to opt for a study group. For a lot of people, the best way to learn is to explain concepts to your friends and classmates, and have them explained to you.

So, get your fellow classmates together—they'll likely come willingly, as they're already studying for the test, too. A good group session in the student union or outside (depending on the weather) is a perfect way to get a lot of work done in the precious few days (or even hours!) that you have to catch up before the exam.

SETTING GOALS

Reward yourself for a job well done—or just done. Setting goals and staying disciplined can help you avoid procrastination. I am less inclined to procrastinate when I know that I can go out to that party on Saturday night only if I have my final study guide ready. Also, let's face it: Facebook stalking and messaging friends is not as appealing as the reward at the end of the road.

Just tell yourself, if I finish reading through four chapters tonight, I can go meet my friend for coffee tomorrow.

IT'S OK TO TAKE A BREAK

A good study session involves some necessary breaks. Breaks can involve food, drink, and sometimes even a little fun. Sometimes the best study break is taking a moment, stepping away from the books and the computer, and blasting your favorite dancing tune of the week. It's like having a mini dance party. Close your eyes, dance your little heart away, and then get back to work. Jumping jacks also work.

> **DID YOU KNOW?**
>
> A 12-oz. coffee from your favorite nearby coffee shop could have *nearly as much caffeine* as a six-pack of 12-oz. Diet Coke.

When it comes to food, make sure to have a balance of healthy snacks and complete crap food. Proteins and healthy fats are a good way to start a long study session (a peanut butter sandwich on wheat bread is simple and healthy), but it's OK to throw in an apple or banana when you need that extra burst of energy.

When it comes to drinks, I know coffee is certainly a tempting option and so is that can of Monster or Red Bull staring down at you from your bookshelf. Resist. When it comes to coffee—and I am sure you've heard it a million times—the higher you climb, the harder you fall. It might give you that initial boost, but when you are trying to stay awake during your exam and the floor starts spinning, those cups of coffee won't seem like such a great idea anymore.

The best and most often underestimated option is actually water. Buy a massive bottle of water or two and just keep drinking it. If the liquid keeps going through your system, it will revitalize and keep you awake without the negative or counterproductive effects of caffeine or taurine, the stuff that gives you wings but turns you into a monster later.

FIND OUT HOW YOU STUDY

Alert, Alert! Tempting beds operating in your area! Move away from all pillows and couches immediately! Your safety depends on it…or at least your studying does.

Possibly the most important step in successfully studying for a final exam is finding out your study style. Study styles vary depending on what kind of learner you are and how well you remember important information. Your study style should determine how and where you choose to study.

One piece of advice that I feel definitely applies to everyone is to get out of your room! Don't fall into the trap of, "Oh I'll just read my sociology book in my bed, it's so comfortable." No matter how enthralling your world history or philosophy book is, reading about fascist dictators or the Socratic method will not keep you awake if you are surrounded by the cloud of your comforter. I'm not saying you won't fall asleep at the library, but most likely the wooden desk where your head would rest is not anywhere near as cushiony, soft, or inviting. If you fall asleep, you most likely won't be there for long.

Library

Your school's library is a good place to get some studying done. Not only are you surrounded by other students who share your study woes, but you are also surrounded by bookshelves. Even if you don't feel the need to grab one of those books for some extra prefinal reading, the sheer power of all of those books should inspire you to get down and dirty with your studies. The library might not be appealing to those who prefer to be invisible during finals time because it will be filled with people, but remember they are all there for the same reason. If you want a good balance between social life and intense studies, the library always works.

Loud/Social Areas

If you are one of those people who find silence way too quiet in a creepy kind of way, perhaps you should opt for a louder and more bustling study area. Sometimes a little

> **U**CHIC Tip!
>
> *How to make the library work?* First, some libraries have more social floors and areas that you can seek out when you head over with your laptop bag and a handy study buddy. Find a nice place to sit with your friends and once in a while stop to ask questions or maybe even chat a little. The best thing about bringing a study buddy with you is that you can pop out to take an ice cream break without having to completely pack up and get off track. You can leave your precious laptop with your trusty friend. When you're studying solo, head to the quieter floors or areas to get some serious studying done.

background commotion is all you need to actually get some work done. Head to a coffee shop or maybe even a student union hangout. There will be tons of people around and you can opt for some breaks while you are there without having to move an inch. Another benefit of this option is that you can eat while you work.

Studying with Others

Be forewarned: study buddies are not for everyone. A study buddy or even a study group can be a great thing for you, but if you are the type of person who wants to chat and socialize all the time, a study buddy could be distracting or disastrous.

Usually, a study buddy is a friend with whom you can get work done. He or she doesn't necessarily have to be in your class or even in your major, just someone you know you can be quiet with and bounce ideas off of as needed. If for some reason, you feel the need to go home or somewhere else to work on your own, don't feel obligated to stay with your friend. Finals are a stressful time and good friends understand. Studying together is not primarily a social activity, so they should not be offended if you have to leave for some quiet time.

U CHIC Tip!

Procrastinated writing your research paper or studying for a test? During your all-nighter, pass on the latte and hit your pillow for a power nap instead. Education.com reported on a study that found *power naps can be a more effective way of staying focused* and concentrating better. And if that isn't enough to sway you, according to the University of Georgia's Student Health Center, students who get seven to eight hours of sleep have higher GPAs than students who get six hours or less. Want to get more sleep? Experts say establishing regular sleep routines and avoiding caffeine at night can help.

Study Groups

Study groups tend to be a little more focused than a couple of study buddies sitting around together. Usually study groups involve people from your class and not necessarily close friends. This is great because you can delegate and divide up the studying work and share it with one another, teaching and learning at the same time without the major temptation to dish on the hottest gossip. Make a list of all the topics you need to know and get ready to divvy up the work. Everyone in the group should have some work to do and report back to everyone else—you can even make a group study guide out of the combined work and give a copy to each person. If you plan to work in a study group for finals, be sure to start way before finals so each group member gets a chance to review everything, and not just his or her part of the study guide.

DEALING WITH THE STRESS

If finals are around the corner, be prepared to accept the fact that it is going to be stressful. There's nothing that you can do about it besides accepting it and moving on; the worst thing you can do is stress about being stressed out.

There are many ways of dealing with finals stress, but some are better than others. The main idea is to take plenty of breaks. Try going to the gym or take the edge off with a swim. Really, any form of physical activity should do the trick. Don't think that exercise will make you tired and leave you too worn out to work. In fact, exercise does just the opposite. It releases endorphins that make you feel better and helps you be even more focused when you sit back down in front of your books.

As for other stress-relieving activities, some schools organize fun events during finals that help chase the stress bug away. Last winter, my friend Hillary and I went to an on-campus event for stressed students in the student union. It was a great idea. Students were getting free massages, taking breaks to play ping-pong with their friends, and much more. Keep your eyes open for similar opportunities on your campus. And if they're not there, seek off-campus ways to pamper yourself during finals, like getting a facial or manicure. The most important thing to remember when dealing with stress is that working too hard or too much might not always be the best strategy for getting a good score on your final exam. Sometimes, all you need is a break or good night's sleep to let all of your hard work sink in. After all, there is only so much you can do.

And the rest? It's up to karma, or something like that.

Insights provided by Olga Belogolova, Boston University

UCHIC ESSENTIALS—
HEAD OF THE CLASS

AIM FOR A WELL-BALANCED SCHEDULE
It's easy to try to take on too much and get overwhelmed. Work with your advisor to plan a balanced courseload so you can keep your stress under control and still enjoy everything that college has to offer.

FIGURE OUT HOW **YOU** WORK BEST
If you're a night owl who learns better when interacting with others, then avoid early morning classes and join a study group. Make an academic plan that supports your personal strengths, habits, and learning style, and you'll set yourself up for success!

REMEMBER TO THINK ABOUT THE BIG PICTURE
Love the classes you're currently taking in humanities? Consider how you can turn that love into a career. And don't be shy about asking professors, advisors, and alumni for advice. Always keep the big picture in mind, and you'll find what you were born to do after college.

Looking for more great advice? Head to UChic.com for even more resources and information—they come highly recommended from our contributors and editors. Be sure to leave your suggestions as well!

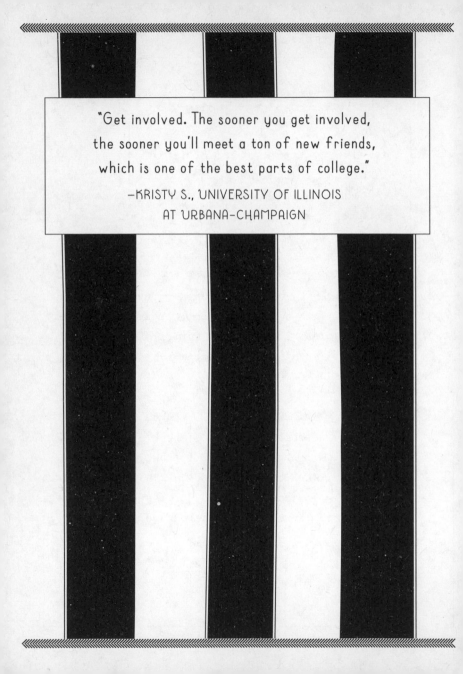

"Get involved. The sooner you get involved,
the sooner you'll meet a ton of new friends,
which is one of the best parts of college."

—KRISTY S., UNIVERSITY OF ILLINOIS
AT URBANA-CHAMPAIGN

4

GETTING INVOLVED

THE PREVIOUS CHAPTER FOCUSED on getting to the head of the class. Well, this chapter is about forgetting everything that was said in the previous chapter and focusing on how to have a life *outside of class*. Just kidding—don't forget *everything*! We just felt it was important to address your extracurricular life, which is equally important to your studies.

When it comes to getting involved in college, just follow your instinct. Find your niche—that special thing that you will do in college—and start it as soon as possible. By carving out time for that niche early on, you're ensuring that this will be a priority throughout your collegiate life, so when the going gets tough (like during finals), you know that you can always come back to your fave activities when the stress dies down. Also, by getting involved in extracurriculars early on, you're giving yourself additional opportunities to expand your horizons, possibly leading to great things like internships and even jobs as you get closer to graduation. Not to mention all the friends you'll make!

One word of caution: watch out for the "buffet effect." With everything that you have to choose from, you may have an urge to try everything and overindulge, so to speak. Don't. Getting involved in too many things can take you away from the main reason that you are in college in the first place—to get a great education. So get involved, but make sure not to put too much on your plate. Read on for some great insights on your life *outside of the classroom*!

DITCH THE DORM,
GET A LIFE!

During your tenure as a dorm dweller, you will be presented with myriad opportunities to socialize with others on your floor at parties, dances, movies, and outings. All these activities are fun, a great way to meet the other people you live with, and a perfect opportunity to relax after a busy week filled with tests and papers. Taking time to have fun is an extremely necessary part of school because, let's face it, you will burn out way before you complete your four or five years in higher education if you don't take time to just chill. Having said that, another vital and rewarding aspect of college life extends beyond the confines of the dormitory—get involved with something, either on campus or beyond.

PICKING UP STORIES AND GUYS

Johannah Cornblatt, Harvard University

When I walked into the newsroom of the *Harvard Crimson* the first day of my freshman year, I noticed instructions on how to open a document for a new story taped prominently on the wall. But after I saw a cute sophomore boy sitting at the desk across from mine, I pretended not to see the directions and, sweetly, solicited his help. I didn't play dumb for long, though. News editors quickly sent me to interview students around campus for a story on e-registration, a new feature (pretty standard these days) that allowed us to sign up for classes online. Halfway through writing my article back in the newsroom, I glanced up at the clock and realized I had missed dinner. Luckily, aforementioned cute sophomore had also lost track of the time. He asked me out to a burrito place across the street, and so began my years-long romance with my college boyfriend—and, that same night, my relationship with Harvard's daily newspaper. I'm definitely not the only *Crimson* editor guilty of what they call "Crimcest." You'd be amazed how good even the nerdiest Harvard boy looks when you're stuck laying out the paper together at 4 a.m.

While the *Crimson* can certainly spice up your love life, another big perk of working on the newspaper for me was the friends. I met two of my current roommates at the *Crimson* during the first week of our freshman year, and we've spent many a late night together in the newsroom since. One is now an executive editor like me, and the other, who writes a biweekly column, is now Harvard's Ann Coulter (although she notes that she's "not insane or anti-Semitic, only conserva-tive and blonde"). I remember how the three of us idolized the senior girls on the *Crimson* when we were freshmen, and it's funny seeing younger girls look up to us like that now. Friendships really cross class years at organizations like the *Crimson*, and girls who have graduated still keep in touch with us, offering advice on everything from boys to careers.

Whether it's for your own pleasure or to enhance your résumé, making an effort to venture beyond the dorm can enhance both your outlook on life and your curriculum vitae. Figuring out how to get involved in a student organization can seem daunting at first. Fear not: there are many tips and tricks to help you negotiate your way into having a fulfilling life outside of class. Branching out beyond the dorm will expose you to new people and activities.

WHERE TO START

When you're first exploring your options in the extracurricular field, think of what interests you. Is it playing a particular sport? Speaking a foreign language? Film noir? Bible study? Whatever it is, chances are there is a club in honor of it on your college campus. And if there isn't, you can always start one yourself. Because there are so many options in college, the difficulty will be in narrowing down the playing field to activities that really interest you.

If you need some help brainstorming what clubs might catch your fancy, here are a few ideas to get you started.

Are Grades Your Thing?

Does the thought of spending more time studying to achieve that latest A or honor make shivers of joy run down your spine? If this is you, consider applying to an on-campus honor society. Many departments have their own honor society or there can be one for an entire class such as Phi Eta Sigma, the honor society that academically inclined freshmen can join at the University of Washington (UW) after achieving a specific GPA and the required community service hours. The benefits of honor society membership are twofold: one, let's face it, they look great on a résumé. It shows that you aim high, achieve the goals you set, and are intelligent and disciplined. Second, your honor society peers are great study partners and the element of positive peer pressure can further your academic ambitions. Third, you may be required to devote time to community service in projects that are for good causes, which can get you out into the world and make you feel great about yourself.

FOR THE FUTURE MADAM PRESIDENT

Alexa Rozell, Georgetown University

You walk onto campus for the first time, ready to make a difference and ready to be a leader. But where to start? I was in your position when I first started college. I was interested in the student government association at my school, but I didn't know how to get involved. After a little bit of effort and seeking out the right connections, I became the chair of the Freshman Class Committee at Georgetown University. Thanks to this experience, I have a little advice to share that can help you access the halls of leadership on your campus.

GETTING INVOLVED IN STUDENT GOVERNMENT

Most universities offer students the opportunity to be involved in different branches of the student government, including the executive board, the senate, and spots on small committees that are dedicated to a single issue. The more public-oriented positions will require a campus-wide election. The smaller committees, on the other hand, are generally appointed positions, especially for freshmen. Don't be afraid to ask upperclassmen in student government at your school how they initially got involved and in what programs they would recommend that you participate.

The time commitment required by student government varies widely depending on the position. I regularly spend around seven hours a week for my Freshman Class chair duties, and I see other student body leaders spending many more hours in their offices. It is an amazing experience and extremely fun, but make sure you know what kind of time commitment you are looking at before you sign on for a project or position.

If you don't want a big commitment, there are many ways to get involved in behind-the-scenes capacities within student government. Class committees are a great example. Generally appointed by the current administration, class committees are responsible for planning events, conducting fund-raisers, and making sure that there is a strong camaraderie within their class.

RUNNING FOR OFFICE

If you're campaigning for student government, the first thing to do is make yourself visible to everyone on campus! Go to meetings of every club that you can, and introduce yourself to its members. Next, make your posters and fliers memorable. The most successful candidates are the ones whose fliers catch people's eyes or make them laugh. Be creative and daring with your ideas and slogans (but remember to keep them appropriate).

If you think you'll eventually want to run for president, you must be heavily involved in student government from the outset. Apply for an appointed position your freshman year, within the executive board if possible.

Being elected is about experience, vision, ideas, and having connections with as many different groups as you can. The entire student body elects you. That means that in order to win, people must believe that you care about all facets of the university, which can most easily be achieved by forging strong relationships with many different clubs and organizations that stand for different issues. Never underestimate the power an endorsement from another organization, or from other important student government leaders, can have on an election.

Even if you don't win, the experience of campaigning is one-of-a-kind and will shape the person you become in the future. Don't get discouraged if you lose a race or aren't appointed to the position you want. There is always time to work your way up through the organization, and every step of the way is a blast!

AND MOST IMPORTANT

Remember to have fun! Although student government can be demanding, it is extremely rewarding. Whether you launch an initiative to beautify campus through recycling or have free movies on Friday nights, you can see the effects of your work all around campus. If you are anything like me, you will catch the "student government bug" and want to be involved for all four years of college.

Do You Have a Deep-Seated Desire to Dive for a Frisbee while Others Give Chase and Tug at Your Jersey?

Or does soccer sound like the perfect way to bond with your fellow man or woman? If the answer is yes, it sounds like an intramural sports team or league is the way to go. These teams range from all-out competition where players vie for titles and trophies to weekend bowling leagues where teams compete for beers and bragging rights. You'll be able to find the level of play you're looking for, and if not, put up some fliers and start a team!

Do You Dream in Different Languages?

Fantasize about traveling to foreign lands? Indulge your inner wanderlust without having to pony up for a pesky passport. Foreign language clubs and language exchange programs are a great way to get immersed in a new language, brush up on skills carried over from your high school French class, and even help an exchange student practice his or her English.

Looking for Ways to Pursue Your Academic Interests with Extracurriculars?

If you're at a point in your studies where you have a good idea of what you'd like to major in, you can also check out meetings or gatherings in different academic departments. Many departments post their clubs and functions in student lounges and places within the department such as study and writing centers. You can also find out about many of these opportunities online.

Best thing about these get-togethers? You don't have to necessarily be a "declared major" to take part. Before I declared my major in English, I often took part in Castalia, a monthly gathering held by the English Department in which students and faculty listened to a group of selected graduate students read their latest works. Even before I was officially in the major, this was a fun way to get to know other undergrad and grad English majors while participating in a function held by the department that I was interested in joining.

ON- AND OFF-CAMPUS EXTRACURRICULARS

Other options for clubs and organizations, both on and off campus, include:

ON CAMPUS
- Student radio shows or newspapers
- Church groups or Bible study
- Student government
- Heritage-oriented clubs (Korean, Native American, African American, etc.)
- Photography
- Political clubs (Young Democrats, Young Republicans, etc.)
- On-campus magazines or journals
- Music groups (choir, jazz, a cappella, etc.)
- Spoken word, poetry slam
- Martial arts
- Lifestyle-focused clubs (vegan, cooking, etc.)

- Seasonal outdoor activities (snowboarding, wake-boarding, boating, etc.)
- Theater and improv groups
- TV show viewing clubs
- Nature clubs (camping, bird watching, saving the wetlands, preserving ocean beaches, etc.)
- Study-centric clubs (become a peer tutor in English, writing, math, or other subjects)
- Volunteer and advocacy groups (Habitat for Humanity, Voices for Planned Parenthood, PETA, etc.)
- Dance (swing, ballroom, etc.)
- Mentorship clubs (meeting with upperclassmen to talk and get their feedback and advice on the college experience)

OFF CAMPUS

- Volunteer as a docent at a museum or art gallery
- Serve as a mentor in a local chapter of the Boys & Girls Clubs
- Join a professional networking group based on your study area; for instance, communications or public relations majors can join the Public Relations Student Society of America (PRSSA). Many of these professional organizations require membership fees but offer lower rates for college students.

THE COMMITMENT

Wherever you think your passion lies, it's important to ask yourself if it's something that you are, indeed, passionate about and interested in. There are things you will tell others you are passionate about because they sound noble (volunteering to help children in Third World countries, for example), and then there are the things you truly love to do. Make sure that you don't neglect getting involved in something that goes into that "truly love to do" category. It will make you happier overall, and thus better able to succeed in and enjoy the other things you are involved in. Also, those activities you sign up for just because you truly enjoy them sometimes end up being the ones that look the best on your résumé—when you do things you are truly passionate about, you will be more willing and likely to rise to a leadership position.

WHY FOLLOWING YOUR INTERESTS MATTERS

Susan Fiorentino, Manhattan College

College is a time to find yourself. You will be around new people and have so many opportunities to try new things. Getting involved is an important way to discover your real interests and start finding your true self.

My freshman year of college, I began getting involved in numerous activities and meeting people who shared my same interests. I was a cheerleader, a coeditor of the communication department's newspaper, a Relay for Life committee member, and I also worked part-time for different departments and interned. Branching out of my comfort zone allowed me to meet people I probably would not have if I'd just stuck to the same kinds of activities or hung out with the same types of people that I did when I was in high school.

I met all different people with different ambitions and dreams, who over four years helped shape my own goals. Without even knowing it, I was building lifelong connections with peers who shared my interests and were looking to build a career from these interests, as well as with mentors who would support me in my own career.

When it comes time to start looking for jobs, it's important to know and communicate your personal brand—what sets you apart from the competition. Because I chose to follow my interests in college, by the time I was a senior I had a clear sense of myself as an ambitious go-getter—which I consider my personal brand. I was passionate about pursuing a career in the communications field for a health-care nonprofit, and I was determined to work for a particular organization. It took time, but I finally landed my dream job the summer after I graduated. And I know that I landed that opportunity because I got involved early on with activities that became building blocks to my personal brand, because I had the support of peers and mentors who helped me cultivate my brand, and because I was able to express my brand eloquently.

So when you're thinking about getting involved in activities in college, remember to be open to exploring new things, to follow your interests, and to always stay true to yourself. It could make all the difference later!

The caveat is to remember to take part in something that you genuinely believe you can commit time to, even if it's just for a few hours a week. If you have a busy schedule with other commitments such as sports or work, make sure that you take these activities into consideration when getting involved. Before getting committed to anything, you need to be fully aware of the expectations for group membership and whether you can meet them before getting involved.

Some groups are more dependent on attendance while others are more laid-back. For instance, to be part of a book club, reading the assigned book before the next meeting is required. If you didn't do the reading, you can't be a star discussion member. Activities like sports, band, and theater require a large, consistent time commitment. So when considering whether to take up a new activity, just make sure you will be able to juggle the timing in your hectic collegiate schedule. You don't want to leave anyone hanging if you're not able to make a meeting, but you also don't want to be needlessly stressed on top of your already busy days. Extracurricular activities are meant to be a fun, bonding experience, not an added stressor.

START YOUR OWN ORGANIZATION

If you've been looking at the opportunities on campus and you can't find an organization that you want to join, why not start your own? Just realize that starting an organization will be fairly time-consuming—you are going to have to find members and work to get the organization recognized (and funded) by the university. Chances are that if you are interested in an area and a club does not exist for it yet, it won't be that tough to find people who are looking for a similar organization.

Getting involved on campus may at first seem overwhelming, but joining a club or volunteer group, and being smart about your commitments and priorities, can greatly supplement your years at school. It's a great way to meet people that you might not meet in class or in the dorm and get exposed to activities that the dorm doesn't offer.

Insights provided by Anna Prestek, University of Washington–Seattle

MAKE A DIFFERENCE

Your résumé is filled with accomplishments: internships, accolades, stellar GPA, and skills galore. But no volunteer activities? Even if you're no Mother Teresa, you should be volunteering! College is known as an arena for opportunity, a place of forward thinking and innovation, free love and revolution. Although career advancement may be one reason for volunteering, there are many other reasons to commit to helping others.

Making a difference in someone's life, whether in your own community or somewhere else in the world, is a great way to experience something you've never done before while promoting social welfare. Also, the things you can learn while volunteering can translate into life and job skills that improve your chances for snagging an internship or job that you really want.

THE NEW WAY TO TRAVEL: VOLUNTOURISM

Ikee Gardner, Duke University

While students have always done study abroad, it seems like more and more of my friends in college have been choosing the volunteer route. In fact, I know girls who've done work in Mozambique, volunteered in South Africa, and rebuilt homes in New Orleans. It's called "voluntourism"— when people not originally from an area do a combination of tourist activities and volunteer work.

"I would do it again in a heartbeat. In fact, I probably will do it again," says Anita, a recent college grad, who volunteered in Belize last spring break. She helped rebuild a school, fixed and varnished furniture, put up drywall, and read to small children.

Where do voluntourists travel? Everywhere, from Uganda to France to New Orleans. Volunteers can do all kinds of activities depending on the location they choose—from building schools to teaching children English to working in wildlife preserves to working in hospitals and orphanages.

Traditional study-abroad programs usually offer academic credits toward graduation and/or a transcript from a foreign university. However, voluntourism has unique perks that you can't get from a study-abroad program.

First, voluntouring is often more affordable. Study-abroad programs include tuition for classes, which can add up to thousands of dollars. It's often possible to do month-long volunteer programs for under $1,000.

Voluntouring can give you a realistic perspective on what life is like for the less fortunate in a specific country. You can do your part to help out the rest of the world. "It's too easy to point to a poor neighborhood and say, 'Oh, isn't that sad,' and then go back to the hotel and back to the States without doing anything," says Itohan, a junior who went to Belize with Anita. "I have two working hands and feet—so in essence, I have no excuse not to help!"

Another great thing about voluntourism is that programs are usually coordinated for you by your school or by organizations that have staff members traveling with the group. You get to meet people, and you still get to be a tourist! Itohan and Anita both saw the Mayan ruins while they were in Belize. Volunteering doesn't mean that you don't get to have fun.

Is volunteering abroad right for you? Each program is different, so do your research and ask yourself if it's a good fit. If you're thinking of traveling to especially rural or remote areas, could you go to the bathroom on the ground or in grass? Could you live without electricity, hot water, phone, or Internet? If so, great! But if you can't live without a hot shower each morning, your makeup bag, and a cup of Starbucks, you might want to think again.

You should also ask yourself whether you have skills or capabilities to contribute in the place you want to volunteer. For example, if you want to teach children English, are you a good teacher? Do you work well with kids? If so, go for it. If not, check out a different voluntourism program where you can make use of your special talents and skills.

Want to be a voluntourist? Check out websites like www .crossculturalsolutions.org and www.volunteerinternational .org. Or just type "international volunteering" into Google and see what pops up. Happy traveling!

MAKING A DIFFERENCE IN YOUR OWN BACKYARD

While there are many people throughout the rest of the world who are in need of help, you will also find people who need a hand in your own community. To make a difference in the world, sometimes it's as easy as getting in a car or bus to travel to a different city in the United States. Check out AmeriCorps or City Year for some domestic volunteer opportunities.

Something as simple as putting a smile on someone's face can be very contagious and truly change that person's outlook on life. Try volunteering at your local soup kitchen or spending time with the sick or elderly. These are perfect opportunities to gain insight into who you are as an individual as well as the truth about the state of American life.

I was able to witness this firsthand while delivering greetings and flowers at a hospital. The power of a balloon or a "Get Well Soon" card is immeasurable. Also, volunteering at a hospital is a great opportunity for those of you planning to go to medical or nursing school.

No matter what you end up doing, the perspective you will gain while helping others will change your outlook on life. To find these opportunities, see what your college has to offer. Most campuses have a community service office (some are even student-run) that connects students with local volunteer opportunities.

NOURISH THE FUTURE

Try being a role model for a child who needs one. You remember what it was like when you were young and had so many questions about life. Now imagine a child without access to successful and secure adults to help guide them along.

Teaching, tutoring, or mentoring a child can make a major difference in his or her life. You can help decrease dropout and teen pregnancy rates. Girls have to deal with issues of self-image and sexual discovery at younger and younger ages. Help them understand what's happening and how to make the right decisions. Believe me—if you can handle the kids of today, then you can definitely deal with difficult coworkers in the future.

If you are looking to make a difference in a child's life, try the local chapter of the Boys & Girls Clubs of America or Teach for America, a two-year opportunity after graduation. Interested in law? Look into volunteering for CASA (Court Appointed Special Advocates—www.casaforchildren.org). The organization, which has grown to a network of more than 59,000 volunteers who serve 243,000 abused and neglected children nationwide, will train you to advocate on behalf of an abused child in a courtroom setting. This is an invaluable experience for someone interested in becoming a public interest lawyer.

SAVING MOTHER EARTH

You've heard it before: if we don't take efforts today to protect our precious ecosystem, the future does not look great for our children and the plants and animals with which we share this world. Try getting engaged in activities that help protect our planet. It can be as simple as setting up recycling in your dorm or sorority house, or even becoming an activist by canvassing for Greenpeace or urging your congressional representative to support legislation that protects the environment.

If you are more hands-on in your desire to save the planet, go out and get local businesses and organizations to plant trees. Or even try to make your next vacation environmentally safe by going to the beach and saving the turtles. Green is definitely the new pink!

SUPPORT AN IMPORTANT CAUSE

The people we meet in our lives can have a major influence on our futures and our decision to volunteer. If your mother has breast cancer or your grandfather is suffering from Alzheimer's, why not get involved in a cause that works to end these diseases? An added benefit: helping the causes that mean a lot to your family can also bring you closer together.

You can do little things like buying an awareness tag or make greater commitments, like volunteering at the March of Dimes or the local American Cancer Society office. You can share a special bond with your fellow participants through similar stories of survival and suffering. The passion and motivation it takes to pursue and uplift a cause will enhance your life in so many ways.

HAVE FUN

No matter what you do, add some fun to the mix by inviting your friends to

U CHIC Tip!

Volunteering with groups can be loads of fun. You get to see another side of your friends, and it can also be a great opportunity to make memories that will truly last a lifetime. I'll never forget shelving dented cans with friends at our local Salvation Army "Grocery Store" and getting rid of the outdated fashions in our closets. Family members especially make great volunteer companions, so suggest it for the next family reunion or when Mom is complaining that you don't spend enough time at home.

join you. Skip the spring break trip to Panama City and instead go with friends on a trip to California to work for Save the Whales. This experience still includes lots of sun and waves, and can offer much more as far as bonding is concerned.

You will also meet many new people you may have never run into otherwise when you choose to volunteer. Who knows, you may come out of a volunteer experience with an entirely new group of friends.

No matter what your background—whether you were born with a silver spoon or not—it's time to get out of your comfort zone to see how others live and think. Pushing yourself to do things you would normally shy away from will help you to gain perspective on what is really important in life.

Insights provided by Jessica Cruel, University of North Carolina—Chapel Hill

TIPS FOR THE BUSY
STUDENT ATHLETE

Student athletes live very different lives from the rest of the student body. From 6 a.m. lifting sessions to six-hour bus trips, time is precious for this segment of the population. Student athletes at every level must carefully balance their sports with academics, relationships, and their careers. It requires a huge commitment, but it also generates great rewards. Here are some tips for the busy student athlete looking to stay on top.

TIP 1: KNOW YOUR PRIORITIES

Life as a student athlete is different from that of the regular student. When you leave home you might think that you are "on your own" and completely free to do anything you can imagine, but that is not necessarily the case if you're playing college sports. Many times, coaches can be just as strict as parents. Like your parents, your coach is not going to want to hear that you've been in trouble for underage drinking or public drunkenness, or that your grades are falling. This is probably one of the most important aspects of being a student athlete. You have to respect what your coach tells you to do. He or she expects your all. Your team expects your all.

Also, understand that your school expects more from you than from the majority of the student body. You represent the university and are expected to act appropriately. This includes Facebook and partying. Be responsible, or your scholarship could be at stake.

TIP 2: ACADEMICS MATTER GREATLY

One of the most important aspects of being a student athlete is your grades. If your grades slip too low, you could be held on academic probation. The easiest way to avoid this is to simply go to class. I knew a girl who always waited until the last minute to get her assignments done. Her procrastination didn't pay off: she ended up with a GPA lower than the academic standards and got kicked off the team. It can happen to anyone, so be sure to keep your grades up. And remember, just like the NCAA commercial says, "Most college athletes go pro in something other than sports."

TAKE IT FROM A GIRL
WHO'S BEEN THERE

I quit playing soccer for my college team just after my junior year season had wrapped up. Every time people ask me why I quit with just one year left, I respond one of two ways: "It's not just the senior year season. It's the spring season. It's summer training. It's preseason. I just could not invest all my efforts into that single activity for one more year." Or, "There were too many opportunities I was missing out on. I just enjoy other things. I had a spring-term internship. I enjoy being active in a sorority, working on my school newspaper, and going on weekend vacations."

Do I regret playing college soccer? No; I had great team-mates and I needed the structure for the majority of my college career. There are no excuses for falling behind when you're on a tight student athlete's schedule, because you just can't. But eventually, I grew out of the desire to play every day, to attend numerous athletic events, and to be held back from other things. The sport I had played since age four had turned into an obligation, not a passion.

TIP 3: VALUE YOUR HEALTH

Make sure to get adequate sleep, eat healthy, and relax. This is important for your sport, but it is also important for your general health. If you don't sleep enough, your playing will suffer, your academics will suffer, and you will probably be upset. Athletes expend a lot of calories, so make sure you eat often and eat healthy. Relaxation is also important. Take the time to slow down and have some time to yourself.

TIP 4: HAVE FRIENDS BOTH ON AND OFF THE TEAM

There is much to be said about expanding your circle of friends. Since you spend so much of your time dedicated to sports, it can be a great stress relief to just chill with friends that have no connection to sports whatsoever. Having trouble meeting people? Join a club or two that meshes well with your practices, but be sure not to overload your schedule. Also, there is always the option of joining a sorority. Sororities, in general, are eager to recruit women that are actively involved on campus and in sports, and are, therefore, willing to work around a busy student athlete's schedule.

Now, I am not saying that you shouldn't be close with those on your team. Your team is practically your family, and with every family comes occasional drama and issues that develop. Cliques will form. But there is good news! You can be one of those rare people that is friends with everyone. Certainly, one can't avoid all conflicts, but it is possible to stay out of most petty arguments by simply refusing to feed into them.

TIP 5: ENJOY!

As a student athlete, your life may be stressful, but sometimes it helps to remember why you play the sport in the first place. As kids, we started playing sports for fun and friends. These two things should still matter most. And if they don't, you should think about doing something else.

Insights provided by Krista Naposki, Elon University
and Amanda Sandlin, Rider University

ŪCHIC ESSENTIALS— *GETTING INVOLVED*

COLLEGE IS YOUR TESTING GROUND

What you learn outside of the classroom can often be more important than what you learn inside. So get out, and get involved! College provides the best opportunity to explore new things, find out likes and dislikes, and test the skills that matter in the real world. It's important to get out of your comfort zone and build these experiences now.

GET SOME STRUCTURE IN PLACE—FAST!

Extracurriculars can help you structure your time outside of class. Busy students are often more productive because they have to be careful about how they manage their time. Plus, getting involved is a great way to meet new friends to hang out with in your spare time!

FOLLOW YOUR PASSION

Get involved in activities that come naturally to you and get you excited. Limit yourself to the few you enjoy most, so you'll be able to dedicate more time to them and make your involvement more meaningful. You might even be inspired to take an all-important leadership role.

Looking for more great advice? Head to UChic.com for even more resources and information—they come highly recommended from our contributors and editors. Be sure to leave your suggestions as well!

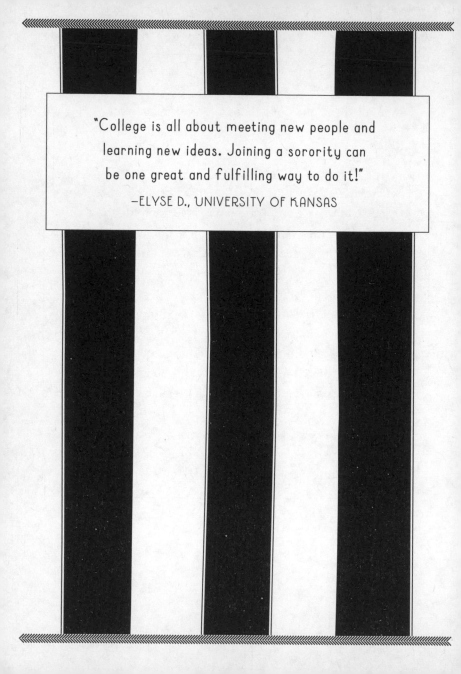

"College is all about meeting new people and learning new ideas. Joining a sorority can be one great and fulfilling way to do it!"

—ELYSE D., UNIVERSITY OF KANSAS

5

SORORITY CHIC

IS THE THOUGHT OF not knowing many people in college completely stressing you out? Or maybe you're trying to figure out how to get to know more people on campus. The important thing to remember is that you're not alone...pretty much everyone—at some point—is experiencing the same feelings. We've already covered several ways to break the ice and get to know people at your new home. One option we haven't covered in detail—and you're probably curious about!—is sorority membership. Known as "recruitment" or "rush," the formal process of joining a sorority is a great way to get to know a lot of people fast, even if you don't end up committing. From the recruitment process to knowing how to find a sorority that's right for you to the secrets of sisterhood—everything sorority—we've got you covered!

LIFE AS A GREEK

As an incoming college student, you probably have had minimal to no experience with sororities, and may be wondering what exactly they do. Is there anything more to it than partying? Yep. Before jumping into the nitty-gritty details of how joining a sorority works, here's an overview of what it means to be Greek, to help you decide if it's right for you.

CHARITABLE PURPOSES

Charity is a big part of any Greek organization, and for my organization, certain events are mandatory. It doesn't mean you get scolded if you cannot attend an event. These events are something we recognize as important to the survival and mission of the sorority. First, you'll most likely be expected to attend community service events. Usually, the sorority will host a philanthropic event like a walk or run, while some events are sponsored by the college. At my school, for example, the Kean University Greek Senate hosts the "Somerset Hills Holiday Party," where we do crafts with kids from a school. The Senate also hosts "Up 'til Dawn," which raises money for St. Jude's Children's Hospital. All Kean University organizations are required to have representatives attend these events whether it's the entire organization

or just two people. A lot of Greeks always show up to these events.
And why not? They're fun!

SOCIAL TIME

You've probably been curious about the social aspect. Being in a sorority does encourage you to be social not only within your own house
but with other Greeks and students at your university as well.

Most sororities have "mixers" with fraternities, which are parties
exclusively for that sorority and fraternity. Mixers are usually big
events, and for the most part, you'll probably be expected to go
(especially those during the recruitment season). In addition to these
mixers and meetings, there are other functions as well, like sisterhood
outings, cocktail parties, and formals that bring back memories of
high school prom. For the most part, these events are not mandatory.

Most colleges have Greek Week to encourage unity among Greeks
with events, outings, games, and on campus activities. At my school,
our version is the Greek Olympics. During the Greek Olympics,
organizations compete against one another for points in events like
softball, pool, basketball, tug-of-war, volleyball, and dodgeball. My
sorority ended up winning third place. It's not all about winning, but
it did feel good for us to get a Greek Olympics trophy for one of the
first times in recent years!

GPA REQUIREMENTS

Other sorority responsibilities include weekly chapter meetings and
having to keep up certain grade requirements. Yes, surprise! Most
sororities do have grade requirements for their members. Your Greek
system may have a minimum GPA of 2.3 or more to join a house!

Some houses may even consider your high school record when deciding to offer an invitation for membership. It makes sense: students who can't obtain satisfactory grades usually won't be able to balance the requirements of belonging to a Greek organization with their school activities. If your grades do meet the requirements to join, but for some reason you fall behind after pledging, your chapter may require that you complete a certain number of study hours per week. But every campus and house is different. It all depends.

MEETINGS AND OTHER ACTIVITIES

Most sororities have required weekly meetings to discuss upcoming events, fund-raisers, new ideas, or other important issues. These meetings are ones that cannot be missed. Besides the mandatory activities, it's entirely up to you how involved you want to be in your sorority. Some members are highly active while others may be less active for personal or financial reasons. When I first joined my sorority, I never imagined that I'd become vice president, later president, and then chosen as Greek Senate Sorority Sister of the Year! It all depends on how much you want to be involved and—like everything in life—your sorority experience will be what you make of it.

SISTERHOOD: A LIFELONG COMMITMENT

Miryam Chico, Kean University

I believe my sorority's motto truly encompasses what sisterhood means to me: "Unity and Sisterhood, Now and Forever, One and Inseparable." A sisterhood is a lifelong commitment and experience. It doesn't end when you graduate college. It's something you work at throughout your life, and gain immeasurable memories and relationships from. Sisterhood has allowed me to not only learn about a different group of women, but also to grow and learn from them. I've gained lifelong friendships that I would not have found elsewhere. Sisterhood has provided me with a network of people who share my joys and sorrows and also act as a source of encouragement and support.

THE FRATS

As previously mentioned, there will be several opportunities to "mix" with fraternity guys either through parties or some type of cohosted charity event. Some houses may even have a brother/sister relationship with one another where they "mix" often, team up for service projects, and support one another with recruitment and pledging.

As for the dating scene, as a Greek I've never dated a fraternity guy so I cannot speak from personal experience, but I have plenty of friends or sorority sisters who have. Based on what I've heard about my friends' experiences, there are some definite pros and cons to dating a fraternity guy.

One advantage of dating a fraternity guy is that you'll both understand what it means to be a Greek member. Some non-Greeks don't understand the reasoning behind all the weekly meetings and events, making it hard to have a relationship during the busy times. Your mutual commitment to being Greek is something that can strengthen your bond.

On the other hand, dating a frat guy can start to feel like overkill if Greek-related stuff is all you ever seem to talk about. And if you're prone to jealousy, keep in mind that your boyfriend's fraternity will have to mingle and sometimes network with girls in other sororities. You might want to also think about the future. For example, if you break up with the guy, what happens? As one sorority sister put it, "It can be as simple as a hookup with one guy from a fraternity to make it feel weird to mix or hang out with the entire fraternity."

Many girls feel like dating a frat guy goes hand in hand with being in a sorority, but it doesn't have to. If it works for you, great! But don't feel pressured to date or hook up with a frat guy if you think it's not for you or may cause problems in the long run.

SISTERS FOREVER

Being in a sorority is not like joining the softball team or choir or student government. While all of those activities are great, your strong attachment to them usually ends once you graduate college. Whereas, in a sorority, you're a sister forever, long after your responsibilities as a student end.

The Bond Forms as Soon as You Join

Many sororities and fraternities adopt the terms "big sister" and "little sister," or in my sorority we refer to it as just "big" and "little." And while the process for choosing little sisters differs from organization to organization, it has the same goal: ensuring that someone is there to guide a new member into the organization and beyond. In my house, everyone has a "big" who picked them when they were "little." And then once you are eligible for a "little," it's your turn to start the process again.

No matter what terminology you use, when picking a "little," you want someone you think you will get along with or have something in common with. When I picked my little, I liked that she was very motivated academically and she seemed to have an easygoing personality while being strong-minded. With time and a little effort, many big/little relationships have transcended college. Of course, not all big/little relationships will be close, but for many they are. In fact, for some girls, it's like having the older or younger sister they never had.

Networking Beyond College

Many girls benefit from alumni interaction. Even in a local sorority like mine, networking is extremely important. One of my alumni sisters was able to get an internship at a magazine, and later a job, through an affiliation with another alumni sister who worked at Time, Inc. Although alumni move on and develop careers and families and other obligations throughout life, a part of them feels a sense of loyalty to the sorority and even to sisters they may have never met. This most likely will be the same case for your sorority. So, don't hesitate to reach out to those who have come before you. They are there to lend a hand.

For me, sisterhood means a support system, a family away from home, and a group of girls who share common goals. Everyone is not the same and never will be, and in any organization, you are bound to be closer with some more than others. But if you stick it out through the good and the bad, your dedication will most likely result in an experience that will provide benefits to you throughout your lifetime.

Insights provided by Donyel L. Griffin, Kean University

GOING GREEK 101

I never planned to join a sorority. As soon as I entered Kean University as a curious freshman, a sorority began recruiting me, but I didn't bite because it didn't feel like it was for me. I spent my next two years of college without even thinking about Greek life. And then one day I realized I wanted to be more involved in my university, but I wanted something more than joining a club or a group. I suddenly decided that I wanted to go Greek.

GREEK SPEAK

A list of definitions that may come in handy if you are considering Greek membership.

ALUMNA/ALUMNUS—Sister or brother of an organization who has graduated.

BID—An exclusive invitation given to individuals who are asked to join the sorority.

BIG SISTER/BIG BROTHER—A member of an organization who

guides/directs a new member through and/or after the new-member process.

EXECUTIVE BOARD—Commonly referred to as both the E-Board or Leader's Council. Typically, this board includes a sorority or fraternity's president, vice president, rush, and social chairs, etc.

GREEKS—The name given to members of sororities and fraternities, which they use to identify themselves by combinations of Greek letters.

INITIATION—A special event or ceremony for new pledges that officially kicks off their membership in the sorority.

LEGACY—A potential new member who is closely related to a woman with membership in a national Panhellenic member sorority. The definition of a legacy varies from sorority to sorority, but it almost always includes a woman whose mother, sister, or grandmother was a member of a particular sorority. Legacies are usually given special consideration for membership, but sororities are not required to invite them to membership.

MUTUAL SELECTION—The process during membership recruitment when the sorority members seek the women who will best enhance their sisterhood and the potential new members determine which sorority will be the best fit for them.

PANHELLENIC COUNCIL—The governing body that controls all sororities and fraternities on campus. Panhellenic officers make all the rules and take action when a sorority or fraternity steps out of line. Members are often made up of executive officers from the many Greek organizations that reside at a specific college or university.

PIN—New sorority members are given a pin to wear that designates them as a member of the sorority. Typically, you receive this pin during an official ceremony.

PLEDGES—New members who have accepted their bids, but have not yet been initiated into the sorority.

PRETTY PLAYBOOK—The rules or guidelines on what to wear during rush. Usually sororities will hand out fliers or post instructions on their websites or Facebook pages to help guide you on what is appropriate for each event.

QUOTA—The number of women to which a sorority can offer a bid during recruitment. This number is defined by the Panhellenic Council.

RECRUITMENT COUNSELOR (RC OR RHO CHI)—Formerly known as rush counselors, these are sorority women who disaffiliate with their own chapters during recruitment in order to help the potential new members with the selection process. They offer impartial support and answer questions during membership recruitment.

RECRUITMENT WEEK—Also known as "rush week." This is when potential members attend parties and meet the sisters of each sorority.

RUSHEE OR POTENTIAL NEW MEMBER—A term used to designate potential members.

SISTERHOOD/BROTHERHOOD—The act of behaving as a family of sisters/brothers.

SOCIALS—Also known as mixers, these are themed parties held by various Greek chapters.

SYMBOLS—A sorority or fraternity's symbol is unique to each organization and has significant meaning to the organization. Often the meaning behind the symbol is kept confidential and known only by the members of that sorority or fraternity.

During my junior year, I was in two classes with a girl who was a member of Lambda Chi Rho, a local sorority founded in 1962 at Kean University. After getting to know her and realizing that not all sororities were obsessed with drinking and partying nonstop (the stereotype we all know) and were actually very diverse, I started attending Lambda Chi Rho recruitment events.

During my rush process, they had open teas or "interest meetings," where we did things like make collages from magazine clippings, throw a Halloween party, make ornaments for a nursing home, and have a mixer with a fraternity. These events helped me see that a sorority could be well-rounded and that I could have fun doing even the simplest things with my potential sisters.

At the end of each interest meeting, the sorority members would ask us recruits if we had any questions about the sorority or Greek life, providing us a platform to express any concerns or raise any questions we had. Having an open forum to ask questions made me feel more comfortable with the current members and with the idea of getting involved with the sorority. As the recruitment process went on, I felt more and more comfortable; Lambda Chi Rho just felt like a good fit. I received a bid and decided to join. It turned out to be a great decision.

If you're considering Greek life, there's a lot to know about how the recruitment process works and what to expect once you've joined. The following advice will guide you through all the ins and outs of going Greek.

FINDING THE RIGHT FIT

Before diving into any formal or informal recruitment process, it's worth putting some thought into what type of sorority you'd like to join. During this process, be sure to seek an organization that focuses on your desires. Do you want a more academic-oriented sorority or one that is more focused on social life? While all organizations must maintain a balance among social, academic, and service in order to survive on campus, some focus on one more than the others.

Go to events at several different sororities and feel out the girls. You want to make sure you like your potential future sisters. It's not enough to join because you know a few people in the house; make sure you can deal with the company of the rest.

FACTORS TO CONSIDER WHEN CHOOSING A SORORITY

How Social Are You?

U CHIC Tip!

If you have a family member who is an alumna of a sorority that you're thinking of joining, call her up! She can give you more details on what it is like to be a member, and she may be able to help you through the rush process by sending a letter to the chapter on your behalf. *Many sororities will take alumnae connections (especially if your mom belonged) into consideration* when making bids. If you aren't a legacy, no worries. These ties will not make or break your chance to become a member.

You will discover that some sororities have more of a reputation for partying than for hitting the books. Now, of course, not every member will fit these stereotypes. But in most cases, the reputation of the house tends to prove true. If you're the honor-roll type and need to go out just once a week to be satisfied, you may find yourself the lone advocate for moderation. And the same goes for the more social gals. Joining an "honor-roll house" may not be the perfect fit for someone needing friends who have an active social calendar.

Are You a Perfectionista?

Some houses aspire to be at the top of everything: top grades, top number of charity hours, top intramural teams, top awards at the annual Greek Award ceremony, etc. If you're the perfectionist type, then these houses are probably a good fit for you. Just remember that you may be asked to commit a little more time than usual to sorority activities, and the expectations on you may be higher.

Are All the Members from the Same High School or City?

It's not unusual for a particular sorority to have several members from the same city or high school—friends recruit friends. If you are in the minority—let's say that you're from a public school in Chicago while the rest of the house is from a top private school in St. Louis—you may feel a little out of the loop. But it all depends. A go-with-the-flow personality will have no trouble fitting in while others may be happier with a little more diversity.

Do You Want a "Popular" House?

If you're leaning toward membership in a particular house for no other apparent reason than it's known for being a good one at your school, fugettaboutit! There is no such thing as a good versus bad house. A sorority will be "good" as long as it's a good fit for you. Focus first on where you feel most comfortable (after all, you'll be spending a lot of time with these ladies). If you're paying attention during the recruitment process, you'll know which houses feel like a comfortable fit, and you'll be less likely to be taken with the "popularity factor" when making this important decision.

Bottom line: if you want to join a sorority, do so for the right reasons—*your* reasons. Don't join something because it sounds good or your friends think you should do so. If you don't follow your gut instinct, you'll end up unhappy with your decision, maybe even dropping out. Don't let this be you. There is almost always a place for everyone who wants to join.

HOW TO LOOK YOUR BEST DURING SORORITY RECRUITMENT

While there are no universal, hard-and-fast rules as to what you should wear, here are some general guidelines on how to look your best without giving off the wrong impression.

YOU'RE RUSHING A SORORITY

I know what you're thinking. "Duh. That's why I'm reading this." But honestly, I can't emphasize this enough—you're not going to a frat party, or a club, or even looking to snag a hot guy. There's no need to show off a ton of cleavage or wear a short skirt that makes your butt look amazing. Just remember, you're trying to impress girls with style—not the male ego. Think pretty, *not* sexy. Also, the little details like manis and pedis *do* count.

YES, THERE ARE LEVELS OF FASHION FORMALITY TO FOLLOW

This may vary at your school, but typically rush starts out casual and gets more formal as the events progress. Jeans will probably work for the first event, and T-shirts might even be provided. Second invites usually require casual sundresses or a nice skirt, while the third invite is typically the most dressy (a cocktail-type number might be required).

TRUST US, MONEY ISN'T EVERYTHING

If you're in love with your oh-so-expensive True Religion jeans and feel the need to wear them for rush, go for it. If you feel more confident and comfortable in your favorite pair of Levi's 501s, that's totally fine too. Don't blow a ton of money on an expensive new dress in an attempt to impress. Just choose what you think best represents your style and personality.

ACCESSORIZE, ACCESSORIZE, ACCESSORIZE!

The members of the sorority chapter who you'll be meeting and chatting with see a ton (like *hundreds*) of girls each day. Outfits start to blend together, and in a time when chain retail stores are everywhere, not everyone can have an original ensemble. That's why it's absolutely *critical* to accessorize with pieces to highlight your unique look and show off your personality and style.

Warning: Don't plan on accessorizing with purses or clutches. These are typically left outside or in a closet during rush for safekeeping.

CHOOSE CLOTHES THAT MAKE YOU LOOK AND FEEL GOOD

So much of what goes into being chic isn't about having the "right" pair of jeans or even the cutest dress—it's about wearing something that makes you look your best. Don't try to squeeze into a size 2 skirt if a size 4 or 6 actually fits you better. Just pick out something that makes you feel good about yourself. That alone should make other people want to know where you got all that confidence (and style!).

HOW TO JOIN

Organizations vary in requirements for membership, but usually you must take part in a recruitment process or "rush" first, which consists of events organized by the sorority to help you get to know them better and vice versa. Each college and university has a timetable for the official recruitment process. Check your school's website or Greek life directory to get this information. Also, be aware that some chapters have an informal process as well that occurs at a different time of the year.

The Formal Recruitment Process

Formal recruitment is different at every school and in some cases every sorority. Some schools have a week set aside—sometimes before school begins in the fall—where all Greeks get to recruit new members. Other schools may extend the process over a two- to three-week time period. Large universities will require everyone who is interested in joining a fraternity or sorority to sign up with the interfraternity council at the university. Once the recruitment process begins, each potential recruit is required to visit every sorority at least once to talk to them and find out what they're about. Schools require this in order to make the process more fair; the hope is that by seeing each sorority and witnessing the diversity among the houses, you, as a potential recruit, will choose a house based on personal preferences rather than joining a house because someone told you to.

Typically, the formal recruitment process is broken into the following stages:

- **First round—open house:** The first round is an "open house" where you, the potential new member (PNM), get to visit all of the sorority houses on campus. This is an informal opportunity to meet women from all the sororities, and it can sometimes take two days if there are a large number of sororities at your school. At the end of the round, you get to select a number of sororities you would like to visit again. The sororities also select the PNMs they would like to return to their home. The Panhellenic Council (Panhel) brings all this information together and generates a list of invitations for each PNM for the next round.

> **U**CHIC Tip!
>
> Preparing for sorority recruitment? It's not uncommon for sorority members to check out potential new members' Facebook profiles to see how you represent yourself when you think nobody's looking, and how you will represent their sorority if you're asked to join. *Ensuring that your social media presence best portrays your ideas, beliefs, and plans for the future is important.* See Chapter 6, Tech Essentials for an Instagram Age, for more tips on managing your digital reputation.

- **Second round—skits:** The second round usually features skits that each sorority prepares to show the PNMs what life is like at their chapter. After you visit all the sororities to which you were

invited back, you again narrow down the list to your favorite ones.
The sororities also narrow down their list of their favorite PNMs.
Panhel once again tabulates the information and generates the
invitation lists for the next round.

- **Third round—philanthropy:** Whew! You're almost done. Each
  sorority has a national philanthropy in which they actively
  participate. During the third round, you will spend time doing
  something that is related to their philanthropy. It usually involves
  crafts or making something and is a casual activity. It is also a
  great time to get to know more of the sisters in each house while
  talking informally. Once complete, you will go through another
  round of narrowing down your list to your faves and the sororities
  will do the same. Panhel tabulates the information, generating an
  invitation to the last round of recruitment.

- **Fourth round—preference:** Now that you've visited all the houses
  and narrowed down your list, you're ready for the fourth and final
  round—"preference." This is a more formal and ceremonial round,
  and everyone will be dressed up. This round usually involves a ritual-
  like ceremony that speaks more meaningfully about the sorority,
  sisterhood, and the sorority's symbols. After attending all the
  preference parties, the PNMs and sororities once again must make
  their decisions. The mutual selection process ends when Panhel
  matches the PNMs and sororities according to the lists provided by
  each. But you're not done yet!

- **Bid day:** The day has arrived when you finally get to find out
  which sorority has selected you! Typically, the PNMs will all
  gather in one location and receive an envelope that includes the
  name of the sorority to which you've been matched. Once you

UCHIC Tip!

Be careful about looking like you're "shopping" too much for the right sorority. Sometimes your indecisiveness, if witnessed by members of a house that you've expressed interest in, can make them second-guess your true interest in their sorority and may affect your chances of getting a bid from them later.

open your bid and know the results, you are then dismissed to find your new sisters. Afterward, you will participate in a pledging ceremony, and an initiation period will soon follow, during which you will be educated in the history and background of the group and become integrated into the sorority. During this period, you will most likely become very close to members of your pledge class, as you work through the steps toward becoming an initiated member of the house.

If You Don't Get a Bid

You might not get an invitation back to your house of choice, or to any houses. If this happens to you, do not take this as a rejection. They're not rejecting "you"; they don't even really know you. There could be any number of reasons why you didn't receive a bid. Maybe your GPA didn't meet the minimum requirements, or there were going to be too many schedule conflicts due to your involvement in other activities. Or maybe it was a factor out of your control, like the number of legacies (women whose family members belonged to the sorority) they gave preference to. Whatever the case, don't take it personally, and don't dwell on the rush process as a negative experience. If you don't receive a bid during formal recruitment, you still have options.

Informal or Open Recruitment

Often after formal recruitment, some chapters will still have open spots and can extend bids. Also, some sororities may "snap bid" the women they want and will not announce that they are still recruiting new members. Other sororities will hold informal recruitment activities in the following days or weeks in order to meet potential new members, even those who didn't go through formal recruitment. It's important to note that not all sororities will be able to participate in open recruitment, as they've already met their quotas, leaving you with fewer chapters from which to choose. But for women who want to join a sorority and are willing to be open-minded about their options, open and informal recruitment can provide another opportunity to join a sorority that year.

Unlike the formal recruitment process, which is typically organized by the university, informal recruitment happens when you befriend members of a sorority outside of the formal period of recruitment. Usually, girls going through informal recruitment were interested in a sorority but did not have the time to pledge that semester, or changed their mind on membership and have expressed an interest in Greek life.

Typically if you are hanging out with members of a sorority— like going to the movies or hanging out at their house—you are participating in the informal recruitment process. There are no time constraints on informal recruitment. The goal with informal recruitment is simply to provide another opportunity for girls who did not participate in formal recruitment, whatever the reason.

Try Again

You can also choose to wait another year and try again at the next formal recruitment. This can work well for women who had a low high school GPA, which hurt them with sororities that had to cut based on higher GPA requirements. If you get better grades your freshman year, you will greatly increase your chances of being able to join a sorority. Another bonus of waiting another year: you get the opportunity to network on campus, potentially meeting and making friends with current sorority members. This can be an asset when going through recruitment next year, since being known (in a good way, of course!) can make a potential new member more attractive to sorority members. One word of caution: if the sororities on your campus are known for extending bids primarily to freshmen, being a sophomore can make it almost impossible to get a bid. As this varies widely from campus to campus, it's important to do your research and know what the options are for rushing as a sophomore or junior.

TAKE IT FROM A GIRL WHO'S BEEN THERE

Even if you're pretty certain Greek life is for you, consider waiting until spring of your freshman year or even your sophomore year to join, if that's an option at your school. I waited until the spring to rush, and looking back, I'm glad I did. Remaining independent for my first semester really allowed me to settle in and figure out who I was before I joined a sorority.

Start a New Sorority on Campus

Avoid going through the recruitment process altogether by starting your own sorority! As you can imagine, starting a sorority is a lot of work and takes a tremendous amount of time and commitment. Also, there are no guarantees it will be a success or that the group will be able to eventually affiliate with a national group. But it is always an option and one to consider if you're a natural born leader.

Embrace the Independent Life

While there are benefits to sorority membership, there are also many other ways to be involved on campus, as you read about earlier in this book. The last option if you didn't receive a bid is to choose to be a proud and happy independent. Explore what else is out there, and you're sure to find new interests, passions, and friends that will make your campus life a fun and fulfilling experience.

PLEDGING

If you receive a bid, it is then up to you to decide which sorority or house fits you best and accept one of the offers of membership.

Once you accept a bid, there will be a new member education process, also known as pledging. Pledging differs from organization to organization, but you can expect to be assigned a "big sister" or "big"—a current member who will serve as your mentor throughout the pledging process. Be aware that going through the pledge process can get frustrating at times, because it can go on for several weeks and will likely take some of your time away from school. If you already have a full schedule, you should find out details of each house's pledging process during recruitment, to make sure that it's worth the time and commitment in order to become a member.

Although it can be time consuming, pledging is important because it bonds you to the other women who are in your pledge class, helping you learn the values, history, and traditions of the sorority. I had two pledge sisters whom I became very close with during the process and they are still good friends today. A pledge sister or brother is the term used most often for mainstream sororities and fraternities, while traditionally African American, Hispanic, and multicultural organizations refer to the people they go through the process with as a "line sister" or "line brother."

Many sororities have taken an educational approach to pledging than making you do silly or harmful things. When I pledged my sorority, there was a lot of tradition, history, and education that I had to learn during the pledging process. I was never forced to drink, walk around in the woods blindfolded, or do anything else that caused me mental or physical harm. You too should be able to have the same positive experience. If not, then it's time to say something to the house leadership or even take your complaint to school administrators. College officials have been enforcing strict rules and punishments to eliminate hazing from the Greek system. In some cases, you may have to speak up for a friend who is being mistreated. Don't be afraid to drop out of a house that is involved in hazing. No one should have to put up with mistreatment of any kind in order to join any organization.

Finally, don't let the uncertainties of the entire recruitment and pledging process prevent you from considering sorority membership. Remember, everyone else is in the same boat. Until you are a member you will not be able to completely understand the entire system and truly appreciate it for what it is.

SORORITY FEES AND EXPENSES

For years one of my friends would say that she'd never join a sorority because she wouldn't "pay for friends." Back then, I agreed with her, although I never put down any of my roommates or acquaintances who were in a sorority. However, after joining, I came to realize that the money you pay is not "for friends" but for financial expenses the sorority will incur for the year.

Sororities have a treasury and treasurer (who is usually on the executive board) who oversees finances. Money from the treasury is usually applied to fund-raisers, recruitment events and T-shirts, "Meet the Greeks"-type campus activities, or other important events. Also, chapters of national sororities pay dues to their national headquarters. National organizations have hundreds of chapters nation- and world-wide, and are basically run like a business at the headquarters level.

Budgeting is very important to maintaining a sorority member-ship. My sorority has payment plans for girls who cannot afford the dues in total, as we all understand that other school expenses can make it difficult to pay at times. In fact, sometimes we will even pay for another sister's dues when she cannot afford it for whatever reason, because, after all, we are a sisterhood and really do feel like family.

LIVING ARRANGEMENTS

A sorority or fraternity house is the house of the organization and is usually located somewhere near the university. Some of these houses are merely for meetings and administrative purposes; other houses are actual homes where members are expected to live at some point in their college careers (usually sophomore and junior year). Some houses can only hold twenty members while some go up to one hundred! At big colleges and universities, recruitment events and bid day are held at the sorority house. However, some schools don't have sorority houses, so the members will instead take up a couple of floors in a dormitory building or apartment complex. The reason for the closeness is because members benefit when they can interact with one another on issues pertaining to the sorority and have meetings and access to one another.

Keep in mind that just because you've joined a sorority does not mean that you have to live in the same house or floor as your sisters. Usually, you will have options for where you live. At my college, there isn't a frat row (an area typical of some colleges where the entire street is lined with sorority and fraternity houses) or an area specifically for Greek housing. However, I know many members of different Greek organizations who have rented or bought their own houses around the college, and it serves as their unofficial "house."

FINAL WORD

So after it's all said and done, is a sorority for you? Even if you're not sure about it but are still curious, go through the recruitment process to try it out. And don't feel pressured to rush a sorority when you first arrive on campus. You're in college to learn, grow, and explore. If joining a sorority is an important part of the collegiate experience for you, then great! If not, that's great too! Seize the moment when you feel it is right. If you don't meet the sorority of your dreams your freshman year, you may discover it later on in college like I did. Best advice I can give: always keep your options open.

Insights provided by Donyel L. Griffin, Kean University

UCHIC ESSENTIALS— *SORORITY CHIC*

FORGET THE STEREOTYPES
Leave the stereotypes about Greek life at the door. Within each sorority, you'll find a diverse group of women from a variety of backgrounds and with different interests. Really, there is no such thing as a cookie-cutter sorority.

TEAM UP AND MAKE A DIFFERENCE
Philanthropy is a central aspect of Greek life that is often overlooked. By joining a sorority, you'll have opportunities to get involved with charities, volunteer, and mentor younger students, first as a big sister and later as an alumna, making sisterhood a truly rewarding experience.

AND YES, GREEK LIFE IS NOT FOR EVERYONE
If after speaking with friends who are sorority members or even going through recruitment you still are questioning whether you should join a house, it may not be the right thing for you. And guess what: that's OK! There are plenty of other things for you to get involved with in college.

Looking for more great advice? Head to UChic.com for even more resources and information—they come highly recommended from our contributors and editors. Be sure to leave your suggestions as well!

"The easiest way to feel at home in your living environment is to be outgoing, introducing yourself to new people and new things, and social media is a great way to quickly get connected. Just be smart about how you do it!"

—COLLEEN M., UNIVERSITY OF CENTRAL FLORIDA

6

TECH ESSENTIALS FOR AN INSTAGRAM AGE

"WILL THOSE PARTY PICS I'm tagged in come back to haunt me someday?" "Am I spending too much time on social media?" "Am I an addict?" Do any of these questions sound familiar?

With smartphones, Twitter, and Snapchat (we could go on), socializing is a whole lot easier these days. But it's also a lot easier for the comments and photos you're sharing—or things other people are posting about you—to get out of hand. And your digital reputation is at stake! You also don't want to get so caught up in social media that you forget the importance of in-person interaction every now and then.

To provide some much-needed rules of engagement, read on for some fail-safe tech essentials for an Instagram age.

HOW TO PROTECT
YOUR DIGITAL
REPUTATION

Get a ton of likes on your newest tweet, status update, or Instagram pic? Congrats—you've got the social media space mastered. What about your online reputation: How is that faring these days? Uh…

In this day and age, we're all about digital media. In fact, we were practically born and bred with an object of digital media in our hands. Growing up in the digital age has been a double-edged sword. On the one hand, we've been able to create the World Wide Web—a.k.a. the Internet—which has been a huge resource we use in our daily lives, from getting our news for *free* to receiving emails and conducting research for schoolwork. On the other hand, some people abuse the Internet and engage in criminal activity. Now more than ever, the digital age has caused us to be less social in real life and more social online. And because it's so easy to post things without a second thought, it can also be *extremely* dangerous to your reputation and can quickly come back to haunt you. Think about all of those celebrities who've had to delete their social accounts because they tweeted out an inappropriate comment or posted something embarrassing on Facebook.

In college, it's essential to have social profiles like Facebook, Twitter, and even Instagram. It's how you find out about everything—parties, classes being cancelled, or the events that are happening around campus. It's become a part of the daily morning routine: wake up, check your social networks to see what happened while you were sleeping, and *then* it's time to start your day. It takes two seconds to tweet a news story that can reach millions of people. And anyone who wants to interact with us has to be online too. More

> ## DID YOU KNOW?
>
> CNN reports that a recent Microsoft survey found that *70 percent of job recruiters and hiring managers have rejected a job applicant based on information they found online.* What kind of information? "Inappropriate" comments by the candidate; "unsuitable" photos and videos; criticisms of previous employers, coworkers, or clients; and even inappropriate comments by friends and relatives, according to the survey report, titled *Online Reputation in a Connected World.*

and more universities and colleges are creating social media profiles to appeal to prospective students. Institutions can contact potential candidates by inviting them through email, connecting with them on Facebook, following them on Twitter, and coordinating live Google+ Hangout chats and events.

THE LATEST APPS SWEEPING COLLEGE CAMPUSES

Ashley Yenick, Merrimack College

For today's college student, social media is a universal language. The evolution of technology has changed how we interact and socialize. Now, we can instantaneously see what our friends are up to...as long as they share it with us. Here are some apps that all students need to have on their radar.

NEW APPS = NEW SOCIAL LIFE

If you didn't Snapchat that wild party on campus, did it actually happen? Social media apps like Snapchat, Twitter, and Instagram help us connect with friends, maintain long-distance relationships, or catch up on the latest event happening on campus. Being social media savvy brings people closer, showing that you can have a supportive #squad no matter the distance!

SWIPING LEFT OR RIGHT: THE ADVENTURES OF ONLINE DATING

Online dating apps can help you find love—or entertainment. Personally speaking, online dating apps made my love life worse! When I was using Tinder on campus, I'd swipe left on a guy and then see him ten minutes later...talk about awkward! However, I have friends that have found boyfriends on Tinder, and they're still happily together. In terms of online dating, it comes down to how comfortable you are pushing yourself out of your comfort zone.

THE ANONYMOUS (OR NOT) YIK YAK

Yik Yak is taking over college campuses. It's a way for students to communicate with one another (anonymously or not) and bond over the shenanigans that happen on campus. When you get votes on the "yaks" you make, it's validation that you're right—there's no harm in that, right?

One of the tidbits of information that people tend to forget is that a social profile can be viewed by everyone. Admissions officers and potential employers search for your name online now as a test to see what information they can find on you. Concerned about what they may find? Even if you aren't, you can never start too early to begin protecting your digital reputation. Because once you lose it, it can be very hard to get it back. Here are some quick tips to help you protect your digital reputation and keep your image squeaky clean in college and beyond.

SEARCH YOUR NAME ON GOOGLE

Searching your name on Google is the first step to assessing your digital reputation. Is there an old social media profile you are no longer using? Delete it. Embarrassing Facebook photos? Untag yourself. A simple search of your name (and any nicknames or social profile names you use) gives you an idea on where you're at in terms of having a great online reputation. Google has the ability to search for things all the way back to when you created your first social profile. Wow. Also don't forget those times your name may have been tagged by a friend in a post or photo; those images might

UCHIC Tip!

*Use Twitter's privacy settings differ-
ently from how you use Facebook's.*
For instance, if you make the tweets
protected, only your friends can see
them and that really limits your ability to network online, which is your
primary reason for being on Twitter.

be there too! You have to search first to know what you're dealing with.

MAKE ALL SOCIAL MEDIA PROFILES PRIVATE

Making every single profile that you have private is ultimately how you can also clean up your reputation. You can usually find privacy features in the "settings" section of social media websites. Having your profiles set to private gives you extra protection of your digital reputation. Keep in mind that although your profile may be set to private, people may still be able to see some basic information on your profile.

NEVER POST PERSONAL INFORMATION

When writing blog posts or posting Facebook statuses, tweets, or Instagram pictures, you have the option of adding your *location*. This feature is great exposure and advertising for the establishment that you're at. It can also tell people where you're located at any moment, potentially exposing you to predators who want to find you. Be safe and don't post your location! Also, please please please do not post your class schedule or any other sensitive information regarding your personal life on your social media profiles.

PROTECTING YOURSELF
FROM IDENTITY THEFT

Megan O'Connell, University of Wisconsin–Platteville

College is a time in your life where you will be giving out a lot of important information to a lot of different sources from banks to schools to loan companies. Giving out sensitive information can lead to trouble if you don't take precautions. For instance, if this information falls into the wrong hands, thieves can use it to steal your identity, leading to debt you're unaware of, benefits taken using your health insurance, money stolen from your bank accounts, and many other devastating possibilities.

Whether you're shopping online, setting up an online bank account, or paying bills online, companies will request sensitive information from you. They usually will ask for your name, address, or Social Security number. Before handing out this information, verify that it is a legitimate request from a reputable business. Do some research before handing it out to just anyone.

Here's what you need to look into:

- If a company you have already given information to emails you and asks you to confirm that information, call them to find out whether that confirmation is necessary (and legitimate). But don't call the number listed in the email; only use the phone number you have saved in your records.

- Never send sensitive information over email; legitimate companies will not ask you to do so.

- Never enter your information in a pop-up or advertise-
  ment that wants private data.

Another thing to bear in mind is the importance of shredding documents. People who commit identity theft will go to great lengths to put back together documents you simply tear apart. Investing in a paper shredder is a very smart thing to do. You should use your paper shred-der to shred bank statements, loan payments, bills, and any other documents containing sensitive information.

Also, if you have any IDs or credit cards stolen from you, do not delay in reporting them stolen and/or cancel-ling them. If you suspect you are a victim of identity theft, reach out to the appropriate government agencies to begin an inquiry. The Federal Trade Commission's web-site has a ton of information on how to handle this situ-ation for consumers and specifically college students. It even has an identity theft helpline at 877-438-4338. For more advice and information, head to www.fraud.org.

By being smart, cautious, and careful when provid-ing sensitive information, you can decrease your risk of becoming a victim of identity theft.

NEVER ENGAGE IN ILLEGAL ACTIVITIES

Ok, let's be honest: statistics show that a lot of underage drink-ing happens in college and occasionally in high school. However, posting a picture or video of you doing a keg-stand or posing with your besties with your red cups in hand won't give you a great image on social media. To colleges and employers, this says you might be a reckless person.

If you catch your friends posting these pictures on social media channels, ask them not to or, at the very least, not to tag you in them. Being tagged in others' photos is probably the number-one way for photos to come back and haunt you later. If you're not tagged in any, you can prevent what will hurt you in the future. I've heard horror stories of students not getting a job or internship because of red solo cup pictures that were on their friends' profiles.

One year at my college, students posted pictures on Instagram of themselves damaging school property during spring break, and they were caught and punished. All of these students were punished because they posted their actions on social media for everyone to see. First, they should never have engaged in such activity, but second, who had the bright idea to document it? Crazy.

DO NOT BASH ANYONE ONLINE

Last but not least, do not be one of those horrible online bullies or trolls. In every school's code of conduct there is an anti-bullying rule. If you bash your professors, school, or a classmate online, your school will find out—whether it's by word of mouth or a direct report from someone. Bullying is unacceptable and you will be punished and maybe even expelled if you choose to post hateful comments via social media. Don't do it.

The bottom line? Don't post or engage in any activity you wouldn't want your family, school, or future employers to know about or see. Stop and think *before* you post.

Insights provided by Ashley Yenick, Merrimack College

SOCIAL MEDIA'S DARK SIDE

Not long ago, many experts felt that spending large amounts of time using the Internet for social interaction was a sign of a personal deficiency in social skills. In other words, people who spent a lot of time socially networking online were doing it because they felt socially awkward face-to-face. However, in the rapidly evolving world of online communications, such generalizations are no longer accurate. Today's students have integrated online communication like Facebook and other social networking sites into their daily lives to enrich, rather than replace, their already existing relationships. But like anything else, it has its drawbacks as well.

YOUR PROFILE SAYS IT ALL

The average college student logs into their Facebook account nearly every day, spending anywhere from ten minutes to three hours a day checking out the latest details on their friends' profiles. You can categorize Facebook users by the number of "friends" that they have prominently displayed on the front page of their profile. If you've got under two hundred, then consider yourself a casual Facebook user, one who thinks it is fun but doesn't quite see its full potential so doesn't waste too much time on it. Have two to three hundred friends? You're the average Facebook user, one who probably checks his or her account and exchanges wall posts with friends at least once a day. For those entertaining three to four hundred friends, congrats. You're popular, one who makes a lot of friends and acquaintances and uses Facebook to keep in touch with all of them. But five hundred or more? You've entered new territory—desperate. Let me guess: you are one of those people who Facebooks everyone, even when you haven't met the person yet!

ARE YOU ADDICTED TO SOCIAL MEDIA?

According to a study conducted at the University of Maryland that challenged college students to go without their phones, laptops, TVs, iPods, and all other tech devices for twenty-four hours, a majority of subjects admitted that they were functionally *unable* to do so. Many students reported withdrawal symptoms similar to those of alcohol or drug addiction, including anxiety, nervousness, and a feeling of helplessness. An overall analysis of students' responses determined that the biggest issue was an overwhelming sense of disconnection from friends and family.

If you worry that you might qualify as an addict, then you most likely have a problem. Ask yourself if any of the following statements sound familiar:

- You're constantly checking updates on your phone, even when you're in class, hanging out with your pals, or on a date.
- You've put off going out with friends and doing schoolwork on more than one occasion to play around with your profile.
- You obsessively keep track of the guys you once dated and the ones you secretly have a crush on.

- If given the choice, you'd choose an hour online over an hour of sleep.
- Your grades are starting to take a hit. Why? With all your free time going to social media, there's little time to study!

Interested in changing? Try documenting for a couple days how often you go on social media sites or use your devices and how much time you spend using them. You might be shocked to learn how much time you waste each day reading up on the details of the lives of your friends and acquaintances. A good goal is to substitute this time with something more positive like going to the gym, meditation, yoga, or spending time with your good friends *in person*. I'm not saying that the solution is to give up social media entirely. We all know that's an impossible suggestion. But just try finding some balance in your life and you'll feel a lot better for it. And if you believe you have a serious problem, consult your school's mental health services center for advice or counseling on how to combat compulsive behavior.

SOCIAL MEDIA AND DATING

Social media has changed the way our generation perceives relationships and interpersonal communication, and that's not necessarily always a good thing. What happens when you're going on a first date with someone, and are only pretending to learn new things about them from your conversations, since you've already memorized their favorite movies and TV shows from their Facebook profile? What you can learn about someone from staring at a computer does not, and should not, in any way, replace interacting with them "IRL."

In the age of the emoticon, people claim that online communication makes dating and friendships easier, but actually, when you look deeper, it can be an obstacle to our ability to interact with people in person. It's easy to come up with witty one-liners online, but more important to be able to improvise in person. Facebook is fun, but it can take a lot away from the process of getting to know another person one-on-one. Don't let this happen to you.

TO SWIPE OR NOT TO SWIPE

Ashley Yenick, Merrimack College

During my senior year of college, dating apps started to become extremely popular. One day when I was having lunch with friends, one of them asked, "Have you used Tinder yet?" My friends were dumbfounded after I asked, "What's Tinder?" They convinced me to download the app by describing it as a "fun new way to date people on and around campus." So, I decided to give it a shot.

I began my quest for a potential boyfriend by swiping left and right. I had a couple of uncomfortable moments where I swiped right on someone I had JUST passed in the hallway...so awkward. It was becoming so popular on campus that when I'd walk by students in the library or sit next to someone in class, I realized they were also on Tinder. It was taking over campus by storm!

Now, this may be a generalization, but some of the guys that I talked to on Tinder were so rude and forward that it really turned me off from using the app. After matching with someone, the guy messaged me and asked, "Do you go to Merrimack?" I immediately panicked and blocked him because I was terrified that he knew where I went to school, even though

I didn't mention it in my profile. Disclaimer: This was before they had settings connected to social media profiles.

I never had the nerve to go on a Tinder date. Since my horrible Tinder encounters, I've tested out other dating apps like Bumble, but I'm currently not using any dating apps whatsoever. On the other hand, I have several friends who have been successful on Tinder, and they even formed lasting relationships.

My experience on Tinder helped me realize that you'll either find a connection online with someone or you won't. For me, it's more exciting to first meet a guy in person and then build a relationship from there. What it comes down to is how comfortable you are in the online world.

FRIENDING AND UN-FRIENDING: THE RULES OF THE GAME

Victoria Reitano, Quinnipiac University

When you connect with someone on Facebook or elsewhere on the Web, you are publicly proclaiming your association with that person. But let's face it: your name is all you have when you communicate online, and the related associations you build are vitally important. That's something you need to remember every time you choose to friend or un-friend someone on Facebook. In my opinion, un-friending someone is an important thing to think about ahead of time. You're always going to have those people you used to talk to, but no longer do, so you need to determine a policy for how you'll deal with these contacts. I generally un-friend anyone I don't speak with in real life—if we're only friends online or I can't remember why we're friends online, then we shouldn't be "friends" on Facebook. Same with ignoring friend requests. The only time I would do this is if I didn't know someone or knew them but never associated with them offline. In the end, it's up to you to decide how you want to deal with these relationships.

MAINTAINING STRONG FRIENDSHIPS

Social media makes it so easy to become "friends" with someone. Within one meeting and a couple clicks of a mouse, you can be listed as someone's "friend," but does this really translate to a friendship? Does writing a happy birthday message on someone's wall once a year really mean you're buddies in the real world? I don't think so. Maintaining a friendship with someone requires a lot more effort than a once-a-year wall post lost among hundreds of others.

It's also easy for those who were once close friends to be relegated to weak online acquaintances. Make sure not to let networking sites like Facebook overtake your social life, and don't forget to maintain your friendships offline as well! When you no longer see someone in class every day or are too busy to hang out with them, it's easy to substitute the occasional wall post or message saying hello, but this is not a good replacement for spending time together in person and won't help build your relationships.

PARTING WORDS OF ADVICE

Social media is a fun and extremely useful tool—there are plenty of people you might otherwise lose touch with in life if they weren't online—but like anything else, use it in moderation. Because I know how addictive Facebook can be, during finals week each year I usually let a friend log into my account and change my password so that I can't log back in until after exams are over. It's just one extra way of making sure Facebook doesn't interfere with what is important to me…like doing well on an exam! Don't let social media take over— remember your priorities and log off of that site!

Insights provided by Nisha Chittal, University of Illinois

UCHIC ESSENTIALS—
TECH ESSENTIALS FOR AN INSTAGRAM AGE

BE SMART ABOUT WHAT YOU POST

You never know who could be viewing your social media profiles. Enable privacy settings and use good judgment about what you post online.

BUILD RELATIONSHIPS *IN* PERSON

Don't let social media or digital devices replace real friendships, in-person connections, and genuine communication. These are the things that make relationships rich and keep them strong and long lasting.

KNOW WHEN TO TURN IT OFF

Social media can be a tempting distraction that can easily turn into an addiction. Set limits, and if you've been online too long, log off, get out, and enjoy life on campus!

Looking for more great advice? Head to UChic.com for even more resources and information—they come highly recommended from our contributors and editors. Be sure to leave your suggestions as well!

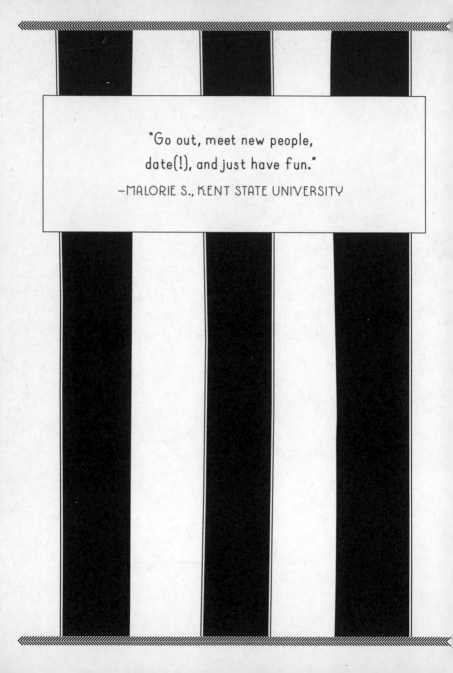

"Go out, meet new people,
date(!), and just have fun."
—MALORIE S., KENT STATE UNIVERSITY

7

LOVE LIFE

IT'S PRETTY MUCH RARE to find a woman in college these days whose primary goal is to get hitched. But it wasn't too long ago that some women went to college solely for their "Mrs." degree. Of course serious relationships still exist in college these days. It's just the way we approach and view dating that has radically changed.

So what to expect? From short-term relationships to long-term relationships to an occasional hookup, be prepared for *anything* when it comes to dating in college. To give you a crash course on the college dating scene, we've pulled together some essential dating advice from college women nationwide. Having been there and pretty much done everything you can imagine when it comes to dating, these women have much to share…

THE SCOOP ON
THE COLLEGE DATING
SCENE

Let's face it. After you've said good-bye to your parents and finished unpacking, you're really excited to check out more than just the campus or your classes.

But as much as I wanted to meet a cute guy and establish a long-term and stable relationship in college, that was not my sole motivation for going to school. After all, this is the age of the independent woman. As an independent woman, you're here to make your dreams your reality, and finding a man should not be your first goal. It's just an added bonus, icing on the cake, when you meet that special someone in college.

Since the rules of dating have changed drastically (even since your older sister was in college), I wanted to share a little advice on how to enjoy the college dating scene without losing sight of yourself, your goals, or your future.

STAY TRUE TO YOURSELF

Let's start with the don'ts: *don't date just to be like your friends*. Before you start dating, make sure you do it for the right reasons. I'm sure your parents have told you time and time again to always act for the right reasons, and now being on your own, it's time to test out your ability to stay true to yourself. Don't make decisions about your own love life based on what your friends are doing. Even if all of them are dating, this does not mean that you have to enter the dating pool. Also, having a boyfriend will not prove anything to yourself or your friends about your maturity or self-worth.

Don't set out looking for a boyfriend. It's so easy to get caught up in a relationship and have your social life revolve around him rather than to make your own friends. And if it doesn't work out, you'll regret not taking the time to make connections with others when you're sitting at home alone in your dorm room trying to recover from a breakup. In college, especially, there are so many new people to meet and interesting opportunities that it can be a bit overwhelming at first. But what should be first and foremost on your new agenda are your friendships. Take the time to get to know your girlfriends before you call anyone your boyfriend. After all, guys come and go. Some may even break your heart, but after all is said and done, your girlfriends will stand by your side through it all.

A friend of mine and her boyfriend broke up after a two-year relationship. They met right when they came to campus, hit it off, and jumped right into a relationship. For two years, her life revolved around him, and she lost touch with many of her friends. When her relationship fell apart, it was hard for a lot of her friends to be there for her since she had cast them aside in favor of her boyfriend. It took some time, but eventually she earned back the trust of all her friends. Her breakup was hard to deal with, but it opened her eyes to the fact that there should always be more than one important person in your life.

OK, I'm done with the don'ts. Once you've made your friends and you are ready to take the plunge into the dating pool, who can you date and where do you meet them?

BOYFRIEND MATERIAL

When starting to date someone, ideally, you want to start with a clean slate. You shouldn't have to pick up the pieces from a previous dating disaster. Guys without girlfriends—meaning they are single but also over any previous girlfriends—are your prime dating material. While everyone comes with their own baggage, fresh baggage is not fun to deal with. It takes time to get over any relationship and the solution is not to jump right into the next.

On the flip side, sometimes guys are just not ready for dating. Not everyone comes to college with the maturity level it takes to be in a meaningful relationship, and the unfortunate truth is that girls mature faster than guys, and some guys still have not caught up even by college.

Another problem you may come across is that some guys are, at times, only looking to hook up. They aren't looking to get into anything serious right away since they are still trying to figure out exactly what they want out of a relationship—almost like window-shopping. But hooking up with someone—with the hope of eventually dating—never really works out the way you want. While there is nothing wrong with wanting to date or wanting a commitment from a guy, you have to be up front about your needs from the very beginning. Otherwise, you may soon discover that you've been wasting your time on the wrong person, and no one likes feeling that she's wasted time.

WHERE NOT TO MEET

At this point, classes can seem like the perfect place to meet someone, but business and pleasure can be a difficult duo. Dating someone you share a class with could work against you—if you break up, you'll still see each other every day. Even dating someone with the same major can be dangerous. My school is by no means a large one, so every year I have the same drama majors in my classes. It's not like you can stop going to classes or really avoid seeing them. I have friends who have dated people with the same major and when it doesn't work out, it can get ugly. The same thing goes for dating in the dorms—the constant close proximity can become an issue. The choice is yours to make, but be sure there is a solid connection between you and your cutie of a classmate or dormmate before you start dating.

BEING A GROUPIE IS NOT THE WAY TO GO

At all cost, avoid becoming a "groupie." Let me describe the typical scene: hanging around at the same place every single weekend with the same group of guys and girls. During my freshman year, my friends and I hung out at one of the sports houses (like a fraternity house for a sports team) every night. We pigeonholed ourselves into the category of girls who only date jocks, which couldn't be further from the truth. Only one of my friends was actually dating a jock; the rest of us just considered ourselves friends with the guys. But not everyone seemed to believe that, including nonjocks whom we were interested in. Once we realized that everyone looked at us as groupies, we got smart and quickly switched up our hangouts. It was too soon in our college career to be affiliated with only one group. Fortunately, we only spent one semester as "groupies" and no long-term damage was done to our reputations.

MORE ON THE SUBJECT OF REPUTATIONS

If there is one piece of advice I could give that you should take to heart, it's that your reputation is extremely important in college, especially at a smaller school. While your college may be bigger than your high school, people still gossip and word does travel. Now, you know that there will always be petty gossip that you just brush off, but when even your closest friends show concern for you, it may be time to take a step back and reflect on what you're doing. Some of us can go a little crazy with our newfound sense of independence and make decisions that we eventually regret. If you come to college fresh out of a breakup and start sleeping around, it can definitely damage your reputation. But don't worry; nothing is permanent. As soon as you realize that you aren't happy with choices you're making, start making better ones. Your reputation may stick for a little while, but once you start making changes, your reputation will change as well.

WHERE TO MEET THE RIGHT GUYS

At this point I'm sure you are wondering where you will meet someone to date. For the most part, many of the guys that my friends and I have dated we met through our friends. Classes *outside* your major area of interest can be a safe place to meet guys as well. Maybe you could take an interesting elective class and see who else is in it. Extracurricular activities afford another opportunity—just beware if it is an activity where you spend a lot of time together. Don't be afraid to put yourself out there. Sporting events and off-campus bars or local cafés are good as well. Make an effort to search out a place that fits your style.

In college, the only real dating rules are those that you make for yourself. There are no parents to check up on you and

enforce a curfew. What you choose to do is completely up to you, so set some rules for yourself and be picky about whom you decide to date. When I say picky, I am not talking about only dating blonds or athletes. I am talking about setting standards for yourself.

WHAT YOU CAN EXPECT TO RUN INTO

Predicting what you'll experience in the world of college dating is just as tricky as predicting the weather. There are times when you'll bask in the sunlight of a new relationship. Other times you'll muddle your way through murky waters of ambiguity. And don't forget about the storms. You have to prepare for the unexpected.

Open Relationships

Perhaps it's human nature, but we usually want what we can't have. You know, the "grass is always greener on the other side" phenomenon. This is especially true when dealing with guys with girlfriends. For your own sake, stay away from the guy with the girlfriend back home. Even if he is in an "open relationship," getting involved with him is just asking for trouble. First of all, the term "open relationship" is a bit of an oxymoron. "Relationship" implies monogamy while "open" does not. If you want to avoid any future drama, be sure to stay away from these guys.

If you do decide to date a person in an open relationship, try not to get too attached. Chances are that if it comes down to choosing between you and his girlfriend, he will choose his girlfriend. You have to admit that it makes sense; he has more history with her and is more comfortable. I have been in this situation once before, and the best advice I can give is to run away if a guy mentions that his relationships aren't monogamous.

What happens when you want more? Here's a little tale to illustrate. I wasn't looking for any kind of relationship, but one night while out with friends I met a really great guy, or so I thought. We had similar interests and hit it off right away. Unfortunately, he and his girlfriend, who was at school in a different state, were having problems. They decided to be in an open relationship. This is the point where I should have walked away, but I thought I had a chance at something with this guy. To make matters worse, he pursued me as if there were no one else in the picture, randomly surprising me, having dinner with me, and basically all the stuff you do when you like someone. Ultimately, he and his girlfriend worked things out and I was crushed. He even had the audacity to tell me that if things didn't work out this time with her, maybe we could give it a shot. It made me realize that I could not date someone who would always consider me second-best.

Rebounders

Like I said earlier, be careful of or even steer clear of anyone who has recently gotten out of a relationship. They are on the rebound, and it might be at your expense. There is no set amount of time that it takes a person to get over someone. Depending on the individual, it can range anywhere from one week to three months or even more. Some guys never get over their ex-girlfriends! Make sure whomever you start to date is still not hung up on his ex—if he's constantly talking about her or comparing you to her, it's best to let him be. To be fair, sometimes he may not even know he's constantly talking about her. Speak up and make him aware of it. When it comes down to it, he shouldn't have to choose his memories over you. But, if he seems to wish his past memories were his present life, it is best to move on.

Fraternity Guys and Athletes

A close friend of mine is dating a guy in a fraternity, and true, at times, it can be frustrating. When there is drama between her and her boyfriend, it seems the whole frat knows about it and she becomes "the bitch." To be fair, many frat boys, athletes, and other boys with "reputations" don't in reality come close to the stereotypes you might have in mind. My motto is to give everyone a chance. More often than not, guys will surprise you.

In all honesty, when it comes to dating in college, you will most likely meet someone when you least expect it. Maybe he lives next door to your best friend or maybe you will meet him at a party. No matter what the situation, just be yourself and live up to your own expectations. The rest will follow!

Insights provided by Jillian E. Sorgini, Hofstra University

DIGITAL RULES FOR DATING

College life comes complete with an array of attractive, educated people at your disposal. Throw in some alcohol, coed dorms, and an ever-growing list of Facebook event invites, and you've got yourself one crazy dating scene. It seems like there are no real rules, and if there are, people sure aren't afraid to bend—or completely break—them.

Let's set the scene. You meet an adorable, delicious boy at a house party, complete with his astrological sign tattooed on his bronzed bicep (and, of course, you totally check your horoscope like every day). You engage in a deep discussion about all your other interests (finally, a guy who will admit to loving reality TV!), and find that you have a lot in common. You're really into each other, so you exchange numbers and go home happy, elated even.

However, it's the next morning and the dilemma sets in. You have his number, now what? What's a modern girl to do when she has two completely viable options for communication—to call or to text? And there is always Facebook to complicate things further.

WHEN TO CALL
If You Have Something Serious to Talk About
My number one pet peeve is when people—girlfriends and boyfriends

alike—decide to initiate a fight, debate, or other meaningful discussion via text message. In the age of texting, sometimes it's easy to forget that some conversations are supposed to be long, drawn-out, and, above all else, meaningful. There are still certain situations, especially in dating, that require you to actually use your voice—and not a keyboard or cell phone keypad—to express yourself. Even if we're talking about your boyfriend of three years, he deserves the chance to actually hear what you have to say.

Also, text messages can be easily misinterpreted when trying to discuss something where emotions are involved—those little smiley faces do not tell all! Sarcasm and other voice inflections are often misread in text messages, causing a whole mess of confusion between the two parties involved. There have been numerous occasions when girls have misread text messages and caused lots of unnecessary drama with boyfriends. If you really want to ensure he understands why you freaked out the night before, discuss the events over the phone, if not in person!

If You Aren't Distracted

My ex-boyfriend and I attempted to carry on many a phone conversation when I lived in the dorm. Let me tell you—living around forty girls did not make for optimum relationship communication time. If you want to chat it up with that new boy in your life or have a quality phone date with your current BF, make sure you are somewhere quiet, free of giggling girls chugging wine and/or discussing the latest celeb gossip. Devote your concentration to the conversation and really listen to what your beau is saying. You'll be surprised how much you will enjoy talking with your sweetie when you give him your full attention.

If You Want to Make Plans

It's tempting to ask your guy to hang in a text message, but wait until you show up at one movie theater and he accidentally goes to another. Confirming when, where, and how you and your dude are going to meet up is best done through verbal communication and will help avoid confusion later. It's faster than waiting for a text message response, which as we all know can take hours—if you get one at all. Solidify special plans over the phone.

If You Want to Show That You're Truly Interested

When you take the time out of your obviously super-busy schedule to actually dial your crush's number, it shows that you have a genuine interest in him and what he has to say. Although firing off a short "What's up?" text is quick and painless, it does not say much, literally.

If You Want to Break It Off

Don't commit the cardinal sin of college dating—the text message breakup. Although I don't think that having a "You-were-the-best-and-worst-thing-that-ever-happened-to-me" tear-jerking conversation over the phone is much better, it at least gives the other person an opportunity to defend himself and spill his side of the story. Breakups aren't easy no matter how you handle them, but a phone conversation is a much more civil way to move on.

THE DOS AND DON'TS
OF ONLINE DATING

Erica Strauss, Kent State University

Considering online dating? You're not alone. According to a recent HuffingtonPost.com article, forty million people in the United States have used online dating sites. But beware—not everyone is who they say they are online. One out of ten users on online dating sites are scammers, and one out of ten sex offenders reportedly use online dating sites to meet people. While these stats shouldn't deter you from trying online dating, you should always keep these safety tips in mind:

- Don't share your address or phone number on a publicly viewed page. Be discreet about who you do give this information to—even in private emails.

- Don't rush into anything. If you think you've met your match, set some ground rules before you meet, like two weeks of emails or texting so you can feel each other out.

- Do provide a close friend or family member with all his information before you go out on a first date together. Things like his name, phone number, email address, where he lives and works, and what he looks like can be valuable information if something bad should happen to you.

- Do suggest grabbing a quick cup of coffee during your lunch break or right after dinner. Picking a crowded safe zone and setting time limits are both good measures to protect yourself against someone with not-so-nice intentions.

- Don't drink alcoholic beverages. Alcohol lowers both your inhibitions and defenses.
- Don't let him pick you up or drive you home. He doesn't need to know where you live or if you live alone. Make sure you park somewhere brightly lit and heavily trafficked, in case he decides to walk you to your car. This may seem overly paranoid, but better to be safe than sorry.

Follow these tips, and your online dating life—if you choose to engage in one—will go off without a hitch!

WHEN TO TEXT
If He Texts First

Take the scenario where you meet at a party. We can argue that chivalry is dead, but let's be honest here—you know that any guy who is truly interested in hanging out with your fabulous self will soon send you a quick, flirty text or call you to take you out (or at the very least, invite you to tag along to a frat party). If the cute boy texts you first, a text response is not only a way to show that you, too, are interested, but it's also polite. Manners are always classy; and classy is always attractive.

If You're Super Busy, Duh

College students are constantly swamped with papers, three-hundred-page readings on thrilling subjects like the principles of formal logic, forty-five-minute presentations, what have you. Between all your activities, it might be hard to find the time for a phone call—especially if you just want to check up. Sending a friendly "How's it going?" or "I love you!" text message—depending on the situation, of course—is totally acceptable. In fact, it might even be the perfect way to go—especially if your partner is busy, too! You can also use text messages as a way to arrange times to communicate other ways. Send a quick "Call me after six!" text message if you miss a call during class so your sweetheart knows you aren't too busy or completely ignoring him.

If You're Already in a Relationship

The rules change quite a bit when you're already attached. While you still shouldn't use the text message as an easy way out (like to break up) or as a way to tackle some serious drama, text messages are a good way to communicate with someone you already know and love. They know your style of speech, they know how your brain works (or at least attempt to understand it), and they will have a better idea about how to decipher your text messages than someone you just met. And when it comes to social networking sites like Facebook and Instagram? It might be OK to occasionally post on your BF's wall, or send him a cute message that you think will brighten his day—but delving into anything too serious using the Internet is an absolutely terrible idea. It's there forever, for the whole world to see.

And Before You Sext That Text

There's flirting and then there's *flirting*, but sexting doesn't fall into either category. What seems like naughty fun now may turn into a nightmare if you're not too careful. One vengeful upload by an ex and you could find yourself blackballed from your career of choice (yes, employers DO Google you before an interview or job offer!).

Flirty text messages are fine. But since texts live forever, steer clear of any revealing pics you might not want your mom, dad, or future boss to see.

Remember that while phone calls and text messages are great ways to communicate with the opposite sex, face-to-face encounters are ideal. In order to establish a real connection, you have to be able to see, hear, and touch the other person. No text message could ever replace a good snuggle session on your comfy couch or a romantic dinner at your favorite sushi restaurant. It's easy to stumble in the fast-paced dating world via smartphones. But with proper tech etiquette, new technologies can make your love life a whole lot easier and more interesting.

Insights provided by Erica Strauss, Kent State University

LONG-DISTANCE LOVE

I fell in love for the first time when I was sixteen. His name was Ryan and he was everything I wanted at that age: passionate, dark, addicted to punk music and cigarettes.

We were high school sweethearts, the couple that made everyone sick with incessant hand-holding and kissing in the hallways. We were inseparable, for five years to be exact. And when the day came that I had to squeeze all my belongings into my parents' minivan and head across the state, I knew that it meant leaving him, and completely changing the dynamics of our once perfect romance. I had to face up to a harsh reality after I started to call Kent State University home. Long-distance relationships (LDRs) take some serious effort, and sometimes it isn't worth it. I had to learn the hard way the ins and outs of what makes a long-distance relationship work—and what can cause it to crumble.

Whether you're trying to make the transition from high school sweethearts to committed college lovers, or you met someone from another university or even another country, having your sweetie miles away is never easy. So, what can you do to make it work? And if it's not working, how do you decide to move on?

TALK ABOUT EXPECTATIONS
Realize That It Will Be Hard Work

First and foremost, realize that in a long-distance relationship, you will experience challenges that new couples in college don't. Sure, you will have to tackle issues of trust, jealousy, and intimacy—just like any couple—but you can't just make it all better with a good-night kiss. However, all is not lost; your relationship can survive. Just make sure from the very beginning of the separation that both you and your partner are ready to expend the extra energy that comes with making a long-distance commitment.

Establish Boundaries

An important word of advice: your lover might see an LDR as the perfect way to have his cake and eat it too. Don't let this happen to you unless you are OK with sharing your guy. Make sure that both of you are clear about the way the relationship is supposed to work. Are you going to remain exclusive or will you be allowed to date other people? If you meet someone you feel you might have a better connection with, will you remain friends? These are just a few of the many issues you'll want to address before the separation. If you take the time to be up front about the relationship from the get-go, this prevents confusion and possible heartbreak later.

TRUST AND COMMUNICATION

Once the boundaries are set, you then have to let go—not of your guy but of your tendency to worry or not trust your partner. Yes, this one seems obvious, but when distance becomes a factor in an otherwise super-sweet relationship, the equation changes quite a bit. In order for your LDR to work, there has to be a very high level of trust.

Don't Bug Your Beau with Endless Phone Calls

Demanding that he tell you where he is every second of every day will do nothing but tear you, and your relationship, apart. You both are in a new place and an exciting time of your life. Let him—and yourself—grow, learn, and have fun without a cell phone glued to the ear. Besides, no one really likes the girl who sits in the corner on the phone with her boy all night. Plus, you'll have much more to say when you can finally talk with your guy without distractions.

Be Honest About Your Weekend Plans

Don't tell your partner you plan to sit at home on a Friday night if you're ready to waltz your way to the local hangouts in your brand-new heels. Even though my BF and I were miles apart, I couldn't bring myself to tell him what I was really doing, and sometimes I'd ignore his phone calls on Friday night just to avoid a fight. I found out the hard way that this breeds mistrust in a relationship; every time I didn't answer, he assumed I was doing something I shouldn't be. He never cared if I hung out with other guys—he cared about me and wanted me to enjoy college—but by me not being honest, I created a pretty sticky situation. By avoiding his phone calls, I created an issue that was hard to resolve.

Learn to Trust Yourself

Do you think you can resist the temptation of going home with the cute boy at the bar after a few Jäegerbombs? Don't put yourself, or your partner, in the position to get hurt. It's always OK to go out, in fact that's one of the amazing qualities about an LDR: you can still maintain your freedom. But if you're constantly tempted to go home with someone else, or always want to go out "just in case" you meet Mr. Right, you need to reevaluate your current relationship. It's natural to miss the closeness that comes with a regular relationship, and you might be eyeballing that hottie just because you miss your own. But if you go out with the sole intention of meeting someone new, you probably just need to break it off with your current beau.

Don't get me wrong. Long-distance love is difficult, but there are benefits to it as well. Unlike other college couples, who can feel smothered when their lover lives down the hall or in the same apartment complex, long-distance lovers can experience the best of both worlds. Not only can you cultivate your own interests and do your own thing most of the time, you can also enjoy the comfort and satisfaction of being in a committed relationship. You can do all the things you love, and you will become a much more interesting person to be with. So trust yourself, and enjoy these benefits.

Get Creative

Communication is key in every relationship—but people in LDRs have to be a little more creative in their approach to keeping in touch. My long-distance boyfriend was a little short on cash, so even though we were only two-and-a-half hours apart, weekend visits were not always an option. I missed his forehead kisses, his calloused hands; I even missed riding around in his disgusting car while he blasted music I absolutely hated. So, I knew I had to do something to keep us connected.

Because you can't see each other every day, you have to form a strong emotional connection in other ways. Buy a webcam or use the FaceTime app and schedule Skype dates. Send each other handwritten letters (doodles of hearts and flowers optional). Decide to read the same books, watch the same movies, or do other activities "together"—like stargazing on the phone with each other. These shared moments will help you to remember that even though he is far away, he is still breathing the same air.

Be Thoughtful

Basically, anything you do to enhance communication in your relationship will help you to feel more connected. Make sure you put thought into every little thing you do. Make him a mix CD of the latest metal songs (even if you detest them!), send him tickets to that concert he mentioned wanting to see, or that basketball game he wanted to watch, etc. Take note of every little thing he says and be creative when it comes to letters, gifts, etc.

TIPS FOR VISITING EACH OTHER

OK, it's been several weeks or even months since you've seen your significant other. Winter break is around the corner or one of you has decided to visit the other in his or her new environment. Will it be awkward?

Be Prepared for Things to Be Different

When you first see your partner again, remember that it might be a little different from the last time you saw him. It's a lot easier to notice changes in people we don't see every day than in the ones we do. Some couples will find that they feel the exact same way about each other, and that their partner hasn't changed much since their last visit. Other couples, who sometimes have to spend months apart, can notice big differences the first time they see each other. Be prepared—you never know which situation you will find yourself in! I had been dating my guy for three years before I even left for college, so I figured that as soon as I did see him, of course, everything would go back to normal. Everything was the same for a while—a few months, actually. But as I became less of a presence in his life at home, he started to fill his time with other things, and other people, as did I. I noticed that we related differently—we were both growing up! The distance gave our relationship some renewed excitement.

The reality is this: people change. The person you started dating six months ago will not be the same person six months from now. In an LDR, you have to deal with this reality and accept the changes both in each other and in your relationship.

Let Your Sweetie Do His Own Thing

Also make sure to give each other some space during visits—after all, you wouldn't spend every waking moment with your sweetie if he lived close. If he comes to visit you and has other friends in the area, encourage him to go out and reconnect with others who are important to him. Just like you'd want to catch up with all your old pals, watch reruns of *Friends*, and drink cheap wine, boyfriends will have their own rituals they want to take part in when they come to visit. If you go to visit him, do the same. Go see some friends or even get up early one morning to grab coffee and explore your beau's new environment. Besides enjoying the opportunity to sleep in, he will appreciate your independence and probably will end up missing you and anxiously waiting for you to return. It's always better to keep him wanting more than for him to feel suffocated by your affection.

Get Out and About

The best way to keep any relationship exciting is to experience new things together. You should make an effort to split your visit between "downtime" with your partner—like lounging on the sofa watching *The Walking Dead*, nestled in each other's arms—and going out. Even if you simply attend a lecture on campus or go out for sushi or a drink, you will have shared a piece of your everyday life and have had a new experience together.

Make a Point Not to "Surprise" Each Other with Unplanned Visits

If you live close enough that you could make the trip to see your sweetie on a whim, make sure you clear it with him first. You wouldn't want your beau to intrude on any important plans you may have with your friends, so make sure that you do not do the same. Besides, would you really want to stumble in on a coed study session or lunch date that may make you jump to the wrong conclusion? Save yourself the drama and call ahead.

FREEDOM OR COMMITMENT: WHICH TO CHOOSE?

If there is one thing that college is universally known for, it's freedom. You are finally away from your parents, your boring hometown, and any restricting rules from the past. You don't need to check in with Mom or Dad before going out with the girls, and there is nobody to make sure that you go to bed on time (or go to bed at all!). Relationships, on the other hand, are all about commitment and, yes, restriction. Relationships in college—especially those long-distance romances—can seem downright ridiculous to some people. Why shun the very freedom that you've been so longing to have?

Even if you start your LDR with the best of intentions, you may find yourself conflicted between wanting to fully enjoy your college life and to stay committed to your significant other. Not every relationship—long-distance or not—is meant to be. So how can you tell if it's time to call it quits? Here are some questions to consider.

Do You Have Your Eye on Someone Else?

This is exactly why LDRs tend not to be satisfying in college. College is the time to explore yourself and your options. You shouldn't feel guilty when you find yourself staring at that cute boy in sociology class with the shaggy hair and Ryan Reynolds–esque eyes. Being in college gives you an all-access pass to plenty of educated, attractive, and ambitious potential lovers. These lovers can teach you a lot about the world, other people, and even yourself. If you feel even a little inkling that you might want to see other people, it's probably time to seriously consider ending your LDR and connecting with someone a little more accessible.

If you're in this situation, break it off with your partner before you start romancing another student. My LDR came to an end toward the end of my sophomore year. I had finally started to feel comfortable around a certain group of people—I found my niche, if you will. I also started to get a little too comfortable with a boy in this group of friends. I noticed that I would get more excited when he called or sent me a cute text than when my own boyfriend did. I knew that this was a sign that I needed to talk to my BF and decide what to do about it. It was crazy—I called him to talk about my feelings for the other boy, and he admitted that he was going through a very similar situation. So we decided, very mutually, to leave the relationship behind. This communication between us at the time of our breakup has made it possible for us to become friends (after a good nine months of no communication whatsoever!). Honesty really is the best policy, and I'm so glad that I was honest with my boy at the time.

Do You Still Believe You're Perfect Together?

Basically, you think that you and your lover are a match made in heaven. You both adore Kurt Vonnegut, playing the guitar, and don't ever get bored when you're together. So why would you want to part ways with someone who seems perfect for you?

This is an all-too-common problem when deciding to continue a relationship or not. There seems to be no real reason to end the relationship besides the distance factor. Sure, your sweetie resides miles away, but your relationship is peachy. Take an honest look at your current situation and ask yourself if it's possible that your LDR is somehow restricting you or hindering your development as an individual in college. You might be surprised.

When I was involved in my LDR, I would try to hang out with new friends in my hall, but I'd always be on the phone with, or waiting for a phone call from, my then-boy. I also made frequent trips home, and even though I'd feel left out when the girls would all talk about their weekend plans for frat parties and trips to surrounding cities, I gave that all up for my boy back home. Eventually, my new friends

told me that all my "Baby-I-miss-you" phone calls were annoying—
and I tried to cut back. But I know now that I'll never get back those
adventures I missed out on with those girls—and I can't say I'm happy
with my decision to choose a boy over new friends.

Would Taking Some Time Off Help You See Things More Clearly?

Rather than completely ending a seemingly great relationship, try
taking a break. Give him—and yourself—some space. Completely
cut off communication for a trial period, say a week or so. You will
probably be tempted to call your boy, but don't. Do you notice any
differences in your relationships with other people? Do you feel more
connected to your school—more willing to get involved in activities and spend your time doing things that don't involve waiting for
phone calls or planning visits? After the trial period is over, call your
BF and discuss how you both felt during your time apart.

No matter what dating obstacles you encounter during your
college years, remember to enjoy every moment and make a conscious
decision to learn from each and every one of your mistakes. Really,
college is the time to explore who you are, so make sure that your
relationship does not restrict this exploration in any way. I cherish
the time I spent with my long-distance boyfriend, but we eventually decided to call it quits. I'm happy with that decision—I'm much
happier in my current situation. If you're certain your long-distance
relationship is right for you, then it will be totally worth the hard
work—just like all good things in life.

Insights provided by Erica Strauss, Kent State University

IS LOVE POSSIBLE IN AN AGE OF HOOKUPS?

My mom is pretty cool, all things considered. Unfortunately, the definition of this term "hooking up" still remains elusive to her, often resulting in hilariously awkward conversations that start something like, "Oh honey, since you're working in New York this summer, maybe you and Jane Morris's son can hook up one evening for dinner." Or, "Honey, here's Benjamin's phone number—you go to school in the same place, and I've been waiting for you two to hook up forever!"

I understand my mom is from a different generation in which courtship and serious dating were the norm, so I can see why she might be a little confused. But how to explain this to my own friends who seem a wee bit hazy on the definition as well? Some refer to a dance-floor make out as a hookup. Others say "hooking up" is an appropriate term to describe any action up to third base, while still others refer to it as the whole (naked) nine yards. Despite the various definitions swirling around out there, the main implication of a statement like "I hooked up last night" is noncommitted, sexual action with a friend, acquaintance, or stranger.

The fact that the phrase "hooking up" has become such a common term says something about today's teens and young adults.

The changing nature of college dating and sexual relationships has dramatically altered the way women view their own sexuality. While the sexual revolution in the 1950s and 1960s brought the advent of the birth control pill and women's lib, the twenty-first century has ushered in a whole new crop of coeds who have casually declared their bodies open for business.

WHAT EXACTLY IS A HOOKUP?

Before diving any deeper into this important discussion, let's first set the record straight on the exact definition of a hookup. A hookup ranges from kissing to intercourse and anything in between. It can involve multiple partners or one partner, and can be as consistent or inconsistent as you choose. The word "hookup" can refer to the actual person that you hooked up with or the act of hooking up. Other than that, there are no rules involved.

One of my friends says she has many ex-hookups but few ex-boyfriends. Her hookups (we're talking about actual people this time, not just the act), which are always monogamous, last anywhere from three months to over a year. If that sounds to you like something more than a hookup, you're not alone. It qualifies as "boyfriend" to me. But to her and her hookups, they were not comfortable using the term "boyfriend" or "girlfriend." Maybe it signified too much of an emotional commitment. As she would always say when questioned about it, "If something isn't broken, why try to fix it?"

As many of us can attest, it's difficult not to get attached to someone after you are physically intimate with him. After all, your brain is wired that way. Touching, hugging, and any other sort of physical contact creates a mental and physical bond with that person. Even if you don't necessarily want a relationship with the person, your body craves that sense of attachment. But here is where the problem lies: when your body is telling you one thing and society tells you another, it's enough to leave anyone confused.

DID YOU KNOW?

Believe it or not, some college campuses have sex toy workshops, erotica weekend conferences, and full-blown "Sex Weeks" (even in the formerly stuffy Ivy League). According to boston.com, one recent study found that *more than 60 percent of college students reported having more than one sex partner.*

THE STAGES OF A HOOKUP

Like long-term relationships, there are several distinct stages of a typical hookup that may be helpful to know. So, I'll try to explain.

The Attraction

Hookups typically don't happen out of the blue. Chances are, if you are hooking up with someone, he has certain alluring qualities that appeal to you. Sometimes it is simply the chase and once you've had your fun, you are done and move on. But sometimes, the hookup can be everything you thought it would be and the thrill of the chase and the unexpected keeps you coming back for more. So you move on to the next stage.

The Pseudo-Relationship Stage

There is a fine line between detachment and attachment. What can start out as an unattached hookup can quickly morph into a pseudo-relationship with real feelings. This is when it gets really confusing. When engaging in any sort of hookup, many of us forget the emotional ramifications.

Is a Long-Term Relationship Possible?

Now, I am not saying that all hookups are wrong and always end badly. In some instances, a hookup can turn into something more, but it can take some time. What I've learned from experience and through friends is that if you gradually ease into hooking up with someone you like, you have more of a chance at having an actual relationship. Easing your way into a hookup gives you and your partner time to establish more than just a physical connection. However, this also means that from the beginning there is some sort of emotional investment before you hook up, so make sure you acknowledge your own feelings and be up front about them with yourself and your partner.

TAKING A STAND ON ONE-NIGHT STANDS

So what do you do when you're over hooking up and ready to look for something a little deeper? The Love Fidelity Network (LFN) is a nonprofit organization that has gained a presence on multiple campuses through the promotion of marriage, abstinence, and the ever-elusive true love among college students. Though this may appear like a tough crowd to conquer, the tides seem to be changing. LFN and other organizations like True Love Revolution are attracting followers in droves, as more and more students start to examine the value of conventional dating and long-term relationships.

Celebrities are also speaking out about the dangers of hooking up and what it can do to your self-esteem. Kelly Clarkson's feminist anthem "I Do Not Hook Up" says it all. Lady Gaga, in an interview, stated that she was embracing abstinence after experiencing some serious hookup action during her college years. "It's not really cool anymore to have sex all the time. It's cooler to be strong and independent," she insists.

While hookups and the rate of sexually transmitted diseases on college campuses are rising, conservative forces are gaining ground as they continue to encourage the search for true love and meaningful relationships. Some say it is empowering to own and wager one's sexuality; others argue that reserving your sexuality for one person is the end all, be all. Only time will tell if my mom's version of the term will ever become a reality again.

THE PROBLEM WITH RANDOM HOOKUPS AND YOUR REPUTATION

The truth of the matter is that there is a definite double standard when it comes to hooking up. No one really cares about how many girls a guy has hooked up with. If it's a high number, in fact, he's viewed as a player—not a bad thing. For us girls, the more guys we hook up with, the more negatively we are viewed. It's sad to say, but even in today's society there is still not sexual equality.

However, hooking up can be empowering for a woman. Rather than settling down or being obsessed with finding a boyfriend, the new hookup culture encourages girls to explore their options.

For those women who can hook up and walk away feeling empowered and unattached, all the more power to you. In certain instances, I completely agree with the fact that sometimes a hookup is all you need. Sometimes feelings and emotions can complicate things, and a hookup can be the perfect solution. With the stress of school and other social activities, it can be hard to find time for dating. Sometimes a hookup is a nice release.

SO IS TRUE LOVE POSSIBLE?

As for finding love in this age of the hookup, it is definitely harder— the hookup culture brings a whole new level of complication to the game of love. However, since the rules are yours to make, do what you feel comfortable with doing. If hooking up is not for you, then wait until you meet someone you care about and prove your friends wrong. Love is out there; you just have to be patient enough to wait for it. While you're waiting, though, never forget the wise words of Janis Joplin: "Don't compromise yourself. You're all you've got."

Insights provided by Jillian E. Sorgini, Hofstra University
and Kylie Thompson, Harvard University

UCHIC ESSENTIALS—*LOVE LIFE*

FOCUS ON YOU, FIRST

College is the time to focus on you first and your love life second. You're going places, and nothing should hold you back from your dreams. If a relationship isn't working out or is even affecting your ability to do your thing, stand strong and make a decision—the relationship either has to change or you have to end it.

HONESTY IS EVERYTHING WITH LONG-DISTANCE LOVE

If you're trying to maintain a long-distance relationship and your eye is starting to wander, don't worry because that's natural. But if you are unhappy or you've taken a serious interest in someone else, then it's time to make up your mind. Without honesty and trust, long distance will never work.

ONLY IF IT'S RIGHT FOR YOU

Casual hookups are a normal part of college for many students, but they don't have to be for you. Be honest with yourself about your feelings, don't forget your values, and decide what's right for you. You don't want to do something you could regret later.

Looking for more great advice? Head to UChic.com for even more resources and information—they come highly recommended from our contributors and editors. Be sure to leave your suggestions as well!

"Find a balance between schoolwork and other activities, and prioritize what's important. You'll find yourself happier, healthier, and more connected to your friends and school."

—SANDEE Y., UNIVERSITY OF CALIFORNIA-BERKELEY

8

STAYING HEALTHY
AND SAFE

MIDTERMS, PAPERS, FRIENDSHIPS, BOYFRIENDS, all-nighters, pub crawls. All of these activities and interactions—some more fun than others—can take a toll on your health in college. And it probably comes as no surprise that your health and happiness are important components of the fabulous college life. This chapter covers health issues you may face in college, but is by no means comprehensive. To completely be up to speed on all health matters, visit your school's student health center or their website for a more complete picture. But to get you started, we've tackled the common issues and concerns that you may face, keeping you ahead of the game when it comes to staying healthy and safe in college.

SEX ED 101

While many of you will be signing up for calculus or political science, there don't seem to be many open sections for talk about the birds and bees. When I told my friend I was writing this section, she laughed, "What's there to know about sex? Use a condom and get in there!" But that's the problem! Everyone assumes they already know everything they need to know about sex, and if not, they always have their latest issue of *Cosmo*.

Although you may think you're the sex guru, even you can benefit from a no-nonsense guide on sex in college to keep all the facts straight. Now, by no means do I purport to be the definitive expert in this field. Heck, people spend years in medical school and residency learning about the more complicated aspects surrounding sex. But thanks to several years in college and having to face the variety of sex-related issues that can come up, I have some real-world advice that can help you prepare. So sit down, strap in, and get your number 2 pencils ready, for you have just enrolled in Sex Ed 101.

FOR THE FIRST-TIMERS

Breathe. Having sex is not as daunting as it seems. First, you must understand what your own expectations are about sex. Even if this isn't your first trip to the rodeo, your feelings toward sex can fluctuate and it's important to be honest about your expectations. These expectations can be physical (*to the left, no right, yeah that's it*) or they can be emotional (*not yet...let's wait...OK, NOW, NOW, NOW I'm ready!*). Each sexual experience you have may not be the same—even if you're doing it with the same partner! So while that McDreamy fantasy is great to keep on standby, don't freak out if it doesn't happen your first time.

Once you've made the decision that you're ready to have sex, it's best to schedule an appointment with your gynecologist just so you know what you're working with. Your doctor can also talk to you about pregnancy and diseases. This includes prevention and detection. The only surefire way to prevent pregnancy or disease is via abstinence. There are also other options you can consider to limit the risks. There's birth control, which if used properly, is over 99 percent effective in preventing pregnancy. Birth control can come in the form of a pill, shot, or an external device being implanted in your body. It's best to talk to your doctor about these options and what may be the best one for you.

If you've already had sex and haven't seen a doctor, you should get yourself checked out. Sex can breed a bunch of baddies that, if ignored, can become a big nasty problem. If you don't have your own doctor, talk to your general practitioner and see if he or she has any information on how to find a gynecologist. You can also check to see if your health center has a women's health services center. My school has a full-service women's health department (with on-call gynecologists). If they can't do it in-house, they'll be able to direct you to the proper place that can.

When you're in your doctor's office, feel free to ask questions, questions, and more questions! Talk about discharge! Talk about pain! If something seems off, bring it up. Don't feel embarrassed; they've heard it all. Your sexual health is one of the most important things to protect. Being uneducated can lead to risky behavior, resulting in problems that you'll have to deal with for the rest of your life. This is the time you can address STDs (sexually transmitted diseases), vaccines, birth control, a change of diet, or even ask about that thing you saw on TV (*can I really twist my body like that?*). In addition to any health concerns, this is also a great place to learn about your body and libido. While a friend is a great resource, it's better to discuss these matters with a physician. It's like cutting your hair—would you trust your best bud or your stylist with a pair of scissors? Think of it that way, but with your vagina, which is a tad more important than a new 'do.

HOW TO PROTECT YOURSELF

The numbers are staggering. According to Stanford University's Sexual Health Peer Resource Center, 1 in 4 college students have a sexually transmitted infection (STI). Sure, you think it can't happen to you, but it can and it just might. So how can you make sure you don't become a statistic?

The surefire way to protect yourself is through abstinence. The next best way to prevent diseases is to use the barrier method. What I'm referring to here is the use of condoms when engaging in both vaginal and anal intercourse. There are different types of condoms, which include male condoms that create a barrier around the penis and female condoms that create a barrier inside the vagina. It's best to try different condoms and brands to see what works best for you. Latex is most popular (they prevent pregnancy about 97 percent of the time if used properly), but for those with an aversion to latex, try polyurethane condoms. (All other condoms—sheepskin, lambskin, etc.—don't perform as well, and you will be doing yourself a disservice by playing with them.) Condoms also come in a variety of sizes, and while there are XXLs, believe me when I say it's all fluff. If you've sat in a sexual-health presentation, you may remember the part when they stretch the condom over their forearm. Snag a free condom from your health center, and try it out yourself.

Condoms can serve as a barrier when performing oral sex on a male. There are even flavored and specialty condoms, for more flair. When performing oral sex on a female, it's best to use a dental dam. Dental dams stretch across the vulva, and create a barrier between the mouth and genitals to prevent disease. Most dental dams can be found via sexual health centers, or at special sex shops. Unfortunately, some infections spread to areas not covered by condoms. Therefore it's best to talk to your partner about their sexual history.

WHAT TO DO WHEN YOUR PROTECTION FAILS

Now that you know how to protect yourself if things go right, what do you do if things go wrong? Although condoms are a medically proven method of protection, there are times when they could slip off, break, or even get stuck inside your vagina. While these things don't happen often, it's important to be careful and make sure you're using it the right way, as incorrect usage leads to faulty results. When using condoms, always make sure you leave space at the tip to allow for shifting during ejaculation. Also, always check the expiration date, as expired condoms can be more brittle and ineffective.

So what do you do when your protection fails? Don't freak! You can engage in a backup method, such as emergency contraception. Emergency contraception pills (Plan B is approved for use in the United States) contain a heightened dose of progestin that acts almost like a supercharged birth control pill. Just as the label says, it should only be used in an emergency, and is only effective if taken within seventy-two hours after sex. Just so you're aware, some colleges do offer Plan B at their campus pharmacy. Cost varies, though a lot of schools will allow female students to secure the pill for free. You can consult your campus health services website to see if the pill is offered. If it isn't, look for a drugstore nearby and speak with an on-site pharmacist. Just remember, the sooner you take it, the more effective it is. Keep in mind, it does have some unpleasant side effects like nausea, dizziness, irregularities in your period, and lower abdominal pain. Remember, it is not 100 percent effective against pregnancy, and is not at all effective against STDs. It would also be best to get yourself checked out by a doctor, because remnants of the condom can sometimes be left inside.

PREGNANCY AND STDS

The best way to find out if you're pregnant is to track your cycle and mark it in a place that you regularly update, like your planner. Once you notice your period is out of whack, make an appointment with your doctor for a follow-up and grab an over-the-counter pregnancy test while you're waiting for the appointment. But it's important to not solely rely on these tests as they can end up being wrong.

Detection for STDs is a little more difficult than just looking at your calendar, especially since many STDs show few to no symptoms. Regular checkups with your doctor will help detect STDs. When you're being examined, make sure that they are testing you for *every-thing*—that includes the standard group of STDs, from herpes to HPV. In between checkups, do your own inspection. Prop yourself up in your bathroom, prep yourself with a mirror, and make sure that there is good lighting. Don't worry about feeling silly. It's yours—why not check out the goods?

If something feels or looks wrong, check in with your doctor. If it's nothing, mazel tov. It's just best to be sure. If you do find out that you have an STD, make sure you talk to your partner(s) and tell them to get tested. Awkward, of course, but it has to be done. Otherwise, they can't protect themselves or others.

TAKE ADVANTAGE OF THE RESOURCES AROUND YOU

No matter what situation you're facing sexually, there are a *ton* of resources on campus. Some schools may offer more services on campus than others, but most provide students with the information they need. Your best bet is to look to your campus health center. These centers are such a huge resource because they cater specifically to the college demographic. As a result, they focus on issues that impact college kids the most, such as pregnancy, STDs, and mental health issues that may begin to show up in young adults. They offer all sorts of resources, and usually provide pamphlets, health guides, free condoms, and peer-education programming.

If you find that your health center on campus does not carry information on sexual health, there are still other resources you can try. First, ask your health coordinator if they work with any particular hospitals or clinics in the area. If they don't have ties to any local centers, hit the Web and look for local hospitals and health centers. Or go to your local government's resource page, or nationally recognized organizations, such as Planned Parenthood. There's plenty of information out there—you just have to find it!

CHOOSING ABSTINENCE

Before we end this class, it's worth mentioning abstinence. When it comes to sex, the first question you must address is whether or not you plan to have sex in the first place. Since sex is such an individualized experience, you need to make sure that you're having it or not having it for the right reasons. It may be helpful to weigh your feelings and see how that corresponds with your values, beliefs, and your life plan. If you find that remaining abstinent is important to you, choose it and embrace it. While the decision to abstain is a personal one, sometimes it becomes difficult when you're surrounded by people who may not relate to you and your decision. But just because they may not share the same ideas doesn't mean that they won't understand. So, don't be afraid to stand your ground in a challenging discussion or situation.

WHY I CHOSE ABSTINENCE IN COLLEGE

Madeline Greene, Minnesota State University

College is a roller coaster of emotions. Choosing your major, meeting lifelong friends, learning about yourself and others, making mistakes, exploring the world, and preparing for life after college can feel like a whirlwind of change.

During my four years, I went through all of those growing pains and still, right after graduation, I continue to find myself looking back on that roller-coaster time, thankful for the lessons it taught me. One lesson, in particular, profoundly impacted my life—the choice to be abstinent in college.

I made a decision in my teen years that I was going to wait until I found the right person to have sex. It wasn't about what my parents wanted or what my religion taught me. It was a personal decision that I made for myself. For me, it was something that I wanted to give to someone I really cared about, and I wanted to make sure that I wouldn't regret my decision down the road.

In college, this decision was tested many times. I thought that I would find Mr. Right and that I would be married (or at least engaged) by the time I walked across the stage to get my diploma. Let me tell you, I couldn't have been more wrong.

Dating in college is difficult because there are two competing things at play. On one hand, you're trying to commit to another person while, on the other, college is really one of the most selfish times of your life (in a good way). The entire focus of being there is about you and finding out what you want for the future. It's important to take this time for yourself. Add in the pressure of explaining your choices—like my choice of abstinence—to that other person, and you can imagine how difficult it was to date at times.

I struggled with this issue in many of my college relationships, and let me tell you, it was not easy to navigate. While some of the guys I dated were understanding and even respected my decision, others found it hard to believe that I hadn't done what everyone else was doing. I found myself questioning my decision, and, at some points, even regretting that I had decided this was what was right for me. Many times, I thought about just getting it over with. But every time the opportunity came forth, something stopped me.

I learned many life lessons in college but this one, above all, means the most to me. I learned that sometimes you have to go your own way, blaze your own trail, and navigate through hard times by following your heart. I am proud that I didn't cave when I was questioned and stayed true to myself. I stayed abstinent in college because that was what was right for me. It caused some heartache and turmoil, but it also allowed be to be confident in my choices and do what was right for me.

As you begin your collegiate journey, I challenge you to sit down and find what is right for you. Don't allow others to weigh in on your decisions if you already know what is best for you. Above all, follow your heart. My choice was to wait for the right person to come along and, while I'm still waiting, I have faith that Mr. Right is out there somewhere.

Most times, your friends will be supportive, but intimate relationships are a whole other matter. What's most important is to be up front about your needs with your partner, and to express your desire to abstain. Sure, there might be some jerks out there who will tease you or even get angry or pushy; don't back down. But by and large, if you're honest and up front with your partner from the beginning, he'll understand that it's a decision that's important to you and will respect you for it.

And don't forget that there are many other ways to be intimate without having sex. Touching and kissing can be just as intense as going all the way. Also, don't underestimate the power of words. Some couples I know who practice abstinence undergo these intense dream sequences where they describe their sexual fantasies in a safe and personal environment. This creates a feeling of physical intimacy without actually having to be physical.

There's so much to say about safe sex that there are not enough pages in this book to cover it, but I hope this crash course has provided a good overview for all you potential sex goddesses out there.

Insights provided by Aja Johnson, University of Maryland–College Park

OVER-THE-TOP PARTY PALS AND WAYS TO DEAL

Perfectly straightened hair? Check. Super-cute new outfit, complete with matching shoes and bag? Check. Your best friend completely plastered before you even head out the door? Uh-oh. Partying with the girls is a great way to de-stress after a tiring week of classes, papers, and exams. And if you haven't heard it before, "College is the time to try everything," and "Hey, you only live once!" While college is known as a time for experimenting, there is still work to be done and, well, embarrassing moments to be had.

Whether hitting a hot bar or club or hanging at a frat party, these moments, although fun, can also pose some challenges if you've got a friend who parties a little too hard. So maybe you're not the drunk girl dancing on the stripper pole, puking in the bathroom sink, or making out with a random stranger—*but what do you do if one of your friends is?*

Whether you're finally checking out the frat house down the street known for throwing killer bashes, kicking it with a few friends on the front porch, or hitting up the bar scene, keep these tips in mind when you're hanging out with a friend who tends to drink a little too much and take things a little too far.

SO, SHE'S EMBARRASSING YOU
You're at a Bar

Is she getting a little too loose on the stripper pole? She might not be the sexiest chick on the dance floor after her seventh beer, but now probably isn't the time to discuss her not-so-suave moves. As long as she isn't popping, locking, and dropping in a way you know would embarrass her if she was sober, let it go. Everyone deserves the chance to go a little crazy on occasion. However, there's a fine line between being a fun drunk and a drunken mess. Use your best judgment in determining that line. If your gut tells you she's gone a little too far (i.e., taking clothes off), don't hesitate to let her know.

You're at a House/Frat Party with Strangers

Is she making out with a dark shadowy figure off in a deserted corner? In college, a few random make-out sessions are almost a rite of passage. But if things look seriously wrong (for example, that guy she's kissing in the corner is twice her age, she's promising to go home with a boy from her English class, or announcing that she's driving home completely smashed), it's time for a chat. In these situations, it's OK to step in to help your friend avoid some potentially horrible consequences. She may drunkenly claim she hates you at the time, but she'll love you for it tomorrow.

DON'T, UNDER ANY CIRCUMSTANCES, LET HER LEAVE BY HERSELF!

Here are a few scenarios that you may face when partying with your over-the-top party pal.

If It's Just the Two of You

So that boy from her class? He says there's something going on at his house later and invites your friend, and you, along. You're tired and so ready for bed—but your friend obviously isn't. Make sure you let her know that you aren't going to follow her and that you don't think she's capable of going by herself. It may seem a little aggressive. But even if you weren't invited, it's still your responsibility to make sure she gets home safely. Offer an alternative: how about a few of you go out for some late-night pizza? The extra calories aren't half as dangerous as heading back to an almost-stranger's house.

If You're Out with a Group

Partying with a group changes the dynamic slightly. You should weigh all the options. Do you or any of your friends know this guy? Do you have any mutual friends? Does one of the other girls want to go with your friend, and is she sober enough to make rational decisions? Don't be afraid to play Mom in the group. Remember that nagging little voice you hear inside your head when you're about to do something you know is wrong? Be the one to speak the truth: going home with this guy is reckless, and could be dangerous.

If You Just Met Up with Her

Say you didn't spend three hours primping with her and didn't even know she was going to be at the same place, but you happen to bump into her at the party. Although there may not be an obligation, a good friend should keep an eye on her intoxicated girlfriend. Offer her the same options mentioned above and advise her as you would any of the girls you came with. If she does decide to leave with a guy she just met in her drunken state, check up on her later. For instance, give her cell phone a ring and make sure she doesn't need an easy out or somewhere else to stay.

If She's Attempting to Drive

The statistics are haunting—seventeen hundred college students between the ages of eighteen and twenty-four die each year from alcohol-related unintentional injuries. This includes vehicle crashes. Don't let your friend become a statistic! Offer to pay for a cab to send her home. Walk home with her and promise a ride back to her car the next morning. Do whatever it takes to make sure she doesn't get her keys in the ignition.

IF THE SITUATION GETS SERIOUS

You've decided to help, but what happens when your friend is not eagerly responding to your advice? Or if she's in imminent danger?

Stay Calm

Remember that your friend is in an altered state of mind. This means that anything you say or do at this point could be blown out of proportion. She might not take your advice too kindly, especially if she's intoxicated. Don't get angry with her or give up. Although she may not realize it, she probably needs your help. Explain that you are only letting her know because you are trying to be a good friend. Leave it at that. There's no reason to fight with her when she probably won't even remember why she was mad in the morning. Plus, no one wants to cause a scene when they're out having a good time.

Now She's Puking All Over the Floor!

You've managed to talk your friend into doing the right thing in choosing to leave the bar and go home. But your job doesn't end there. If she is extremely wasted, don't leave your plastered pal passed out on the tile. Get her some water and hold her hair back. Then get her in bed on her stomach. Don't forget that she could possibly choke if she is lying on her back. She'll thank you in the morning, even if she's über-hungover.

Your Friend Is Completely Wasted and Now You're Really Worried

If her breathing slows, she appears unconscious, or her skin is cold and clammy, she might have alcohol poisoning. Don't hesitate to dial 911 or find a Resident Assistant who will do it for you. At Princeton, the university policy require that students help severely drunk people by contacting local medical or safety personnel or local police. And don't worry. Neither you nor the people you help will be disciplined for intoxication. Even if your school does not have this policy, always take care of a friend in need.

A COMMON OCCURRENCE?

People can develop psychological and physical dependency on alcohol, and alcoholism can occur in people as early as college. It's not uncommon at all. In fact, 31 percent of college students meet the criteria for substance abuse and 6 percent meet the criteria for alcohol dependence. Everybody likes to have fun and relax in his or her own way after a long, stressful week. But if your friend is drinking every night, drinking alone, or can't control or stop herself while she is drinking, she could be developing alcoholism. You'll be doing her a favor if you sit down and talk to her about her drinking.

Need More Information on Alcoholism?
Check out alcoholism.about.com for tons of information about alcoholism and other forms of substance abuse, including an Alcohol Abuse Screening Quiz.

Insights provided by Erica Strauss, Kent State University

DEALING WITH A DISABILITY ON CAMPUS

Leaving home for the first time is an incomparably nerve-wracking experience. You set off for school with your shower caddy and laundry tote, expected to face a brand new world solo. The experience seems daunting enough on its own, but add in the responsibility of balancing a disability and suddenly the whole thing seems terrifying. As a student who made it through college with a couple of her own, I can promise you—as long as you are open and honest about needing help (and DON'T try to handle things alone)—you will manage with no problem.

I was born with severe food allergies to egg, peanut, tree nut, and shellfish. If I ingest any of these allergens, my body is prone to enter anaphylactic shock—a complex way of saying *I could die*. My parents were terrified to leave me fending for myself in the dining hall and eating at strange restaurants, but I wanted to play it cool.

In my tiny hometown, despite many attempts to downplay my condition's severity, my allergies were considered "common knowledge" by those around me. College, however, provided me an opportunity to start with a fresh slate. No one had to know! When my school offered me accommodation housing (my own kitchen) and disability services, I was adamant about remaining a "normal student"—whatever I thought that meant.

Unfortunately, it didn't take long for me to learn the importance of being up front and honest about my allergies. I'd find eggs mucking up the feta cheese in the salad bar, and watch the sandwich station attendants repetitively reuse knives with mayo and nut bread. I got unhelpful responses from staff and spent a lot of time feeling frustrated and embarrassed. Fruit is a major part of my diet due to my allergies, and I repeatedly got in trouble for taking an extra apple or banana back to my room for a snack.

My sophomore year I moved into an on-campus apartment with a kitchen, and it was one of the best decisions I ever made. I also started asking the dining hall questions via email, allowing them to address any questions when they weren't super busy. And furthermore, my doctor spoke to the dining hall staff about my needs—and no longer was I punished for "stealing" an apple.

That was one big issue I had to handle. College can also be a time when mental illness can take shape and begin to cause issues for many young people. I was officially diagnosed with a fairly typical "disability" for students—Generalized Anxiety Disorder (GAD)—my junior year of college. Stress and new surroundings often exasperate existing conditions. I denied many of my symptoms for quite some time. I pushed them away and suffered in silence until it became obvious to my loved ones that I was dealing with something. I've probably had GAD my entire life, but it didn't really start to show itself until I was off on my own.

It wasn't until I sought help from services on campus (and eventually off campus) that I realized how important it is to be honest about your needs. I will probably always have to seek a little side help for my anxiety, but I'm prepared to deal with it and confident that I can.

I'll admit: I had a long-standing stigma about talking to a therapist and was convinced my anxiety was just something I needed to deal with myself. It's hard to explain exactly how crippling true anxiety can be—it removes any sense of rationality and logic and can really prevent you from living a healthy, normal life. I was caught under this sense of floating panic at nearly all times, and could not turn it off despite my many attempts.

I am now a strong advocate for counseling. *Seriously, go talk to a therapist!* In my therapy sessions, I never lie on a couch and receive clichéd advice like you see in the movies. Instead, the conversation is typically pretty free-form, and I often find myself coming to realizations and resolutions on my own. My therapist likes to tap into my favorite creative outlets like writing to help me express myself, and that was really important to me. I honestly believe journaling to be one of the most therapeutic practices in the world. Looking for a good fit when seeking a psychologist, therapist, or counselor is key in creating an environment in which you feel comfortable.

No matter what's wrong or what disability you may face, if you ask trusted individuals—like the staff in the Student Accessibility Services department on your campus or the Student Counseling Center—you'll find it's pretty easy to be connected to proper on-campus support. For example, tutors are all over campus, and often offered at no additional costs. Extensions can be given barring certain circumstances, and some students are able to take tests in quiet rooms or for extended periods of time. Professors can be pretty understanding, so be sure to let them know when something personal is getting in the way. Overcoming challenges is definitely nothing to be ashamed of, as I've learned (albeit the hard way).

Untreated or "ignored" issues can become huge barriers to success over time. It's important to be honest about the situation you're in, and seek the proper help. Talk to your peer advisor. Talk to your faculty advisor. Check out the counseling services on your campus. Seek disability services on your campus (at my school, food allergies were handled under this office too!). Don't be embarrassed; be proactive. College is too expensive (and stressful) to suffer unnecessarily. So don't. Plus, college is the perfect time to learn how to cope with your disabilities. When the "real world" comes (and it comes fast!), you'll want to be on the right path.

Insights provided by Emma Martin, Ithaca College

STAYING FIT IN COLLEGE

Everyone fears those evil, infamous "freshman fifteen," but are they really fact or just fiction? Leading a healthy lifestyle can be hard in college when you are always on the run and Mom isn't there with all three of your daily meals prepared. Classes, jobs, extracurricular activities, and your social life can cause your eating habits to go haywire.

Last semester when I was an intern, I'd come back from my internship and feel the urge to devour something easy and quick. I'd rarely eat lunch during the day, as I was busy on my feet, working on projects and helping editors into the early evening. When I arrived back on campus, I was tired and hungry. My solution? I would grab the easiest food, like a greasy Hot Pocket or fries for dinner. Sometimes I'd try to be healthy with a sandwich or salad or something sensible. But most of the time I used my crazy workload as an excuse to eat certain "bad" foods a little too much. As an incoming college student, you too will be busy. However, if you take control early on, you can develop great habits that can last a lifetime. If you want to win the "Freshman Fitness Test," here are a few tips to help you stay fit and be healthier overall.

YOUR FIRST YEAR

As a new college student, it's only normal that you will have a million questions. Simple things like where to get food, where to work out, and how to stay on top of things can seem overwhelming when you first arrive at your new home. So let's get started.

Eating Right

Most likely, you will have a university cafeteria, and the majority of you who live on campus will have meal plans included in your tuition bill. As a freshman at my school, I was required to have a meal plan of $1,200 per semester because fresh-

> ## DID YOU KNOW?
>
> Research studies have proven that *the average female college coed only gains two to three pounds during her first year of school*; it's actually her male counterparts who are more likely to pack on the weight! If you want to ensure that the freshman fifteen remains a myth, cut down on carbs and fatty foods, amp up your fruit and vegetable intake, and set aside at least two to three days a week for an hour of cardio or strength training.

men dorms did not have kitchens. These days, college students access their meal plans through their university identification card, which swipes almost like a credit card in cafeterias and dining halls. Some universities have dining halls that are like cafeterias but are all-you-can-eat buffet-style. Proceed with caution with buffets! Sometimes too many food options are not a good thing; overabundance can lead to overeating. But rest assured that you can eat healthy with minimal effort—these places almost always have vegetarian dishes, salads, and fruits for health-conscious students.

Some colleges have perks or points options where you can go off campus to local restaurants and they will deduct money from your meal card, while others have student discounts at nearby restaurants. Here's a healthy tip: instead of going crazy at the nearby McDonald's or KFC, look for other options like Saladworks, Subway, or alternative restaurants like sushi bars and Thai food, which offer healthier meal choices and place less of an emphasis on fried, fattening foods. But watch out for that shrimp tempura at the sushi restaurant! Check to see if the restaurant has nutritional guidelines so you can find out just exactly how many calories are in that delectable item you're getting ready to order.

Working Out

During your first week, find your school's gym. Recreation hall or gym facility fees are usually included in your tuition bill, so you might as well use them! I cannot tell you how excited I was my junior year when my university finally completed our new gym. It was closer to the dorms than the previous gym, and the new state-of-the-art treadmills with TVs were definitely an upgrade!

Did you know that you can even get school credit for working out? At most schools, you can. Have you always been curious about Tae Kwon Do or wanted to become a better swimmer? Check out your school's course offerings and sign up for an easy A and better body next semester.

What if you don't live on campus? Sorry, no excuse. You still have access to the gym before and after class or on the weekends. Even though you may not have the opportunity to work out several times a week, a regular routine of two or three times per week will help you see results.

Make use of what you've got, whether it's your school's running track, the gym, or your own dorm room. One year, my roommate and I did weekly Tae Bo workouts in our dorm room (we were lucky to have a spacious area that year). Bottom line: find a routine that works with you and your schedule and stick with it!

Don't Freak Out

So you've been at school for a few months and really haven't gotten into a healthy routine yet. If you look in the mirror and don't like what you see, stop the negative feelings! Don't freak out if you're not at the same weight you were when you first started high school. What many women fail to realize is when you first enter college at seventeen or eighteen, your body is still developing physically. So you can't compare your body to how it was a few years ago or sometimes even a few months ago!

Take a deep breath, and refocus your efforts on starting a healthy routine of exercising and eating right. Also, being healthy isn't just about the numbers on your scale; there are several other tests that are used to determine how fit you really are. Body mass index (BMI), is a guideline used to judge whether you are at risk for health problems associated with your weight. Rather than relying on the bathroom scale, experts say that you should also know your BMI, a figure that takes into account not just weight but height to indicate body fat. In general, experts say that you should aim for a BMI that's over eighteen and under twenty-five. (To check your BMI try the online calculator at www.healthcentral.com/diet-exercise/index-1688143.html.) You may be surprised to find that you are underweight when you consider your height and body frame.

MAKE A PLAN

OK, so you've made the decision to get healthy. Now the question is how to do it.

Some of you may end up living off campus or in apartment-style dorms. If you have a kitchen with a stove, jump for joy! Your options are endless. All you need to do is visit your supermarket right away and start cooking your own meals. Cooking your own meals has two benefits: it's generally healthier *and* it's cheaper. Sometimes it will be tempting to go to Applebee's or the local diner for a quick bite, but don't cave in to a quick and unhealthy fix. And don't forget that ordering Chinese food and pizza can become really pricey on a student's limited budget.

TAKE IT FROM A GIRL WHO'S BEEN THERE

Sometimes you can become unhealthy by association. One of my close friends started dating her boyfriend over a year ago, and since then, she's noticed she gained a few pounds from eating out more often. The problem? She feels the need to clean her plate just as he does, and most restaurants are notorious for their extra-large servings. It's not a myth that men can eat more than women and still maintain a reasonable weight.

It's cool to dine out with your boyfriend or even a bunch of your guy friends, but realize that while he can scarf down eight slices of pizza and seem not to gain a pound, it's definitely not a habit to acquire. However, don't be too afraid or shy to eat around your guy. Most likely, he'd rather see you actually enjoy food and eat well than pretend you hate food. In fact, your good habits might inspire him to make a few positive changes for himself!

Make cooking at home fun! Invite your friends to your place for a low-cost and healthy dinner. One of my former roommates and I used to occasionally cook dinner together and make a recipe of baked chicken with breadcrumbs and usually a vegetable like green beans or broccoli to go with it. It was filling, full of flavor, and more health-friendly than eating pizza and french fries. For other recipes, check out websites or apps from Allrecipes or Epicurious for delicious options.

Find a System That Works for You

The best way to get healthy is to establish a routine and stick with it. Take your daily planner or even a blank piece of paper and write down your schedule. Include class, work, and any other obligations you have. Next, find spots where you could fit in a workout; it doesn't have to be every day. You'll probably have some Monday/Wednesday/Friday classes with breaks in between. Just pencil in an hour at the gym at the same time for each of these days, and treat it like a class. When you set a routine, you'll be more likely to stick to your workout plan. Also, don't worry if you go off track. Maybe that's an indication that you need to rethink your schedule, and you shouldn't be afraid to readjust. Since I hate the word "diet" (and you'll find out why later on), think about a program that doesn't tell you what to eat, but encourages you to make better decisions. My friend currently is on the Weight Watchers plan and says it works for her because she can eat all the foods she likes but just in moderation.

Working out with friends is a great way to stay motivated. You will be much more likely to go to the gym when someone is depending on you to be there. But just make sure you first discuss your goals and what type of workouts you are going to do. For example, I had a friend who inherited her workout routine from her boyfriend who was involved in track. Needless to say, her complete routine was difficult! It consisted of a long warm-up, and then a lot of running on the track. Now, I had no qualms about warm-ups and doing exercises, but I have always despised running. This is an important thing to remember. Having friends to help you exercise or eat healthier can be a huge motivator, but you have to make sure not to lose track of your *own* goals. A friend may want to lose a few pounds while you'd like to lose twenty. That's a *big* difference. Or maybe your roommate can eat whatever she wants and still maintain her hourglass figure with just exercise while you have to exercise and eat better to stay in shape. Everyone's body type is different, so before you try to mirror your friends' habits, find the system that works the best for you!

Be Realistic

Finally, the trick to being healthy and fit in college is getting rid of the word "diet" and substituting the words "moderation" and "exercise." I know that the latest diet crazes are everywhere—in gossip magazines, the news, and commercials. I don't care how often you read about it because dieting is not a healthy way to eat long-term. You may lose a few pounds initially, but they always come back unless you change your lifestyle. UCLA researchers recently found that one year after starting a diet, people were no better off than before—in fact, about half of them ended up gaining weight.

Get rid of the word "diet" because restricting your eating is not healthy in the long term!

Make realistic changes to your lifestyle over time, and do everything in moderation. Only you know what you can handle. For instance, if you entirely abandon a food that you love because it's unhealthy, your supposedly healthy change may not last long. It's very difficult to give up favorite foods. It might make you more likely to binge or go overboard later.

I'll give you a quick example of what I mean by moderation. You're going to make a sandwich. Instead of a glob of mayo to top it off, use something healthier like mustard or even fat-free mayo. Or try eating only half the sandwich. And when it comes to snacking, instead of having a candy bar every day after class, cut down to giving yourself this treat once a week while filling yourself up with tasty fruits and vegetables on the other days. If you find yourself eating out every week, cut it down to maybe once or twice a month.

Be Safe

Being healthy is great, but don't go to the extreme and acquire an eating disorder. Eating disorders such as bulimia, anorexia, binge eating, and overeating can happen to anyone. Actually, 5 to 7 percent of women in the United States will suffer from some type of eating disorder during their lifetime. Also, something else to watch out for is over-exercising. Some warning signs of a compulsive exerciser are the following: exercising even when you don't feel well, basing your daily diet on how much you exercise, constantly worrying you'll gain weight if you don't exercise every day, forcing yourself to do multiple workouts during the day, or becoming depressed if you miss a workout. If you think you've acquired any of these unhealthy eating or lifestyle habits, seek out professional help. This is something you do not want to ignore, because it may become worse over time, negatively affecting your collegiate experience and your health.

LAST BIT OF ADVICE

Remember that you're in college, so expect late-night pizza orders or times when you'll pig out on ice cream and cookies. Food is not to be feared. Your best bet to ensuring a successful college experience is to enjoy your faves in moderation and exercise throughout the week. With this approach, you will be the best you can be academically, socially, and physically.

Insights provided by Donyel L. Griffin, Kean University
and Kylie Thompson, Harvard University

STAYING SAFE ON CAMPUS

A few months after I moved into the dorms, a young woman was sexually assaulted in my housing complex. My friend Hailey and I were concerned that not enough information about safety was getting out to the rest of the campus and decided to try to do something about it on our own. We spent a whole day running around campus, being sent from office to office trying to talk to the right person who would help us get the word out. Luckily, we were able to convince campus police to make us hundreds of copies of the crime report. Hailey and I proceeded to post them in every housing building, on every door. This was an unfortunate crash course introduction on the importance of being safe on campus.

WHY SAFETY MATTERS

College students, especially female college students, need to learn how to be safe on their campus. Why? From the news headlines to music videos, physical violence—especially against women—is just a part of everyday life in our culture. The result of this is that the college campus is not always a safe place for female students. In the face of this, we need to take control of our lives and our safety, and learn how to be as safe as possible. Now this does not mean that women have to walk around scared or live in a state of fear. I believe it is possible for women to live their lives fully and be safe at the same time.

Before I dive into the practical areas of campus safety, let me say that although there are ways to ensure one's safety on campus, any type of violence against women is *never*, in any circumstance, their fault. Women don't deserve to be assaulted because they left a window open, walked home late at night, or wore an extra tiny skirt. Violence against a woman is never her fault. With that noted, here's how you can make your college experience safer.

BE AWARE OF YOUR CAMPUS RESOURCES AND SURROUNDINGS

When you arrive on campus, one of the first things you should do is familiarize yourself with your campus's safety system. It's there for you, should you ever need it. A good thing to keep in mind is that every college campus has a campus safety system in place and campus police.

In addition to the safety system, the "buddy system" is another way to stay safe. Always walk with a friend, classmate, or a roommate at night, whether it's to the library or to a late-night class. Most campuses also offer shuttle systems at night in case you find yourself without a buddy. And if—for whatever reason—you have missed the shuttle and/or need to walk to your car alone, don't hesitate to call campus security and have them walk you to wherever you need to go.

TAKE IT FROM A GIRL WHO'S BEEN THERE

One time, I was on campus after eleven working on a project.

I didn't even bother considering how I could walk home safely alone. Instead, I called campus police for an escort, and they actually sent an officer in a police car to drive me down to my dorm. Program the number for the escort services on campus into your cell phone, so you are never stuck walking alone at night.

If you do walk alone, there are a few measures you can take to be safer. Experts say to avoid being on your cell phone while you're walking alone. This way, you're more alert and are paying more attention to your surroundings. You can also call a friend or family member when you are leaving the library and tell them you'll call them when you are safely back at your dorm, apartment, or car. Give them an estimate of when you'll get home, and ask them to call you back if they don't hear from you by that time. Carrying pepper spray or mace is also a good idea.

SMARTPHONES AND SAFETY: AVOID PROVIDING TMI

Ashley Tripp, University of Alabama

Imagine that someone is able to track you no matter where you are and at all times just because you're using your cell phone. This isn't a bad dream—it's reality. Thanks to mobile apps like Foursquare and social media sites, they may already be tracking you.

As you likely already know, Foursquare enables you to "check in" to particular locations like stores and restaurants, and in exchange, you receive points, badges, and even dis-counts to your favorite spots. Great perks, right? Even though Foursquare says that only your select friends can see your activity, creepers such as hackers, stalkers, burglars, and potential sexual predators can still track down your location, especially when you link your Twitter or Facebook accounts to Foursquare. By doing so, you're broadcasting your location to a larger network of people.

When using Foursquare or similar apps, be cautious about what you post so you can avoid privacy issues and potential crimes. Don't share your phone number, email, hometown, or any other personal information on your Foursquare pro-file page. Also, NEVER check in to where you live—that is just TMI. Still want to rack up those points at your favorite bar? Try "checking in" to your location after leaving the site instead of beforehand. And don't add anyone you don't know or don't feel comfortable with seeing your profile. Add people that you trust. Last but not least, while on vacation, avoid "vaca-tion shout-outs," which puts you at risk for burglary and other safety issues.

The best way to ensure you're staying safe on Foursquare and other apps is to keep your profiles private and limit your posts.

There are several other things to be aware of when considering your safety on campus. Be aware of the lighting on your campus. Are all areas of the campus and your dorms well lit? Are there large dark areas? You want to be in lighted areas at all times of the night. It's better to take the long way if it helps you to stay safer! And if there are major areas lacking sufficient lighting, make a stink about it. It will take persistence to get these things fixed, but you deserve safety. Your campus should also provide emergency phones. They should be sporadically placed around the campus for you to grab and call in case of any emergency. Know where they are. Finally, be aware of any large bushes. Are there large bushes and shrubbery that would make the perfect hiding place for someone? Knowing where these bushes are and the potentially dangerous situations they may present is important to keeping yourself safe. Bottom line: trust your gut and don't place yourself into a dicey situation that you didn't have to be in in the first place.

DORM-ROOM SAFETY

Now, regarding the dorms, keep windows and doors locked. End of story. This may be tricky to do, as people are always going in and out of other people's rooms, but it's essential to keeping yourself safe. And don't be afraid to ask your roommate(s) to do the same. Roomies should look out for one another. My last bit of advice on keeping yourself safe on campus: have your campus police number programmed into your cell and if you have a landline, on the speed dial. My speed dial number seven says "Campus Popo." This way the police are always at your fingertips in case of emergency.

PREVENTING THEFT ON CAMPUS

Ashley Yenick, Merrimack College

No college student wants to be a victim of a crime, but the

truth is that it does happen to normal people like you and me, and it is a real concern on campuses nationwide.

All campuses are required by the Clery Act to report crimes that have happened on campus, so you should be able to find this information pretty easily. The United States Department of Education has set up a website where you can check crime that has happened on your college campus for the past three years. It's called "The Campus Safety and Security Data Analysis Cutting Tool" (ope.ed.gov/security), and it's pretty simple to use. You just type in your college campus name, city, and state, and the public records show up. This is important to check because it can be helpful to see what the potential risks and threats are—which crimes were committed and where on campus. Having this information in your back pocket will help you avoid obvious safety missteps.

Here are some simple steps you can take to protect yourself from theft on campus.

IN YOUR DORM ROOM

- **Always keep your door locked:** The only people who have keys to your room should be residence life staff members, your roommate(s), and you. That's it.
- **Invest in a personal safe:** Limit the valuables, keepsakes, and expensive tech devices that you bring to campus. Costume jewelry is a lot easier to replace than a family heirloom. Store the valuables you do bring with you in a safe, or consider other options like a door alarm or hide-away items.

- **Buy a laptop lock:** Laptop locks are easy to use, inexpensive, and can be found at electronics stores. Use it whenever you leave your laptop unattended.

- **Choose combinations and passwords that are tough to crack:** Combinations like "1111" or "0000" are not safe. Also, it's better not to use your birthday or any personal information in your passwords and/or combinations. One nifty trick I use: Choose a password that serves a dual purpose of locking your device *and* setting a goal for yourself like "runamarathon2013" or something that you want to achieve. That way, you'll be constantly reminded of your goal, and you'll remember the password!

IN THE LIBRARY AND OTHER CAMPUS HUBS

- **Perform a bag check:** Before you go to the library, take an inventory of things that you have in your bag. Then check your bag before you leave the library to make sure you have everything you brought in. If you find you're missing something, retrace your steps to make sure you didn't misplace it, and if you still can't find it, notify campus security immediately.

- **Keep your things with you at all times:** When in the library, cafeteria, or other busy campus buildings, always take your belongings—purse, backpack, or wallet—with you even if you're just going to search for a book or making a quick trip to the bathroom. You can ask a study neighbor or friend to watch your stuff, but do realize they are not ultimately responsible if anything goes missing.

PREVENTING CAR THEFT

- **Always, always, always keep your doors locked:** Always. I don't think I can stress it enough. If your car is locked and alarmed, there's less of a chance that it will be broken into, or worse, stolen.

- **Leave all belongings in your dorm or apartment:** Don't leave any valuables in your car, especially items like laptops, tablets, GPS devices, or iPods. If you do have something valuable on you, store it in your trunk. Out of sight, out of mind.

- **Remember where you park your car:** If you go to a big university, you might have a huge parking lot where the entire student body parks. Keep track of your car. If there's a long stretch of time where you don't use your car, check on it every couple of days to make sure everything is OK. I would also suggest moving your car to a different spot every now and then. That way, even if you're not using it for a few days, a thief won't be able to tell the difference.

Follow these tips to avoid finding yourself a victim of a crime that didn't need to happen. If you want more information on campus safety, check out Collegestudentsafety.com.

TAKE A SELF-DEFENSE COURSE

If you have not already done so, sign up for a self-defense class as soon as you arrive on campus. Now, I'm not claiming that if you take one of these classes that you will have the ability to beat the crap out of every person who steps in your path. However, it does equip you with the tools to defend yourself, to fight back, to get away from an assailant. Also, it isn't just about the physical aspect of defense—like how to use a man's strength against him so you can get away—but there is also a psychological component. After taking the course, I felt stronger and more confident in my ability to defend myself. It's not just how to drop and elbow some guy in the cajones when he bear hugs you from the back. It's empowerment. My campus offered Rape Aggression Defense classes in the dorms, and also a Women's Self-Defense class through the kinesiology department. Look into your resources on campus. See what's offered and take advantage.

NOTHING SAYS CRAZY LIKE YOUR VERY OWN STALKER

While it may seem like only celebrities deal with freaky overeager fans, real people can and do encounter stalkers. In many cases, the stalker will start out as a friend, boyfriend, coworker, or familiar face from class. In fact, 77 percent of female victims and 64 percent of male victims know their stalkers.

How do you know if you're dealing with a stalker? Someone is likely stalking you if:

- he or she repeatedly follows or spies on you
- he or she repeatedly calls you at home, work, or during class
- he or she repeatedly sends unwanted letters, texts, emails, etc.

- he or she leaves unexpected gifts for you to find
- he or she threatens you or someone close to you
- he or she vandalizes or damages your property
- he or she repeatedly shows up for no legitimate reason at the same places you do

It's important to communicate a clear "NO" to your stalker from the moment his or her behavior becomes suspicious. Don't encourage his or her behavior by responding to phone calls, texts, Facebook messages, emails, etc. Change up your routine if you notice that somebody is closely following you. If the stalking continues and you start to feel unsafe, notify campus security or the local police department right away. Whatever you do, don't make the mistake of trying to handle the situation on your own. Take immediate action to keep safe.

You deserve to feel safe on your campus. Be aware, know what resources are available, and take those self-defense classes—every last one of them! Safety is a major issue on college campuses that women have to deal with in a way that men don't. So educate yourself, and be empowered. We college women are completely capable of being safe, fun, young, adventurous, and wise all at the same time.

Insights provided by Monica Taylor, California State University–Los Angeles and Ashley Yenick, Merrimack College

UCHIC ESSENTIALS—
STAYING HEALTHY AND SAFE

LISTEN TO YOUR BODY

College is the time to do anything and everything. But be careful not to overexert yourself. Take time to rest and rejuvenate. It will remind you that you are important, hardworking, and deserve to be pampered every now and then.

USE YOUR ON-CAMPUS RESOURCES

From the campus health center to disability resources to the fitness center, your university has fantastic resources created specifically for you. And you're paying for them, so why not use them? Your body and mind will thank you.

TAKE SAFETY SERIOUSLY

It's so easy to get comfortable in your campus surroundings and think that nothing bad will happen to you. But campus crime and violence does happen. The best thing you can do is be proactive about your safety. Please, don't take it— or yourself—for granted.

Looking for more great advice? Head to UChic.com for even more resources and information—they come highly recommended from our contributors and editors. Be sure to leave your suggestions as well!

"It is important to try new things and learn how to become independent, but it's just as important to stay true to who you are and what you believe, and to not lose sight of those things."

—BLAIR B., UNIVERSITY OF MIAMI

9

IF THE GOING
GETS TOUGH

THERE ARE BOUNDLESS OPTIONS in college. No curfews. No limits on alcohol. No reminders to do homework. We could go on, but you get the picture. The only hard and steadfast rule is that you are in charge, so you may naturally feel a bit stressed to make the right decisions when it comes to some very tough topics and temptations. Sometimes, it's not your own temptations that should be of concern. Your friends, a boyfriend, a guy you just met at a bar, and maybe even a professor will face their own temptations, and might drag you into situations you never had planned (or wanted) to be in. Taken too far, something that started out as innocent could end up being a disaster for all. With these freedoms comes the fact that the going can and will get tough on occasion in college, especially when you are surrounded by so many temptations making it hard to always do the right thing. Follow the advice in this chapter, and you'll learn how to not only survive but also thrive in college—no matter what challenge(s) may be ahead.

OVERCOMING MENTAL HEALTH ISSUES

When I first went away to school, it was like an experience I never could have dreamed up. It was four hours away from my old stomping grounds, and my first time away from home. As a girl with such a strong social circle, it was weird being light-years away from everything that was familiar to me. Don't get me wrong; I was no wallflower. I was busy buzzing around campus, meeting new people, staying out late, getting in trouble, and doing all of the great things that could only go on in a college setting (where else can you get fresh brownies delivered at the drop of a dime, or partake in a midnight round of freeze tag?). But between the food and the fun, I noticed something missing. While I was doing things that were fun, new, and exciting, there was a part of me that felt I was drifting into the background…that somehow my self-confidence was losing out.

One of the best things about college life is the ability to get caught up in anything. It's spontaneous, it's crazy, and it can put you completely out of your element and comfort zone. Although fun, it can also be a bad thing for your self-confidence.

A CULTURE SHOCK

As I drifted from party to party, running into girls from my hall and guys from my classes, I found myself bending to complement each situation. I was paranoid that I wasn't smart, pretty, or cool enough. I thought I was talking too much, saying too little, and I was afraid they would find out about me. I was afraid they would know I was cheating, applying a smile with each swipe of my lip gloss. I wasn't being fake, but I was stretched too thin. I began blending into the background and found myself not knowing who I was anymore.

Over time this tore at me, since I didn't realize what was happening. The littlest things brought me down; I overanalyzed, and because of it, my self-confidence all but disappeared. I began doubting myself and my individual shine became lackluster. How could this happen to the girl who once made everyone laugh? This wasn't just because I wanted to fit in; it was so much more than that. It was more like culture shock, and I wasn't prepared for it. I thought I could seamlessly be the same me as I was in high school. Yet in retrospect, it sounds ridiculous. How could I be the same me when everything was different? Even through this angst, I was growing. I was getting out there and challenging myself. It was simply ridiculous to cling to the past. I wasn't that version of "me" anymore.

When I finally realized how I was sabotaging myself, I felt so embarrassed by my behavior. I thought I was so much stronger than that. But I was completely worn out. My spirit was silenced (as corny as that sounds). So what did I do? What could I do? I pulled back. I asked myself what I needed to do to get back to smiling, back to laughing, back to just breathing easy. I figured out this was much larger than what I could handle and looked to every resource I could find. I found out that I was struggling with my self-confidence and needed an extreme boost to my self-esteem. The more information I

read, the more I realized how many girls go through the same thing—
and they were just like me. Suddenly, I didn't feel alone.

DEALING WITH DEPRESSION

Janine Camara, University of North Carolina-Greensboro

We all face periods of sadness. From the "winter blues,"
which can be caused by a lack of sunshine during the winter,
to a period of sadness after a breakup with a boyfriend, it's
common to have times when you just don't feel like your
normal, more positive self. But how do you know if it's merely
a fleeting case of the blues or something more serious?

According to Dr. Kala Annambhotla, staff psychologist of
the Counseling and Testing Center at the University of North
Carolina-Greensboro, "It's normal for people to feel sad,
anxious, or discouraged from time to time. These feelings
usually lift within a few days to a week, as people find solutions and support from friends." Annambhotla continued,
"Students should seek professional help when they notice
that their low mood lasts too long or occurs frequently, when
symptoms feel severe, when they notice that their mood is
causing academic, social, or other problems, and/or when
they feel stuck and can't seem to solve the problems causing
the depression."

If your feelings do not subside and they are starting to
affect your work and everyday life, you may be suffering from
clinical depression and should consider seeking professional
help. Now, before you start freaking out that there is something

horribly wrong with you, you need to know that you're not alone. According to HalfofUs.com, an online portal for college students coping with mental health issues, "nearly half of all college students reported feeling so depressed that they couldn't function during the last school year." That's a lot of people!

Depression isn't something you should keep hidden or feel ashamed of. The best way to deal is to be open about what you're going through. And seek professional help. The World Health Organization (WHO) reports that treatment such as psychotherapy and antidepressant medication has proven to be helpful for between 60 and 80 percent of people suffering from depression.

Annambhotla's advice to depressed students: "I advise depressed students to talk with supportive friends and professionals and be patient with themselves as they recover. They may want to simplify their life while still pursuing goals that are important to them. Learning to accept yourself and taking pride in your accomplishments is so important."

Annambhotla also said that antidepressant medication may also be an option for students who are experiencing decreased levels of energy and disrupted eating and sleeping patterns. By taking the steps to get the help you need, you can help put yourself on the road to recovery and the reclaiming of your sense of self-worth.

For more on depression, check out these resources:

1. Your Campus Health Center—Your campus health center is staffed with knowledgeable and understanding professionals who have experience helping students

deal with depression. You can call ahead to make your appointment and stop over on your way to bio lab.

2. HalfofUs.com—This website is dedicated to helping college students deal with a range of mental and emotional health issues, touching on topics like depression, cutting, and drug and alcohol abuse. The website includes information about depression, testimonials from celebrities and college students about their struggles with depression, and an online assessment called "Check Yourself," that allows you to screen yourself or a friend for a mental health disorder.

3. CampusCalm.com—This website is geared toward college and high school students and offers tips and articles for dealing with academics, self-esteem, and self-worth. The site offers a free online "Stress Less" kit, and has other valuable information.

4. MayoClinic.com—The website of this nonprofit medical practice has detailed information on depression. It outlines the signs and symptoms to look for, the possible causes of depression, and the different methods for treating depression.

A SELF-CONFIDENCE OVERHAUL

First step, get outside your head. Reach out to your campus health center and see if they offer some form of mental health service. If they don't, ask if there are organizations on campus that do. Therapy is one of the greatest resources. It's great to have an outside element that you can spill your guts to. Plus, let's face it: you may not be hiding the world's greatest secret, but you still may not want your friends to know exactly what's going on. Heck, you may not even know what's really going on! Working with a therapist will help you understand your anxieties in a tangible way, so you can work on them, instead of experiencing a mess of emotions trapped inside your head.

Therapists can suggest ways to work with your issues and provide strategies to overcome difficult situations. They also help you focus on what's really troubling you, and will troubleshoot for specific problems instead of giving a general diagnosis that might not actually make the problem go away. If you're unsure if you "need" therapy, chances are you do. Therapy isn't for the "crazy," the weak, or the otherwise helpless. It's for the everyday girl who may be punishing herself for things she can't control. A friend of mine once told me she didn't think her problems were "big enough" to seek outside help. Don't think that way! There are no silly questions, and the important thing to recognize is that therapists are there to help you. They provide an extra hand when you feel as if you're juggling a basket load of issues.

Many experts say to try out one session. And keep in mind that choosing a therapist is like choosing a great pair of sunglasses—not all will fit. Sometimes you have to try several pairs, but when it works, it works. Some therapists just don't click with your personality and that's OK. Some people like their therapist to be very strict and straitlaced; others like to feel as if they're talking to a friend. Try out a session with someone you like, and if you still leave uneasy, at least you can say you tried.

There needs to be some concrete work to build up your mind and your self-esteem, but there also needs to be something to speak to your spirit. Remind yourself that you are fabulous and carry your own set of idiosyncrasies that make you who you are. Embrace them! These are the things people love about you. When you're feeling down, try to find something positive to affirm about yourself. Finding something positive will remind you that there are things that you love about yourself, which will combat the hate-speak you may say on a daily basis.

Believe it or not, the more times you say that you're a screwup, the more likely you are to end up believing it. At the very least, ask yourself, "Would you talk to a friend the same way you talk to yourself?" Chances are if you did, you wouldn't have any friends. People who suffer from low self-esteem issues judge themselves to such a high degree that they don't realize that they are their own worst enemy.

WHAT TO DO IF YOU OR A FRIEND IS SUICIDAL

Amanda Ferrara, New York University

Do you know what you would do if a friend was suicidal? What if you were? What would be your next step toward getting help? If a situation arises where you or someone you know needs to get help, do not let yourself be unprepared. Take ten minutes to visit www.suicidepreventionlifeline.org to read about the warning signs of suicide and to find crisis centers in your area.

If you ever encounter someone, perhaps even yourself, displaying the warning signs, there is also a number you can call for assistance: 800-273-TALK. And don't forget about resources on campus like mental health centers, which are there to help in situations like these. Remember: when it comes to someone contemplating suicide, every second counts.

TYPICAL ROADBLOCKS

Once you have hammered out a system that works for you, it's time to apply it and see how it holds up in the real world. A lot of work goes into recognizing the damage we do to ourselves, and then figuring out the best way to repair the damage. However, the work doesn't stop once you've figured out the equation—now it's time to apply the system and test its effectiveness.

HOW I FOUND THE HELP I NEEDED

Sanah Jivani, University of Texas at San Antonio

As I walked back to my dorm after my first week of classes, my mind was racing. A million questions ran through my head: *Why wasn't I enjoying college? Was there something wrong with me? Why couldn't I just be happy like everyone else?*

I walked into my room, threw my stuff on my desk, and collapsed onto my bed. I couldn't see through my tears as I tried to work through all of the emotions. Transitioning to college was clearly affecting me in ways that I couldn't handle. I began to acknowledge the heavy feeling in my chest was not okay. I had a problem. I was always extremely independent, so it was hard for me to accept help—but it was necessary.

I soon realized that asking for help is a strength, not a weakness. I started seeking out professional help by contacting the student health services department at my school. I was then referred to the counseling center and immediately scheduled sessions with a counselor. Talking through my emotions with a trained professional helped me finally cope with my depression.

There are many resources available that college students may not be aware of. There was so much help available to me, from support groups to free counseling sessions. *All I had to do was ask.*

The most important thing you can do is realize you're not alone in your struggles. The university staff, especially, will be there to support you.

While we may sometimes need a major self-confidence overhaul, often it's the little things that can have even the most confident chicas checking their self-esteem at the door. There are moments when you just sort of hit an emotional snag, and need some extra support to get you through it.

Post-Breakup

We've all been there. The sniffling, the Facebook stalking, the masochistic viewing of *The Notebook*. Breaking up sucks and it often gives your self-esteem a beating. After a breakup, the most common things women look for are answers. We try to categorize blame, we scrutinize our faults, harp on our shortcomings, and it really does a number on us. During this time, try to celebrate your newfound single status. Make a list of all the qualities you love about yourself. Sure, it's easy to list all the bad qualities of your ex, but it isn't about him, it's about you. Take the time to get to know yourself better, and enjoy the spontaneity of being single.

BFF No More (Breakup with a Girlfriend)

Breaking up sucks, but what happens when you break up with a friend? I'd rather sit through a million sappy romantic comedies with a best friend than watch my favorite movie alone. Breaking it off with a BFF can be really rough, especially since we rely on them when things aren't going right. During the college years, relationships will be tested, and you and your true blue may drift apart or come to a breaking point. Just like any relationship, take the time to mourn the loss of your bond and get it out of your system, but also start reaching out to the other friends in your circle. Then try to reach out to people you may not have talked to before. Ask the girl down the hall about the song she plays that you totally love, or hang out with your lab partner after class. Get involved in your student government or your campus paper. While it sucks to lose the Selena to your Taylor, it doesn't mean you've lost all the cool things that make you who you are.

Change in Physical Appearance

College is a time where you'll be testing your mind and your body, and you may notice your body changing as you spend more time away from home. If you see yourself losing or gaining an alarming amount of weight, try to reflect on your routine and your eating habits, as stress eating may point to an underlying issue. If you're concerned, talk to a nutritionist or a doctor about a healthy diet, but remember nobody's perfect, and no one is expecting you to be either.

THE DANGERS OF EATING DISORDERS

The concept of eating disorders is probably not new to you. You might have learned about them through a high school health class or even during a "very special" episode of your favorite teen sitcom. While you might know what eating disorders are, it's important to understand how they function on a college campus and what to do if you or someone you know suffers from disordered eating.

WHAT IS DISORDERED EATING?

Eating disorders are extreme eating patterns that have a psychological dependency on control. There are three main types: anorexia nervosa, bulimia nervosa, and binge-eating disorder. Anorexia nervosa is excessive starving or limiting of food. Bulimia nervosa follows a routine of bingeing— eating a large amount of food in one sitting—followed by purging, which is ridding the body of this food in an extreme manner (via vomiting or through the use of laxatives). Binge-eating is using food as a means of comfort, consuming large amounts of food rapidly in one sitting, but there is no purging process.

There are also new variations of these behaviors that are becoming more common. For instance, exercise-bulimia involves an excessive amount of exercise, with a woman (or man!) working out for hours and hours on end. In this case, exercising works just as any other traditional form of purging, with the intent to work away any food the individual consumed. Other dangerous forms of disordered eating involve the use of drugs or binge drinking, where controlled substances are used as a way to numb the body of its need for food. The drugs and alcohol respond to the depressive state the individual is in and compound the effects of the lack of eating, which can destroy the body at a much quicker speed.

With any eating disorder, it's important to recognize and address the psychological motivation behind the behavior, especially because the person with the disorder might not even realize that they've developed eating-related issues. Eating disorders arise from depression, anxiety, low self-esteem, and overwhelming feelings of being out of control, and they are often accompanied by extreme feelings of guilt, sadness, anger, or remorse. The disorder isn't about food, but the satisfaction of completing a goal, attaining a certain ideal, or adhering to a larger standard of beauty.

It may be hard to spot someone who is suffering from disordered eating, as they don't always look extremely skinny. Sufferers of bulimia especially may look overweight, and may view bulimia as a "weight maintenance" practice. People can develop a combination of these disorders, jumping from one to another at any given time.

WORRIED ABOUT A FRIEND?

If you suspect that a friend suffers from disordered eating, be on the lookout for unusual behavior, such as suddenly becoming withdrawn, secretive, or moody. If you hear her making negative remarks about her body, idolizing or glorifying thinness, and you notice a shift in her behavior, then she may be suffering from a disorder. If she has had a history of depression, physical/sexual abuse, or weight issues, she may be more at risk to engage in or relapse into disordered eating. While it may be awkward to approach a friend about her eating habits, it's important to confront disordered behavior before it spirals out of control.

Meet with your friend in a comfortable place, and be direct with your concerns: "I've noticed you've been feeling down lately. I haven't seen you eat much, and I'm concerned." This addresses the behavior without attacking her. Avoid blame or guilt, and just stick to your own observations. Present options for help. If the direct approach is too difficult, frame it as a hypothetical issue. Expressing your support in this "hypothetical" situation may clue her in that you're a safe person to talk to. Be sure to follow up, and let her know that you're there to help in any way you can.

YOUR OWN BEHAVIOR

If you feel that your eating habits are sliding toward the unhealthy, try to assess what your behavior means. Recognizing disordered eating is the first step on the road to recovery. There are plenty of resources out there to help you understand and overcome your disease. Talk to a therapist about your behavior. If you're truly unsatisfied with your appearance, talk with your doctor and discuss healthy alternatives for weight loss and weight management.

If you are concerned about yourself or a friend, contact the National Eating Disorders Association Helpline, at 800-931-2237. Other useful links include:

- **Anorexia Nervosa and Associated Disorders:** Provides support groups, resources, and candlelight vigils around the United States. www.anad.org
- **Eating Disorder Hope:** An informational site about eating disorders. www.eatingdisorderhope.com

Failed an Exam/Class

Remember that all-nighter? The one last week, where you had to miss your best friend's band and the midnight waffle sale to spend the entire night cramming for that bio exam? Yeah, it just came back, and you totally bombed. So, not only did you miss the killer encore but it was all for nothing. Yikes! Nothing is worse than putting your all into an assignment and finding out you failed. The first thing you should do is find out why you bombed so you can put it to rest. Look over your paper or your exam and really review your work—learn what mistakes you made so you don't make them again. If you feel shortchanged, schedule a time to talk with your professor to discuss your performance. The most important thing here is to make the progress tangible. In most cases a makeup test isn't an option, but the work you put into understanding your mistakes will help you with other assignments down the line. Reviewing your test or paper and learning from it helps channel your stress into something productive, which is way better than just throwing in the towel.

FINDING AN EQUILIBRIUM

When I finally pieced myself back together, I was able to see the person I was truly becoming. It's easy to get over a cold, but not so easy to recover from being emotionally under the weather. You can't just snap back to "normal"—and really, why would you want to? You've made it through the hard part, so try to think of how you can make your newfound strength work for you. We mess up, we goof off, and it's all just part of life. The important thing is to learn from your mistakes and take time to laugh along the way.

Insights provided by Aja Johnson, University of Maryland–College Park

DEALING WITH DRUGS AND ALCOHOL ON CAMPUS

I'll never forget coming back to the dorms one night my freshman year and seeing someone from my floor being carted off on a gurney while an ambulance's blue and red lights flashed outside.

I was on my way home from Dillons (the local grocery store) with ice cream for the girl's night my suite-mates and I had planned. I saw the lights flashing, but I kept walking up to my room on the second floor. Unaware that the paramedics were right inside, I walked into our hall entrance and came face-to-face with my friend on the gurney. She had drunk way too much alcohol. Her face was pale, her hair matted, and there were remnants of vomit on her face. She wouldn't respond to the paramedic's questions; all she kept saying was she was okay. I was so worried and scared for her. I remember asking the paramedics if she was okay, but they shooed me away and told me to go back into my room. We all went to visit her in the hospital later that night. She was lucky, only having to get her stomach pumped, and was able to come back two days later.

I wish I could say that was the only time I ever saw something that scary, but the next year, I became an RA, and over the next two years, I saw the same thing many Thursdays through Saturdays. The only difference was now I was the one calling the ambulance.

Friday nights, I loved watching students get involved on campus and go out to have a good time. I enjoyed watching friendships and relationships build as timid students broke out of their shells to try new things. I enjoyed watching students walk by decked out in costumes they created for ABC and Gatsby-themed parties. But then there were the nights they would come home too drunk to talk. And the times I would find them passed out in some random location in their own vomit. I would have to be the one to call an ambulance. And when the paramedics came, I would have to relay as much information as I could to them.

Parties in themselves aren't bad things. They can be great ways to meet friends. And you should have fun in life. But when drinking turns from fun to risky to an excessive habit, you can find yourself in serious trouble. So take the following advice on dealing with alcohol and drugs in college from me, a former RA who has seen a lot.

DRINKING IN A DORM? FORGET ABOUT IT

If you're thinking about pre-gaming or just drinking in a dorm, don't. Take your activities somewhere off campus. You're not fooling the RA when you carry around a flask or bottle filled with pink liquid while wearing that cute, short dress. And, if an RA catches you, you'll usually receive some sort of disciplinary action that will most likely include a fine, which can range from $50 to $500. RAs aren't out to get you (the paperwork is ridiculous), but they have a job to do. There are a lot better things you can buy with that money instead of paying a fine, I promise. And that's not counting the huge bills that come with a trip to the hospital, if you're in such bad shape that you're showing signs of alcohol poisoning.

THERE'S NOT MUCH JUICE IN JUNGLE JUICE

Stay away from the jungle juice! This is a common drink at parties, but you never know exactly what substances are in it. This concoction usually has a high percentage of hard alcohol, but it can also have other things mixed in to enhance the effects, such as NyQuil. If you're already intoxicated, adding a sleeping agent can be deadly. I've seen so many girls at parties just fill those red solo cups up without even thinking about it. Please, just take a moment to think about what you're drinking (if you're choosing to drink). One moment of reflection can truly save your life.

DANGEROUS DEPENDENCY: PRESCRIPTION DRUGS

Erica Strauss, Kent State University

Between five-page papers, exhausting lecture halls, endless pages of math problems, and weekend road trips, the life of a college student can be overwhelming. There are lots of ways to reduce stress: exercise, yoga, meditation, writing, to name just a few. But some college students turn to prescription drugs instead. Need to get that paper done in an hour? Pop an Adderall. Want to unwind after a nerve-racking presentation? Try a Xanax. Have a few aches and pains? Vicodin will do the trick. Bad idea. For one, it's illegal to use these drugs unless you're the one with the prescription. And two, they're incredibly addictive.

A junior fine arts major, let's call her "Marie," takes Adderall, a popular prescription drug, for her ADHD symptoms. Adderall is a stimulant that affects chemicals in the brain and controls hyperactivity. "I take it because I can't concentrate without it," she said. Adderall has been described as the drug for overachievers, and the side effects—including increased energy, ability to focus, and inability to sleep—sound like a miracle pill for the busy, hectic, fast-paced life of a college student.

"Whenever I have a paper due, I won't stress about it because I know I can take Adderall and get it done fast," said a freshman who wishes to remain anonymous. "It also helps when I pull all-nighters to study for exams." Adderall also suppresses the user's appetite, and many students, especially young women, enjoy that extra side effect. Not only will you get an A on your exam, but—hey!—you could even drop a dress size.

Xanax, Valium, and Vicodin—which treat anxiety, pain, and insomnia, among other ailments—are also college favorites. Just ask the kid sitting behind you in psych, your hall-mate, or even that gorgeous girl in your sorority—one of them probably has a prescription to your drug of choice, or knows someone who does. "People know I have a prescription, and I get phone calls all the time from people asking for it," Marie said. "I don't need them all, so usually I'll just give them away."

Marie isn't the only legally prescribed drug user who chooses to sell or give away her pills. A study conducted in 2008 by a Massachusetts psychopharmacologist reported that 11 percent of students surveyed who had prescriptions to Adderall XR sold their pills. Another 22 percent reported misusing their prescription and didn't take the pills when they were supposed to.

THE DANGERS

Although Marie is prescribed the drug, she can still see the many dangers of drug misuse. She feels not only physically but also psychologically dependent on the drug. "I feel like I can't do my work without Adderall now," Marie said. For others, the drug becomes a crutch—an easy way to avoid a bigger issue. The problem is that once the drugs wear off, the real issues are still there.

Many students don't see the harm in popping a pill that is prescribed to someone else. People mistakenly believe that it's OK to take the drugs because they have been prescribed by a doctor. But you never know what kind of reaction your body might have when you introduce a new medication, especially one that hasn't been specifically prescribed to you. Not only are there health risks involved, but addiction is another very real side effect.

Yet prescription drugs don't carry the negative stigma that street drugs like cocaine and heroin do. You don't cringe to hear that a friend is taking excessive amounts of Adderall or Vicodin the way you would if they were hooked on cocaine.

"I take it to do better in school," said the same anonymous freshman. "It's not like I'm buying it off the street."

But getting caught with Adderall is just like getting caught with marijuana, since police can charge you with drug possession. And if you're caught selling your stash? Same deal: you can be charged with drug trafficking.

The bottom line? If you do not have a medical condition requiring treatment, you should not touch prescription drugs. If you think you might be suffering from ADHD or Generalized Anxiety Disorder, make an appointment with your doctor. And if you have been prescribed drugs as a legitimate medical treatment, use them only as directed.

AVOID DRINKS LEFT UNATTENDED

You may be thinking, "Duh," but I mean it—don't leave your drinks unattended *ever*. True, you're not going to be drugged with Rohypnol (roofie) every time you leave your drink unattended, but it does happen. And if you're at a party with a gracious host, they may keep refilling your cup for you. While this is a generous offer, it also makes it really hard to track how much you've actually been drinking. And again, it is hard to know what is in your drink. Be mindful of what you put into your body.

THE POWER OF PAIRS

Always go to a party with at least one other person so you can keep an eye on each other and walk home together. I remember a girl who came home one night without her best friend and told me she was tired and had left her friend at the party because she wanted to keep drinking and flirting with guys. This was so frustrating to me. Her friend was now alone, in an unfamiliar environment, highly intoxicated, and with people she didn't know. One of the other girls on the floor ended up taking her home, and everything worked out okay. But please, always go with a pair or a group, and don't leave a girl by herself at a party.

WATCH FOR SIGNS OF ALCOHOL POISONING

A lot of people believe it's fine to "sleep it off" when they or their friend is really intoxicated. How can you tell when "sleeping it off" is actually a dangerous situation? Some signs of alcohol poisoning include mental confusion, stupor, vomiting, seizures, less than eight breaths per minute or irregular breathing, bluish or pale skin caused by low body temperature, and being passed out and unable to be awakened. If you notice yourself or a friend having any of these symptoms, get help immediately and get to a hospital.

RESOURCES FOR SERIOUS HABITS

Are you or a friend dealing with an alcohol or drug addiction? Most campuses have counseling centers or programs you can visit. There are counselors you can talk to free of charge. If necessary, they can also point you to off-campus resources. If you aren't comfortable with going to a counseling center you can talk to your RA. RAs cannot tell anyone what you're going through besides those who absolutely need to know (i.e., the paramedics are need-to-know personnel). RAs also have been trained on your campus-specific resources, and can point you in the right direction for more help. Additionally, if you are worried about a friend, don't hesitate to seek advice. It may feel uncomfortable, but in the end, it could help your friend end her night safe in bed rather than wrapped up on a gurney.

Insights provided by Katie Jones, Missouri State University

FACING SEXUAL HARASSMENT

"Sexual harassment on campus? That so does not happen anymore. Well, at least not to me anyway!" Does this sound like something you think when anyone mentions sexual harassment? Well, before you decide to skip to the next chapter, consider this: a recent research study by the American Association of University Women (AAUW) found that 62 percent of college women had experienced some form of sexual harassment. Surprised?

WHAT IS SEXUAL HARASSMENT, EXACTLY?

Before we dive any deeper into this discussion, it is worth asking what sexual harassment is in the first place. Definitions of sexual harassment vary depending on the source. I'm going to provide a definition from my own alma mater, California State University–Los Angeles, that is pretty standard and comprehensive.

Sexual harassment includes but is not limited to

1. Unwanted sexual advances, requests for sexual favors, and other verbal or physical conduct of a sexual nature.
2. Any act which contributes to a workplace or learning environment that is hostile, intimidating, offensive, or adverse to persons because of the sexual nature of the conduct.

3. Conditioning an act, decision, evaluation, or recommendation on the submission to or tolerance of any act of a sexual nature.

So to make it clear, sexual harassment is any form of unwanted sexual advances—touching or otherwise—which can be anything from someone grabbing your butt to making a sexual joke. It can also be any sexual act that interferes with your college environment or routine. For example, it's that guy who constantly talks about inappropriate sexual stuff around you, so you leave your dorm a few minutes early every morning to avoid seeing him. And finally, it includes someone who holds authority in your life, conditioning your success or advancement on your participating in anything sexual. So, for example, you have a professor who puts his hand on your thigh in his office and insinuates that your A in the class is dependent on you responding to his sexual advances. In short, anything sexual and unwanted by you is sexual harassment.

Sexual harassment presents a unique problem for women these days, especially since our culture tends to downplay the fact that it still exists. The college campus is no exception. Sexual harassment is common on college campuses, and women experience it in a distinct way. According to the same AAUW study previously mentioned, women are more likely to be harassed through physical contact such as being touched, grabbed, or pinched. They are also more likely to receive sexual comments, gestures, jokes, or looks.

Bottom line: sexual harassment is not something that happens to other women somewhere out there. It happens to us—to you and me. Hopefully reading this will get you more informed and help you recognize it and know what to do when it happens.

MY PERSONAL EXPERIENCE WITH SEXUAL HARASSMENT

Sanah Jivani, University of Texas at San Antonio

"Hello, this is the campus counseling center. We wanted to talk to you about the recent sexual harassment experience you reported to campus police..."

My hands suddenly began to sweat, and I could barely hold on to my phone. My mind was moving in a million directions, and I could barely speak.

"I'll have to call you back," I said quickly, and I immediately hung up the phone.

I replayed the experience in my head. I sat in a cab, the driver stopped a couple blocks away from my destination and tried to kiss me. I said "no" several times but he was extremely persistent. Thankfully, I was able to get out of the car before the situation escalated.

After the experience, I felt like I could not speak. I did not want to tell anyone. I did not want to leave my room. I decided I wanted to deal with the situation on my own.

Thankfully, I had wonderful roommates who encouraged me to speak up. They helped me call the cab company and then brought me to the campus police. The campus police officers filed a report and assured me that they would be looking out for me. They also referred me to the counseling center.

However, when the counseling center called to follow up, I felt guilty. Did the term "sexual harassment" even apply to my experience? Should I feel guilty for talking to the campus counseling center about my situation? What would people think of me?

Now I understand that "sexual harassment" has different meanings, and every individual has the right to ask for help, regardless of the severity of the situation. I eventually did reach out for support and used the resources on my campus.

The first and most important thing I did was talk to someone I felt comfortable with. After that, things began to fall into place. Having the support of my campus police department was very comforting. They called several times to follow up and make sure that I was doing OK. With their guidance, I also received group and individual counseling.

After my experience, it's evident that there should be more dialogue about sexual harassment on college campuses. I wish I had not felt that initial shame when I was thinking about reporting my experience. All people who face a similar problem should feel more comfortable talking about it and take advantage of the available resources.

DON'T BE AFRAID TO SPEAK UP

If you do face a sexual harasser at some point during college, people are probably going to try to make you feel like sexual harassment isn't that serious. They are going to tell you to let it go, to just ignore it, to stop complaining. They are going to tell you that it's excusable for this reason or that, and they are going to tell you that it doesn't really matter. Well, I want to tell you that those are all lies, absolute untruths, falsehoods that perpetuate our society's belief that disrespecting women is excusable. We live in a culture that views women as sex objects and devalues women constantly. Some men think they have a right to women sexually as if they are possessions, and that sexual harassment is excusable. Well, it's not. Period.

Regardless of circumstances, please know that no one has a right to touch you, speak to you, or manipulate you in any unwanted sexual way.

RESPONDING TO SEXUAL HARASSMENT

So what in the world do you do when you're being sexually harassed? Part of the answer depends on who the harassment is coming from. Often sexual harassment is student-to-student. If it's happening in your dorm, tell your RA, or your Resident Director. If it's from a staff member like a professor at your college, then many campuses have a designated person who receives sexual harassment complaints. Explore your university website to find contact information for that person and reach out to him or her as soon as possible. The longer you let it go, the less likely you'll find the courage to speak up. The common thread here is that you say something. Otherwise, they will continue violating your right to a life without harassment and most likely the rights of other women just like you. Reporting sexual harassment is just plain hard, especially when the offender is a peer or someone you have to see regularly. Being scared of retribution is commonplace. If the person you report is a peer, then you will proba-bly see them around campus, but don't be intimidated. You don't have to address them or talk to them or argue with them or explain yourself if you're not comfortable.

In my opinion, the best way to deal with this is by finding support in the community. Friends, family, even staff on campus can offer you great support and encouragement when it seems like it's just too hard to deal with sexual harassment. Some friends may discourage you but real ones will stick with you through it. No one has a right to sexually harass you in any way, and you have every right to defend yourself against inappropriate sexual behavior. Assert yourself. Don't be scared.

Even though sexual harassment seems like something that doesn't happen anymore, it's still a reality for many women in the workplace and on college campuses. But now that you have the info, you'll know what to do if it happens to you.

Insights provided by Monica Taylor, California
State University—Los Angeles

SPEAKING UP AND SPEAKING OUT: ENDING SEXUAL ASSAULT ON CAMPUS

Sexual assault has been a growing issue on college campuses in recent years. According to a 2014 *Washington Post* analysis of data reported by nearly sixteen hundred colleges, reports of forcible sex offenses on college campuses increased by 50 percent from 2010 to 2012. To some degree, this drastic increase may indicate that the efforts of some colleges to promote campus safety have made some students feel more comfortable stepping forward and reporting incidents. But this alarming statistic also demonstrates that sexual assault on campus is a much more widespread problem than colleges have previously acknowledged.

As of August 2014, the federal government was investigating seventy-six colleges nationwide to determine whether their handling of sexual violence reports followed the rules established by Title IX. President Barack Obama even named a White House task force to develop proposals to prevent sex assault, and Congress is considering legislation.

DITCHING THE VICTIM LABEL

Monica Taylor, California State University–Los Angeles

Did you know that one in six women will be sexually assaulted during her lifetime? It's almost too hard to believe. Even more startling? College women are four times more likely to suffer sexual assault. Why? The college coed environment of easily accessible alcohol and casual campus hookups places many young women at risk and makes them more likely to be victims of unwanted sexual encounters. Unfortunately, it often goes unreported because the victim was under the influence at the time of the attack, sometimes blames herself, and is unclear as to whether the situation can truly be classified as a crime.

You can significantly decrease your chances of becoming a victim of rape or sexual assault at your school by following a few simple guidelines:

- Don't engage in binge drinking. This is one of the easiest ways to find yourself in a scary situation and not be able to do anything about it.
- Never put your drink down at parties. It's very easy for someone to slip a date rape drug like GHB or Rohypnol into your beer when you're not looking. The same holds true at the bar. Never accept a drink from a stranger unless it's directly brought to you by a bartender or server.
- Use the buddy system when out with your friends. Don't ever let a pal go someplace alone with a stranger or walk back to the dorms by herself.
- If you feel uncomfortable in a situation, don't ignore your gut instinct. Who cares if your friends or that hot guy in your lit class thinks you're crazy? If you get a bad vibe from someone, leave immediately. It's always better to be smart and play it safe than to find yourself hurt or abused.

The good news is that more and more college and government officials are taking a stand against the terror of sexual assault and are making campuses safer. Many colleges are starting to put sexual assault policies and direct actions plans into place for when an assault happens on campus. And you can be part of this movement.

USE YOUR VOICE

If you are in a situation and you do not feel comfortable, speak up. If there are other people around you, let them know that you are not okay with what is happening and get yourself out of the situation as soon as possible. It may not be easy to do, but *use your voice*. Many people are sexually assaulted not by strangers, but by people they know and thought they could trust. This is another reason to speak up. Say something to this person and let them know that you say no and that they have to stop. If you see someone in a bad situation, help them out of it. Walk up and pretend to know the person or even speak to the abuser directly, telling them to cut it out and get away. Do whatever you can without putting yourself in danger. Report any funny business you may see. It's better to speak up and misinterpret a situation than to be a silent bystander and allow a sexual assault to occur or go unpunished.

WHAT TO DO IF YOUR FRIEND HAS BEEN RAPED

Ashley Tripp, University of Alabama

The fact is that college women are at a higher risk for sexual assault. A study conducted by the National Institute of Justice found that completed or attempted rape happens to between one in four and one in five college women during their college years. And according to the Rape, Abuse, & Incest National Network (RAINN), 80 percent of rape victims are under the age of 30. These are sobering statistics for college women.

If the worst happens and you or a friend ends up a victim of rape or attempted rape, it is important to seek medical help immediately, even if you think you don't need it. According to UCLA's Rape Treatment Center, this is crucial, as you can discuss the possibility of exposure to an STI and the possibility of pregnancy with the health-care provider.

Having a medical exam immediately following the assault is also a way to preserve physical evidence. And one important point here. According to UCLA's Rape Treatment Center, you should "not shower, bathe, douche, eat, drink, wash your hands, or brush your teeth until after you have had a medical examination. Save all of the clothing you were wearing at the time of the assault, placing each item of clothing in a separate paper bag."

Rape survivors experience different reactions and responses, so you or your friend may want to also consider counseling. Seeking counseling from a trusted source is an important first step in the process of recovery. You or your friend can decide whether to notify the local and campus police or contact a campus-based resource center such as a Women's Center, Student Counseling Center, Student Affairs Office, Student Health Center, or a local or national rape hotline like 800-656-HOPE. The Rape Crisis Center also offers a twenty-four-hour hotline at 210-349-7273. Websites like www.rainn.org and www.911rape.org are additional resources for support.

The best thing you can do for your friend is to offer words of encouragement, respect their decisions, and be a good listener. And for yourself, do not hesitate to reach out to friends and family. They are there to provide the love and support you need.

Reporting incidents of sexual assault, seeking support, and raising awareness are necessary steps. Join your student government, petition to school administrators, or join an activist group on campus to spread the word. For more information on how to report incidents of sexual assault and for resources you can go to for support, visit www.notalone.gov.

Use your voice, and don't stop using your voice after an incident has occurred, whether to you, to a friend or loved one, or to any young woman on your campus. Together, we can put an end to sexual violence on college campuses.

Insights provided by Ana Berkovich, Missouri State University

WHAT TO DO IF
YOU'RE FAILING

I was sitting in Chemistry 171, learning (well, I was *supposed* to be learning) about stoichiometry and all its real-world applications. Stoichiometry, the calculation of relative quantities, was a mandatory class for my cellular and molecular biology major. I was going to be a doctor. So there was no escaping it. After college, my plan was to travel to sub-Saharan Africa and work for Doctors Without Borders. I didn't want to let go of this dream. So, I was going to force myself to love stoichiometry, counting fruit flies, and filling out Punnett squares.

As it turns out, in that excruciatingly long, four-hour lab, I learned a lot more about myself than about chemical reactions. I was struggling in all my classes related to my major. I wasn't interested in the topics, and I wasn't trying. I didn't want to try. It's not that I wasn't capable of the work. It just didn't excite me and hadn't captured my attention. So, I took a step back and refocused. What if this dream I'd had since I was a child wasn't my dream anymore?

I was also taking an English class and a psychology class—and guess what, those were far more interesting to me. And soon enough I switched my major to professional writing and psychology. I dropped my Chemistry 171 class, and I don't miss it. I changed my minor to creative writing to help fulfill my creative endeavors. And although

Doctors Without Borders wasn't in my future anymore, I found other ways to volunteer and make a difference. I created my own club. It's called TOMS Initiative, and it's based around the ideals of the for-profit company TOMS. We volunteer in the community and hold events to raise awareness for children without proper foot- and eyewear.

In my case, struggling turned out to be the best wake-up call for me; it told me that something needed to change. But no one expects to struggle with or even fail the coursework required for their major or dream career, and finding yourself in that situation can be scary. You need to ask yourself why you are struggling. Are you genuinely interested in the subject and just having a hard time with some of the concepts? Or is your lack of interest in the subject resulting in a lack of effort? Is it worth sticking it out, or should you drop the class? Here are some resources that can help you seek answers and determine the best course of action to change the situation.

ACADEMIC ADVISORS ARE A GREAT RESOURCE

If you're struggling with classes, you're not alone, and it's not too late. Before you make any decisions, talk to your academic advisor. If it's early enough in the semester, you may be able to drop the class. I don't want you to think dropping a class is the go-to answer. It may not solve everything. If you drop a class, you may have to take it later on, or it may show up on your transcript in a negative way. Always consult your academic advisor first.

If you are genuinely interested in the subject, or if dropping isn't an option, your advisor or professor can connect you to on-campus resources that can help, often for free. For example, many schools have learning centers with tutors. Missouri State University, where I went to school, offers a learning center for math, chemistry, biology, foreign language, and writing.

Your academic advisor has a great deal of information he or she can share with you to make your experience in college smoother. Visit him or her often, and visit early in the semester. Usually until your sophomore or junior year, you will have to meet with your advisor each semester before you enroll in classes. If you are concerned and worried that you may have chosen the wrong major, or that your struggles are a sign of a bigger problem, bring your advisor a Starbucks drink and just sit down and discuss your plans, struggles, concerns, and questions. My freshman year I thought I would be a failure if I dropped a course, but my advisor helped me see that wasn't true, and in the end it was the best decision for me.

PEERS CAN PROVIDE A SUPPORT NETWORK

Learning centers on college campuses are often staffed by fellow students who can serve as tutors and mentors to you, offering academic help and advice. Many colleges offer other opportunities where your peers can actually form a larger support system. Living-learning communities are a great example of that.

If you aren't in college yet, but you are enrolled or are still researching or choosing a university, I'd strongly recommend that you look into living-learning communities (LLCs). LLCs are created in dorms. Each floor of the dorm is linked to a specific interest like business, agriculture, health, fitness, or volunteering. Students are grouped based on interests. You will also usually have a professor or a few professors assigned to your floor. Missouri State University, University of Iowa, Syracuse University, University of South Carolina, and Yale University are just a few schools that offer this program.

I was in an LLC all three years that I lived on campus, first as a student on the health and human services floor and then the next two years as an RA for the first-year female floor. Living on the health and human services floor was great, but that's when I learned that science wasn't my forte. That being said, we did a lot of neat experiments. The most memorable experiment was working with a science professor and taking cultures from random objects in our dorm. We let the specimens grow over winter break, and the results were shocking. I will never look at a water fountain or purses the same way. The next two years, my LLC did a lot of things. We had a paint-tag war, a luau, went ice-skating with professors, and more. Even though I wasn't a freshman anymore, I had an absolute blast on this floor.

If you're in an LLC and find yourself struggling academically, you're already surrounded by a group of peers who can offer advice and may be willing to lend a helping hand. It can be a great support network to remind you of why you got into your major or future career choice. On the other hand, if you feel like you don't fit in with your LLC because you're not as passionate about or engaged in your major as you expected to be, it might be a sign that you need to consider a new area of study.

GET TO KNOW YOUR RESIDENT ASSISTANT

Resident Assistants can also be a resource. Contrary to popular belief, they aren't just there to bust you for alcohol and tell you to turn down the music. Your RA has knowledge of your university, so use him or her. If you want to know about more resources that would be applicable to you and your major or interests, ask your RA.

My last piece of advice is to take classes that inspire you. And remember dreams evolve. Be true to yourself. Don't be afraid to change plans. Because maybe, just maybe, there is a better major out there for you.

Insights provided by Katie Jones, Missouri State University

HOW TO DECIDE IF TRANSFERRING IS THE RIGHT DECISION

If you're one of the lucky ones, and transferring colleges has never entered your mind, stop reading now. Move on while the rest of us plot, plan, and cry on the inside.

There are some of us, actually a lot of us, who doubt we made the right decision when we chose to attend our current school. We expected it to be *The One*, but now that we're here, we're not so sure.

My doubts started around the end of my first year. I was super involved and had made amazing friends. I volunteered at the children's hospital and in a lab. I joined the cheerleading team, as well as a sorority. Yet somehow, I felt like I wasn't in the right place. It wasn't that I didn't put myself out there. I did. I just never felt right. It just wasn't home.

Second year came, and I went back to school thinking that it was something I was doing wrong. I tried to become even more involved. I became the orientation week leader, held a vice president position in my sorority, joined the varsity rowing team and was elected as an executive of Greek Council. Even with everything I had going for me, I *still* couldn't feel at home. I hated my major, and I wasn't happy. Finally, I decided that I was going to start looking into transferring schools and programs.

Now, more than a year later, I am at my new school and in a new program. I couldn't be happier! So, how did I decide that I should transfer? Transferring colleges is a huge decision that shouldn't be made lightly. You really need to spend some serious time thinking about *why* you want to transfer, and whether transferring is truly the best way to solve the problems you're having now.

First of all, if you're thinking about transferring schools, the biggest question you're probably asking yourself is, "How can I be sure this is the right move for me?" The thing about transferring schools is that you will *not*, in any way, be able to know whether it's the right decision until you get to your new school. You will think it is, but you will not *know* until you've made the move. So keep that in mind while you are going through this process—no matter how sure you feel about transferring schools, choosing to transfer is still choosing to take a risk.

Here are some of the most important points and questions to consider, to help you decide whether to take that big step.

SOCIAL LIFE
If You Don't Make Friends Very Easily

Is loneliness the main reason you're considering making the trade? If making friends is the problem, chances are that problem will follow you to a new school. So before you make any decisions, take advantage of opportunities on campus to meet people that you haven't tried before (see Chapter 4 for some ideas). Talk to someone new. What's the harm in reaching out? A new friend could make all the difference.

If you've made a genuine effort to meet people but you still aren't connecting with the students at your school, then you might want to think about transferring. Keep in mind, when you're a sopho-more, junior, or senior transfer student, you don't get to go through Orientation Week again. And as we know, this is where many people make a good number of their long-term college friends. So if you do transfer, make sure that you join lots of extracurricular activities or live with roommates. Find ways to get involved and meet people. That way you won't feel lonelier at your new school than you did at your old one.

If You Don't Like the Campus Atmosphere

The biggest problem I had with my old college was the lack of school pride and events, so I made sure my second college valued and encouraged traditions and school spirit. Make sure to consider what exactly it is that you don't like about the atmosphere at your current college. Every college has a different personality, and it's really hard to know what a college is actually like without being there. If you're serious about transferring, visit the campuses of the top two or three schools on your list. Location or finances can sometimes make that difficult to do, but I'd strongly recommend campus visits if at all possible. Also, talk to current students, and ask them specific questions about the things you're looking for in your new college environment.

If You're Only Staying for Someone Else

Relationships are hard, and long distance is even harder. But if that person isn't willing to come with you or to let you go, then maybe it is not meant to be. After all, you're only young once. You have the rest of your life to be married. You can reinvent yourself at this new university. And hey, maybe you will meet someone new! Focus more on building yourself as an individual and making yourself happy before you try and make someone else happy.

ACADEMICS
If You're Struggling with Your Classes

Adjusting to college-level coursework can be a big challenge for many students. It's not unusual to be overwhelmed by your classes at first. If as the semester goes on you continue to struggle academically, talk to your advisor and try to figure out why.

Is class size an issue? Some people do better in smaller classes, while others do just as well in a class of four hundred as they would in a class of forty. Most high school students have never been in classes with hundreds of other students before, and it's hard to know if that will work for you until you've tried it. If you're finding that your current school isn't meeting your desired class size needs, consider transferring to a smaller school. A benefit to smaller class sizes is more one-on-one time with your professors.

Maybe it's the subject matter that's the problem? If you're doing poorly in courses required for your major, it may be a sign that you need to switch majors, and you might be able to find something you love at your current school. If you're struggling across the board, and tutors or other academic resources aren't helping, it may mean that your college is just not a good fit academically, and you should look seriously at transferring.

If You're Switching Majors or Programs

During my second year, I decided that I wanted to switch programs, and go from biochemistry to nursing. This was the perfect time to switch schools. If you're going to have a fresh start in a new major and really don't like your current college anyway, why not try out a new school too, especially one with a better program in that field? But first, talk to an advisor to make sure your credits transfer. You don't want to end up on the five-year plan.

MONEY MATTERS
If Tuition Is Too High

You don't want be drowning in student loan debt when you graduate. If your school is too expensive, why not transfer to somewhere a little cheaper? Again, make sure that your credits will transfer. If they don't, and you end up having to retake classes you've already earned credit for at your current school, you won't be saving any money in the long run. Do your research on your new school of choice. You want the quality of your education to remain the same (or better). Keep in mind that the cost of a college does not necessarily correspond to its academic quality. Besides, many employers are more interested in a candidate's experience than where they went to school, so don't get hung up on prestige.

If you are in a situation where you love your current school, and the only reason you're considering transferring is because you think you can't afford it, don't make any decisions without researching your financial options. Go to the financial aid office and ask if there is anything else they can do for you. Ask about scholarships. Academic departments sometimes offer scholarships to sophomores or upper-classmen that you weren't eligible for as an incoming freshman. Talk to your advisor. Maybe your school has an accelerated degree option that will help you graduate in less time. Find out if your school accepts college credit from other sources that cost a lot less money—like CLEP exams or online courses, for example. If you really don't want to leave your school, there are people who will do their best to help you try to find a way to stay.

OTHER CIRCUMSTANCES
If You Have Reasons for Needing to Be Closer to Home

Life happens. Someone close to you may become seriously ill or even die while you are away at school. In this case, if you can't cope at a school away from home, consider transferring to a college that is closer to your sick loved one.

On the other hand, if you're dealing with a special circumstance that may only be temporary or short term, you may not need to go so far as transferring schools. Look into your college's policy on leaves of absence. Going on a temporary, approved leave of absence for a semester or two could give you the break you really need to deal with the situation and then allow you to come back to school when you're ready and pick up where you left off.

If after giving careful thought to each of these points, and talking them over with advisors, mentors, family, and friends, you feel strongly that transferring schools is the right decision for you, then it's time to get planning. Do your research on potential new schools. Work with your academic advisor to map out the best course of action and for help with the application process. Before you know it, you'll be ready to transfer schools.

Saying good-bye to the friends you've made at your current school can be difficult, and you might get pre-move jitters, but be confident in your decision. You've put in all the personal reflection and hard work to get to this point, and you're ready for the change.

So how will you know if you've made the right decision? There's no way to really explain it. It's a feeling that you get in your gut that the move just feels right. Congratulations on putting your needs and happiness first! Give yourself that well-deserved pat on the back and enjoy your new college!

Insights provided by Claudia Romkey, Queen's University

UCHIC ESSENTIALS—
IF THE GOING GETS TOUGH

SEEK HELP WHEN YOU NEED IT

If something is troubling you, talk to someone about it. Get help. Don't try to deny that something is wrong, and don't be ashamed. No issue is too small. Remember that you're never alone; in college, you're surrounded by resources and people who will support you and help you get through tough times.

RECOGNIZE WHEN IT'S TIME FOR A CHANGE

From majors to relationships to life goals, your needs, interests, and priorities might change while you're in college—and that's OK. Sometimes things just don't work out, and the best answer is to take control of the situation and make a change. It's a sign that you're growing. Ask for advice from people you trust, and find out how to put yourself on the path to the future you desire.

BE FEARLESS

Take the lead in defining your values and setting limits on drugs, alcohol, and other dangerous behaviors. If you see something happening that you know is wrong, speak up. Reach out to friends in need. Don't be afraid to take actions that will make a positive impact on yourself, on your friends, and on your campus community.

Looking for more great advice? Head to UChic.com for even more resources and information—they come highly recommended from our contributors and editors. Be sure to leave your suggestions as well!

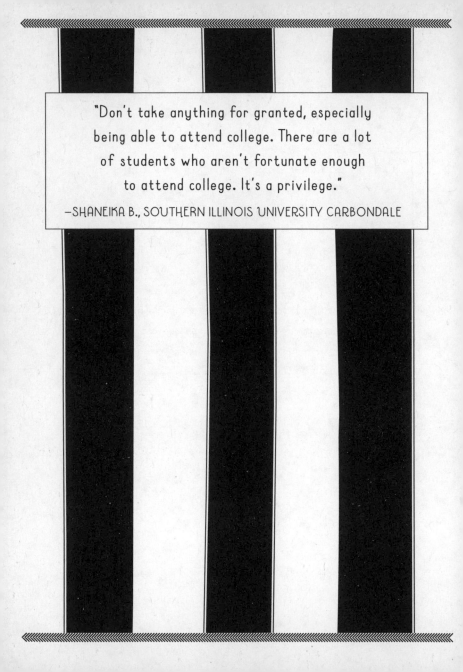

"Don't take anything for granted, especially
being able to attend college. There are a lot
of students who aren't fortunate enough
to attend college. It's a privilege."

–SHANEIKA B., SOUTHERN ILLINOIS UNIVERSITY CARBONDALE

10

MONEY MATTERS

PAYING FOR COLLEGE, LIVING on a budget, hunting for an apartment, staying on top of credit card bills: these are just a few of the "real-world" (well, sort of real-world) responsibilities and experiences that you'll face as an independent woman in college. On the surface, they don't sound like much fun. And when you consider how recent economic challenges may have already impacted your college experience, things might look a bit tricky at the start. However, by taking charge of your life at an early age—whether by setting and sticking to a budget or getting a jump-start on the financial aid search—you are guaranteeing yourself a bright future no matter what. On top of that, you'll develop a sense of pride, and more than anything, these good self-management habits will last a lifetime. Bottom line: this is definitely a chapter that you do not want to skip. Read on to get inspired with advice from other college women who discovered their inner money diva by successfully pursuing the independent life.

THE INS AND OUTS OF FINANCIAL AID

College, as you no doubt know, is an expensive investment to make. With the cost of tuition skyrocketing, most students and families today have to borrow thousands of dollars in loans. The result? Students can expect to spend a good chunk of their adult lives paying off their college debt. Given these high stakes, it's important to take advantage of the resources available to you and stay on top of the financial aid process while you're in college.

You may be used to having your parents or older relatives remind you about important things like money. Maybe they even took care of the whole financial aid process for you when you applied to college as a high school senior. That is about to change.

College is about claiming your independence, and along with that comes the responsibility of taking your future into your own hands, including your financial future. Now, your family will still be there to help guide you along the way, but they will not be able to update your calendar or keep track of deadlines for you. These things will be mostly up to you. So let's get started!

SOURCES OF AID

Financial aid is the primary way for you to receive assistance to help pay for higher education. Sounds great, right? However, wading into the financial aid waters can seem like a daunting task, with all the options that exist and the hoops you have to jump through just to get funding. Consider this your cheat sheet to this complicated process.

According to Kiplinger.com, a business publication, the federal government provides the majority of financial aid for college—more than $100 billion a year. But you can finance college through a variety of sources: federal or state agencies, private lending institutions, and scholarships.

Here's a quick snapshot of the various types of funding options:

1. **Federal and state aid:** Includes loans, grants, on-campus work-study programs based, for the most part, on financial need rather than scholastic merit.

   There are three types of loans: Direct student loans, Perkins loans, and PLUS loans for parents. Perkins loans, as well as the Federal Pell Grant (which doesn't have to be repaid) are usually awarded only to undergraduate students with very high financial need. To find out what your state may offer, check out your state's education department website.

2. **Private loans:** Used to fill in the gaps left by federal programs. Unfortunately, according to Kiplinger.com, these are more expensive and harder for students to get, given today's economy. To get a private loan, you will need to have good credit and a creditworthy cosigner, typically your parent. Ask the financial aid office at your school for a list of preferred lenders. You can also compare lenders and loan terms at FinAid.org to avoid securing an overly expensive college loan with high interest rates.

3. **Scholarships:** To uncover potential options, check with your high school guidance counselor, college financial aid offices, and scholarship directories at your library or online, as well as your

UCHIC Tip!

Beware of scammers who will offer to complete your FAFSA form for free. Be sure that you go to www .fafsa.ed.gov to fill out the official FAFSA form via the government's website. Now, we know this process is not easy. If you need assistance with your FAFSA form, most colleges have a financial aid office that will happily guide you in the right direction, so don't hesitate to reach out and ask for assistance on any questions.

employer, community organizations, advocacy groups, or associations related to your field of interest. Education loan provider Sallie Mae's free scholarship database at SallieMae .com contains more than three million scholarships worth more than $18 billion in funds. Free sites such as Peterson's, the College Board's Scholarship Search, FinAid, and Fastweb also provide a host of options.

To learn more about your financial aid options, including how to apply, head to www.studentaid.ed.gov.

THE PROCESS

To get started with the financial aid process, it is important that you first find out all deadlines and write them down in one place that you will look at on a regular basis. Do you have a homework calendar? Make sure to include when the applications are due, when your tuition is due, when the loan money will be available to you, and the term limits of the loan, such as the length of time the loan money will be available to you.

Don't forget that in order to qualify for federal aid, you have to file the FAFSA (Free Application for Federal Student Aid) form at www .fafsa.ed.gov *each year that you're in college.*

DON'T MISS THOSE DEADLINES!

Don't delay in getting started. The deadlines for loan applications come a lot earlier than you think, and they are strict. You may not be eligible to receive any loan money until the next term if you miss a deadline. Staying organized is crucial.

An added benefit of staying on top of the process? According to a spokesperson for Sallie Mae, as quoted in a Kiplinger.com article, students have a "better chance of securing cheap loans for college by completing the application early and in advance of state and school deadlines."

FINDING SCHOLARSHIPS IN SURPRISING PLACES

While government aid and private loans do help ease the monetary pain of paying for college, some students do not qualify for financial aid, and, in most cases, the financial aid package does not completely cover the total bill. Scholarships are the next major source of financial aid, but full-ride awards from colleges are hard to come by, especially if you didn't pull off a 4.0 or master every extracurricular activity when

U CHIC Tip!

What happens when it's time to pay your tuition and you don't have your loan money? Don't fret! Take a trip to the financial aid office, which will most likely already be aware of the situation and have set *special deadlines for people who are still waiting on their federal loan money to come in.* They will be able to fill you in on these deadlines or other options. Don't wait until the last minute—you don't want to miss out on any opportunities.

you were in high school. So what are you to do? What other solutions might there be that can combat the rising price of a college education?

Well, first of all, you need to stay positive. While you may not have received the big-name, top-dollar prizes, an innumerable amount of smaller, often unheard-of scholarships are only an application away.

B-average student? There's a scholarships for that. Tall? There's a scholarship for that one too. Good at duck calling? It's hard to believe, but there's even a scholarship for that! You name it, there's probably some scholarship somewhere for it.

To help you find these lesser-known opportunities, here's a quick list of resources you should have on your radar.

If You're an Athlete

The National Collegiate Athletic Association (NCAA) is a great resource for exploring scholarships. Its website (www.ncaa.org) has in-depth details on the recruiting process, research on graduation rates, and access to athletic statistics. Keep in mind that the NCAA itself does not offer scholarships, but its Division I, II, and III member schools do.

For more information about athletic scholarships, check out the following websites:

- www.athleticscholarships.net
- www.guidetoathleticscholarships.com

If You're a Minority

Underrepresented minority groups, like African Americans, Hispanics, Asians, and Native Americans may be eligible for a wide range of scholarship opportunities. These scholarships often involve strict guidelines or restrictions pertaining to your ethnic makeup, so read the scholarship criteria thoroughly.

One fantastic resource to be aware of is The Gates Millennium Scholars (GMS) Program. We're all familiar with the Gates family and their commitment to education through philanthropy. GMS provides significant financial help to thousands of outstanding minority students with undergraduate and graduate scholarships. For more information, check out www.gmsp.org.

For more information on scholarships for minorities, visit the following sites.

AFRICAN AMERICAN STUDENTS
- www.thesalliemaefund.org
- www.4blackyouth.com
- www.oedb.org/scholarship/african-american

NATIVE AMERICAN STUDENTS
- www.catchingthedream.org
- www.nrcprograms.org
- www.oedb.org/scholarship/native-american

HISPANIC STUDENTS
- www.hsf.net
- www.oedb.org/scholarship/hispanic

ASIAN AMERICAN STUDENTS
- www.apiasf.org
- www.asianpacificfund.org
- www.awib.org

If you identify yourself as a lesbian, gay, bisexual, or transgender student, you may also be eligible for a plenitude of scholarships. Consider the LEAGUE Foundation, which annually awards up to seven scholarships to individuals who have demonstrated involvement in their communities and who boast a strong GPA. For more information, check out www.leaguefoundation.org.

If You're a Legacy Applicant

Many universities offer financial incentives not just to children of alumni, but also to grandchildren, siblings, nieces, and nephews. The University of Virginia, for instance, has a well-known legacy scholarship program that benefits children of alumni. The George Washington University also has a family grant program that offers half-priced tuition for an undergraduate sibling of a current undergraduate. Talk about a great investment!

Universities are not the only institutions that award legacy scholarships. The Elks National Foundation Legacy Awards for the Children of Elks offers $1,000 renewable scholarships to children or grandchildren of living Elks based on good standing. Similar opportunities are also offered for children and grandchildren of Masons and Shriners.

If You're Considering a Career in STEM

Women are rising through the ranks in the traditionally male-dominated industries of science, technology, engineering, and mathematics, commonly referred to as STEM. If you aspire to be one of these inspirational women, there are many scholarships out there for you.

- **Science Scholarships:** The Association for Women in Science (AWIS) offers many grants and awards to undergraduates pursuing a science major. For more information, visit www.awis.org.

- **Technology Scholarships:** The Vanguard Women in Information Technology Scholarship Program strives to assist junior and senior college females pursuing degrees in computer science, computer engineering, web design, and other IT-related disciplines. Annual scholarships of up to $10,000 are awarded

based on academic merit. Visit www.sms.scholarshipamerica.org
/vanguardwomenintechnology for more information.

- **Engineering Scholarships:** The Society of Women Engineers
  (SWE) awards scholarships to women pursuing engineering,
  engineering technology, and computer science at the undergraduate
  and graduate levels. In 2011 alone, SWE awarded 188 scholarships
  valued at $540,000. Wow! To find out about the extensive list of
  scholarships offered, visit societyofwomenengineers.swe.org.

- **Mathematics Scholarships:** The Association for Women in
  Mathematics (AWM) awards the Alice T. Schafer Prize to an
  undergraduate woman who excels in mathematics. The prize is
  named after founder and president, Alice Schafer, who promoted
  and supported women in mathematics. For more information,
  check out sites.google.com/site/awmmath/programs/schafer-prize.

By doing your research, tapping the resources that are available
to you early on, and staying on top of deadlines, you should have no
trouble getting through the financial aid system and getting on with
your unforgettable college life.

*Insights provided by Kelly Leslie, San Francisco State
University, Megan O'Connell, University of Wisconsin–
Platteville, and Laura Iglehart, Georgetown University*

AVOIDING THE CREDIT CARD BLACK HOLE

Every time I dig up my mailbox combination and check my mail on campus, usually hoping for a new edition of *Glamour* or a postcard from my BFF abroad, I end up with dashed hopes and a ridiculous number of credit card offers. Even when I come home for Christmas break, my dad hands me a pile of envelopes from creditors who are just preying on young, presumably financially irresponsible students like me. But whose place is it to assume young adults can't manage credit? Some students are responsible for paying for their own tuition, board, and life's little incidentals and haven't depended on their parents for years. Other students appropriately manage their finances and know not to go crazy on $5-margarita night by buying a few rounds for the table. Many teenagers and young adults are perfectly capable of spending, swiping, and saving in measure. Right?

Unfortunately, some irresponsible spenders have given young adults a bad rap, and recent credit card regulations have forced adolescents and college students to give up some of their financial independence. Since February 22, 2010, individuals under the age of twenty-one have been unable to apply for a credit card unless they have a source of money that they can document, like a part-time job, or a cosigner on the account, most likely a parent. For most students, it really isn't that difficult to prove employment or find a parent or family member to authorize credit, but the fact that there are constraints on young adults' ability to secure credit is frustrating. Learning to manage finances on one's own at a young age is crucial to becoming an independent adult. In a time of economic uncertainty, it is vital that the next generation knows how to invest, save, spend, and support the American market economy.

NO CREDIT CARD? NO PROBLEM

Did your family decide that a credit card isn't a good idea for you this first year in school? Even without a credit card of your own, there are a few ways that you can learn to budget and start to build some financial savvy. Using strictly a debit card or cash can prove to be a safe way to manage money, although it will be more difficult to start building a credit history. You can also sign on as an "authorized user" to your parents' credit accounts, so that parents can keep a watchful eye on your spending. Or parents could simply act as cosigners, as required by law, and give you a trial period, allowing for a margin of error. In a time of "helicopter parents," where grown college students take their laundry home on weekends and call Mom each morning and night, giving young adults free rein with credit may seem scary. However, financial education is crucial to (eventual) independence. Discuss these options with your parents and determine a plan that everyone is comfortable with. Just remember to keep calling Mom daily after she gives you the go-ahead with the Visa.

TAKING THE PLUNGE

Have a job and want to take the plunge and get a credit card? If used wisely, credit cards can be a useful tool for helping you manage your money. They also help you build good credit that can help years down the road when applying for a mortgage, but only if you pay your bills on time and in full. Use the following strategies to prevent yourself from ending up like the countless thirty-something women still paying off the thousands of dollars of credit card debt they racked up during their teens and twenties.

Do Your Research

First, make sure you do your research. Pay attention to interest rates before signing a contract; credit card companies are not afraid to take advantage of students who don't read the fine print on their contract. Three of the features that credit card companies use most often to entrap students are low credit limits, low income requirements (if any), and high interest rates. A Bankrate.com survey found that the average interest rate on a student credit card is 17.51 percent—ouch! Try aiming for a rate lower than 8 percent. For more info on common credit card terminology, visit the Adventures in Education website: www.aie.org.

No matter what, don't let yourself get tricked into signing up for a card advertising "low student rates"; make sure to read the fine print very carefully and make sure that low means low. And limit yourself to one card at a time, rather than opening several different ones; it will be easier to keep track of and pay one bill a month.

Really, using a credit card is no different from walking into a bank and taking out a loan for "entertainment expenses." It is way better to only use a debit card, which draws money automatically from your bank account, so you will never pile up any debt for items you didn't have the cash to buy.

Get a Low Limit

Most reputable creditors will offer only very low credit limits to students who have little or no income and little or no established credit history. This is usually a good thing, since it acts as a built-in check to keep your spending under control. However, not all creditors are this kind; some are willing to give you credit limits of thousands of dollars. My first credit card, which I still have today, gave me a $4,000 credit limit from the day I signed up. Thankfully, I have never racked up more than a few hundred dollars at a time and have been able to pay off the balance each month, preventing a buildup of debt. But in retrospect, being handed that $4,000 credit limit as a naïve, inexperienced freshman was a potential recipe for disaster!

Pay Your Bill Electronically

The credit card companies make a lot of money off late fees, and off raising your interest rate when your payment is late. The best way to avoid this is to set up "automatic payment" from your bank account, so you will never be late with a payment.

Pay It Off Every Month—On Time

Credit card statements will offer to let you pay a minimum each month, which is just a small portion of the total bill—sometimes around $20 to $50. If you're only paying the minimum, interest will accrue on whatever part of the balance rolls over to the next month and you may only be paying on the interest and not the original amount that was charged. The result? You actually end up paying the credit card company to hold your debt for you. Credit card companies are making enough; they don't need any additional help!

Pay off the balance in full every month before the due date or try to pay off more than the minimum payment if not the full balance. You have the option to pay late, but you'll also face penalties like finance fees ($30 a pop!) and the potential that the card company will raise your interest rate.

Build Up Good Credit

By paying off your bills in full each month on time, you will begin to establish a good credit history. This is extremely important in life—having a good credit history allows you to make large purchases like a house or a car, take out a loan, open certain types of bank accounts, and even apply for certain jobs. While it may seem boring and unnecessary to worry about now, women who neglected their credit scores while in college have regretted it for the rest of their lives when they weren't able to get a house, a car, or go on the vacation of their dreams! Sure, the "live in the moment" strategy seems great today, but you'll be sorry tomorrow.

Pay with Cash or a Debit Card

Once that credit card is in your wallet, sometimes it's just difficult to resist the temptation to use it. So many things are available to you now! It's tempting when walking through the mall, or even down a shop-lined street off campus, to stop by and pick something up and come up with all kinds of reasons to justify it to yourself. (I just aced my exam! Or I just bombed my exam and need to treat myself!)

As you already know, college is a drain on your finances. You can work a part-time job for thirty hours a week and still feel like you don't have enough money to keep up with your rich friends or sorority sisters. But don't let credit cards get the best of you. Though it may seem hard right now to have an outdated wardrobe or to have to skip your spring break with your friends (believe me, I know!), it's not worth getting drowned in debt that will haunt you for the rest of your life. If you're going to use credit cards, think smart and only buy what you can pay off at the end of the month. Don't let your credit cards control your life!

Insights provided by Kylie Thompson, Harvard University

LIVING FABULOUSLY ON A BUDGET

If you haven't done so already, you'll soon be making the clichéd reference to yourself as a poor college student. I will be the first to admit that college can be tough at times—having to worry about grades, extracurriculars, working for low pay—all while trying to be trendy and up on the latest iPhone or other gadget that all our friends seem to have these days. Well, it's time for us to stop feeling sorry for ourselves for being financially challenged and start living fabulously despite our limited monetary possessions. Living the fabulous life on a budget is all about budgeting for your life, not your best friend's, and not your parents' either.

THE B WORD: BUDGET

The first part of achieving this fabulous life is making a fabulous budget. Start your "fabulous financial budget" by recording all of your monthly expenses and due dates and then compare that to your projected monthly income. When writing down your expenses, include things that are bought on a regular basis like gas, groceries, etc. Once you have your monthly budget set, limit your weekly expenses to whatever you have left over after taking into account your monthly financial goals.

If one of your goals is to save money, consider your monthly

savings goals as part of your monthly expenses, and don't dip into your
savings when spending your weekly allowance. One trick that can
help (because we all have
those days when an extra
grande mocha with whip
would solve everything) is
what I call being "blind" to
the savings—having money
automatically moved into
your savings account each
pay period, whether each week or month. Sometimes it's easier to
save if it's done automatically for you at regular intervals.

UCHIC Tip!

Don't forget that *budgeting has to be more than just a monthly occurrence.* You must think about your budget on a daily and weekly basis.

Now, if your monthly expenses are greater than what you make
each month, you're a bit further behind in staying on a budget.
However, no matter how far behind you may be in being financially
responsible, it's never too late to get organized and headed in the
right direction.

WAYS TO CUT COSTS

If there is one thing that can't be emphasized enough it is to always
pay your bills on time to avoid those unnecessary late fees and other
charges. If you find that you are having trouble keeping up on your
payments, contact your credit card company(s) or other creditors to
work out a payment plan. These entities are willing to work with you,
but you have to make the effort to stay in touch with them and let
them know about your situation.

Also, if your annual percentage rate on your credit card is high
and you're carrying a balance every month, it never hurts to call your

credit card company and ask for a lower interest rate. To get them to deal, threaten to switch card companies if they will not give you a lower rate. Despite what you may have heard, credit card companies really do work with their customers and, more often than not, will come up with ways to help you pay your bills more easily. See the article in this chapter on credit cards for more tips on using credit cards wisely.

HOW I MANAGED SCHOOL AND A PART-TIME JOB

Rachael Smith, Radford University

If you're on a budget like most—if not all—college students are these days, there is no better way to supplement your income than from a job.

Luckily, my university offers work-study programs, and I got approved to participate. The Free Application for Federal Student Aid (FAFSA) offers qualifying students the option of a work-study program that pays you an hourly rate, in exchange for a certain number of hours of work per semester. Getting approved for work-study meant I could apply for a job on campus. Since I had always wanted to work at the school's post office—it looked like such a fun place to work—I chose to apply there.

I have been working at the post office since my sophomore year, and for the two years I have been there, it has been the best part-time job I've had so far. The post office is a family, and we all joke that it is because the working atmosphere is

so laid-back. I have made great friends with my student work-
ers and supervisors.

Despite the fun, there are times when I resent it. Having a
job means having to be responsible and show up on time. Of
course, I love the positive impact it has on my bank account,
but it has prevented me from doing some of the fun things I
want to do in college. There have been many times when my
friends send me texts like, "Let's get lunch and go to the mall!"
I hate telling them I have to work. It's the worst feeling being
cooped up at work when you know your friends are having a
great time.

And let's be honest. Having to "serve" the underclassmen at
my school is occasionally no picnic (especially when they don't
know how to address an envelope properly!). But you have to
be polite to everyone at all times, even when your eyes are
drooping and you want to take a nap after partying a little too
late the night before.

There have also been some stressful days when I've had
a major project or paper due and had to go to work instead.
My boss will never forget the day when I had to go around
campus interviewing students with a digital recorder. I was
already late for work when everything got deleted by acci-
dent! I was so paranoid about calling in to work to explain
my absence that I had my mother call for me. It was such an
embarrassment, but luckily one of my supervisors answered
the phone with sympathy. I was a joke around work for a
while, but I was thankful my boss understood that school
comes first.

Despite these occasional downsides, I'm getting a taste of the real working world, and this experience is invaluable. After all, the reason you go to college is to find that dream job, and for most of us, that's a nine-to-five gig. This job is teaching me how to learn to support myself without having to rely on Mom and Dad for everything.

I've never regretted picking up my job at the post office. I've met some great friends and am proud to say I can stand on my two feet while juggling classes, extracurricular activities, friends, and a job. If you have to work or are considering a part-time position for similar reasons as mine, embrace it. Find a job that interests you.

It might end up being the best thing you do for yourself in college.

FABULOUS BUDGET-SAVERS

Now we can chat about the fun part of living fabulously on a budget—finding ways to cut corners and spend less money while still being utterly fabulous. You know how sugar gives you a little rush when the chemical dopamine gets released in your brain, boosting your happiness level? The same thing can happen when you find great ways to save money! I call these happiness boosters "budget-savers." They can help you save a little or even a lot of money each day, week, and month.

One big budget-saver for me is investing in sandwich-sized storage bags and filling them each morning with snacks like almonds, Cheez-Its, Chex Mix, or other little snacks to eat during the day to satiate my hunger. It prevents me from buying snacks from those overpriced student stores on campus. Also by having a little snack throughout the day, I can spend less money on lunch because I'm not as hungry.

Another place that you can easily cut costs is grocery shopping, for those times when you're able to get off campus to do so. Always make a list before you go, and follow the old saying "Never go to the grocery store hungry." When you're shopping on an empty stomach, everything looks appealing and you'll end up buying things that you don't need. The same thing happens when you shop without a list; having a list to follow when you grocery shop helps you focus on buying the things you need and helps prevent useless spending each month. Searching for coupons online or in the local newspaper is another quick thing you can do, and those savings add up more than you might think.

Another great budget-saver for me has been to learn how to do a lot of things for myself rather than having to pay someone else to do them, like cutting or coloring my hair, basic manicures and pedicures, and waxing. The list goes on. You end up saving so much more money in the long run while learning a useful skill.

TREAT YOURSELF

What's a fabulous budget without the fabulous part? The most important part of maintaining a great budget, without going totally insane, is treating yourself with little things every now and then so the undeniable urge to splurge won't build. For instance, small treats like a movie or a magazine once a week or a new pair of shoes or purse at the end of the month should keep you satisfied to resist that dreadful urge.

BE THRIFTY!

Shopping at thrift stores or heading for the sales racks is a great way to save money while still being able to shop. Learn some basic sewing skills so that you can buy that ultra-cute dress with the missing button for half-off and fix the button later. Try making thrift store or sale rack shopping a special outing with your friends on a regular basis. Who's going to resist the opportunity to shop *and* save money? There are so many ways to live fabulously while being on a budget. By mapping out your expenses and financial goals, finding budget-savers, and treating yourself every now and then, you'll not only be living fabulously on a budget in college, but you'll be living a fabulous life as well!

Insights provided by Lativia Jones Bolarinwa,
University of North Carolina–Chapel Hill

UCHIC ESSENTIALS—
MONEY MATTERS

EDUCATE YOURSELF ON FINANCIAL LITERACY

There's a lot to know about things like paying off loans and good credit habits; even a small misstep can set you back big-time financially. We've only scratched the surface here, so take the initiative to educate yourself. Government websites are a good place to start, and your school's financial aid office can point you to even more financial literacy resources.

MAKE A BUDGET—AND STICK TO IT!

The key to financial success is having a budget in place that is easy to follow. By knowing what your limits are ahead of time, you are more likely to not overspend. It may seem hard now, but it will pay off in the end.

EMBRACE YOUR INDEPENDENCE

You're in college, on your own. Even if your parents are still providing some financial support, it's time for you to start taking charge! Embrace your independence by establishing good money management skills, and you'll be setting yourself up for success not only in college but beyond.

Looking for more great advice? Head to UChic.com for even more resources and information—they come highly recommended from our contributors and editors. Be sure to leave your suggestions as well!

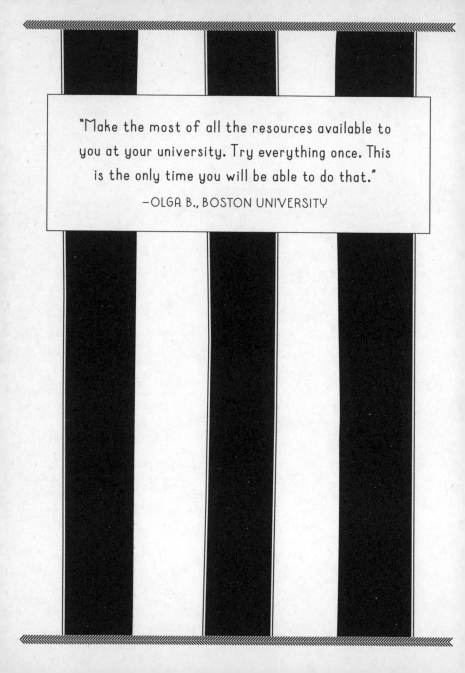

"Make the most of all the resources available to you at your university. Try everything once. This is the only time you will be able to do that."

—OLGA B., BOSTON UNIVERSITY

11

THE COLLEGE PERKS

COLLEGE TUITION IS EXPENSIVE these days. Sometimes you have to wonder where all of this money is going. Well, if you already are spending the cash on attending college, why not try to maximize all your opportunities while you're there—a surefire way to get a bang out of every buck going into your college's pockets. From finding internships to networking and reaching out to alumni to studying abroad, your school has a range of services, or as we like to call them, "college perks," set up to help you find your path in school and life. So what are you waiting for? Read on to learn about all the opportunities that await you in college.

SECRETS FOR
LANDING THAT TOP
INTERNSHIP

If there is one piece of advice I have to pass along it has to be that internships are a must-do during college. They help you figure out your interests and can even land you a job right out of college—which is a key reason you're in school. I have many friends who worked at the State Department, Department of Homeland Security, and Congress right after college because they impressed their bosses during their internships and utilized the connections they made. Internships are simply the best way for you to gain professional experience while still an undergraduate. Bottom line: you really need to check out and take advantage of these opportunities.

BUT WHERE DO I BEGIN?

The process of finding an internship can potentially be daunting, but above anything else you must keep a positive attitude through the *entire* process, from rejection to rejection to finally an offer. Be excited by all the possibilities! Be open to exploring different areas. It is just as important to know what you don't want to do as it is to know what you do want to do.

Although you may not realize it, you already have access to a treasure chest of resources that can help you snag that hot internship opportunity.

A good first step would be to drop by your university's career center. You can talk to a career counselor or review the school's database to see if your university has any established relationships with certain programs. The counselors can also provide feedback on your résumé and cover letter.

In addition to the career center, don't be afraid to ask your professor, academic advisor, or teaching assistant if they have any recommendations. They may be able to directly connect you to an organization. If you haven't heard it already, connections really do matter!

For those looking for advice for specific internships, here are some tips for you.

> **U**CHIC Tip!
>
> *Twitter is home to several different internship-focused "tweeters" who regularly put out job search advice* that you can follow. How to find these like-minded individuals? Run a simple search for your profession, using a Twitter tool like TweetDeck, and then "follow" those with information on jobs and internships in your area. A personal favorite of mine is the "Intern Queen," which is very helpful for many different types of nationwide internships.

Want to Work for a Not-for-Profit?

Looking for nonprofit work experience? You're in luck. There are many good websites such as Idealist.org that focus on posting internships and jobs, so check them out regularly and get on their mailing lists. In the nonprofit world, internships are like entry-level positions that often lead to a job afterward. But be prepared to work for free; it's a short-term sacrifice that can eventually land you a paid position.

For the Corporate-Minded

Want to work for an investment bank or a Fortune 500 company? Take the initiative to thoroughly research the company by checking out their career or internship websites, which can provide a lot of detail to give you a sense of the corporate culture and opportunities for advancement. Many companies have college recruitment programs that involve campus visits and career fairs, and they likely have established internship programs with set deadlines for which you will need to plan ahead to meet.

Interested in the Government?

If you are interested in politics, you should definitely consider interning in Washington, DC, whether on Capitol Hill, in a think tank, or at a nonprofit organization. Politics is all about networking and connections, so definitely take advantage of any personal connections you may have (family connections, professors' connections, alumni networks, etc.). You can also join organizations or participate in programs to add credentials that can help you get internships. For example, the Public Leadership Education Network (PLEN) is a national organization whose sole mission is preparing women for public leadership (www.plen.org).

If you want to intern on the Hill, you should apply to multiple offices and not just those from your home state to increase your odds of getting one of these coveted spots. Make a point of applying to the offices of congressional representatives who support issues you are passionate about, and showcase related experiences in your cover letter and résumé. Prepare a succinct one-page résumé and make sure you comprehensively research the office before you interview. Ideally, it's preferable that you intern full-time rather than part-time, so you gain a better understanding of how things run day-to-day and your organization or institution gets to know you better (think future letters of recommendation).

For the Budding Young Journalist or Media Maven

If you're considering a job in the media, there is no better time to start than now. And with the Internet, you can start as soon as you finish reading this chapter. Pick a topic that you love, start a blog, and post frequently to start building a following. Write for your college paper or even local newspaper during school. If you're interested in PR or marketing, join your campus organization for these careers, like the Public Relations Student Society of America (PRSSA; www.prssa.org) or the Society of Professional Journalists (www.spj.org), and aim to become a leader in the organization. When you are applying for internships in the field, highlight your experiences with your blog, campus paper clippings, and your involvement in campus organizations.

Dreaming of a Job in Medicine?

Medical school admissions offices like to see that you have clinical experience and are seriously interested in the profession. Volunteer in a hospital or clinic or become an emergency medical technician (EMT). Participating in undergraduate research is a great way to help you secure internships in medical fields and prepare for medical school. Nothing shows more interest in medicine (well, a top grade in organic chemistry doesn't hurt) than conducting outside research and even getting it published in a medical or scientific journal.

No Clue What You're Interested In?

That's fine! College is about taking your time to figure yourself out and discover your likes and dislikes. Apply for an internship in an area that you are interested in. Who knows, you could love it or hate it, but you'll never know your preferences unless you explore different areas.

INTERNSHIPS: IT'S ALL ABOUT THE SMALL STUFF

Harmony Haveman, Pacific Lutheran University

Internships will be your ticket to a job at the end of senior year when all of your friends are frantically searching for any job they can find. I had the most incredible opportunity to do three internships abroad thanks to networking and using the connections I had made along the way. I was able to intern at CNN International in London and MGM Television in London, and I also did an internship with the United Nations in Geneva, Switzerland. These experiences changed my life and paved the way for my career.

So how did I swing these fantastic opportunities? It's all about the small stuff. I went to every event that had anything to do with journalism. I was fortunate to get the internship at CNN International in London thanks to attending one of the many seminars about journalism at my university. It took being one of just a handful of college students to show up at an event to get my name out there. It was there that I met someone who worked for CNN. Because I was only one of a few students there, I had a great opportunity to talk about my future with this professional. After meeting with me and learning about my passion for journalism and my future, she said she'd help me get an internship at CNN in London. Those little connections make all the difference in the real world. I am a firm believer that it's a lot about who you know and even more about how to treat people.

APPLY, APPLY, APPLY!

Put yourself out there to the universe! People fear rejection, and this can prevent them from applying for multiple opportunities. One friend applied for two internships and got one offer. Another friend applied for ten and got only three offers. That's a lower success rate, but she has three times as many opportunities as my other friend—three versus one.

Timing and Follow-Up

Ideally, the goal is to plan ahead and apply to internships before the deadline. However, if you're like most of us, you get busy and may end up missing a deadline for an internship that you would have loved to have had. Don't be afraid to just go ahead and apply even if the deadline is close or has passed. Write in your cover letter that you are aware the deadline has passed, but you are still interested and available (this works especially well if you live near the organization). For example, toward the end of the spring semester, I finally decided I wanted to intern somewhere in San Francisco during the summer. I sent my résumé to many nonprofit organizations, even if they were not advertising an open position. I finally received a response from Greenpeace and interned there for the summer.

The Waiting Game

Don't be shy when going after something you want. Follow-up is a door-opening technique that can land you that great internship or job. If a decent amount of time has passed (use your judgment), it's definitely OK (actually, more like mandatory) to make a follow-up email or phone call. Keep it simple, "On April 10, I sent you my application for the summer internship. I am still interested in the position and would like to please check the status of my application." This worked for me when I landed a graduate internship at the United Nations. I applied for a summer internship and received an email from the UN saying that my application was still under consideration but they recommended that I apply again for a fall internship. So I applied again for the fall session but soon received a similar email. This time, I responded directly to this email, asking about the status of my application. I was told that the department I originally applied to no longer accepted applications, but if I was able to move to New York in the next few weeks, they would forward my information to other departments. Since I had good girlfriends from college whom I could indefinitely crash with, I was able to move from Los Angeles to New York immediately. So I asked them to please forward my information, and I quickly received a phone interview and an internship offer. I sent the follow-up email, and within a month, my dream came true of finally interning at the UN. The point of this story? Be persistent and your dreams can come true!

DON'T PUT ALL YOUR EGGS IN ONE BASKET

Have faith that it will all work out for the best, but at the same time, don't be too emotionally attached to a single application. I applied to Teach for America twice, the first time during my senior year and then a year later when I was in graduate school. I was rejected both times. The first time I made it to the final stage of an interview; I thought it went really well, but I was not accepted into the program. I applied again a year later and was not even given a phone interview. Both times I got rejected I felt really bad

> **U CHIC Tip!**
>
> Sometimes an internship can sound great on paper, but the actual experience may be less-than-stellar thanks to a poorly managed internship program. How to avoid this? *Track down people who have previously done the internship, and check for satisfaction surveys in your university's career center* to help you better understand your options.

about myself. My partner was accepted to Teach for America during our senior year. I hate to admit it, but initially I was really jealous. How silly was I! You should never compare yourself to anyone else! Everyone has a different life path. Reflecting back, I realized all the amazing things I have been able to do during the two years I would have potentially been in Teach for America. I volunteered in Kenya, lived in Egypt, got a master's degree, interned at the United Nations, and did a fellowship in the United States Congress. In the end, it all really worked out, and as much as I wanted to do Teach for America during the times I applied, I truly believe things worked out for a reason.

A WORD ON UNPAID INTERNSHIPS

At most universities, unpaid, for-credit internships are the norm. However, depending on what kind of work you do at your unpaid internship, it could actually be an illegal arrangement, according to a U.S. Department of Labor ruling. The Labor Department is afraid that these illegal situations—such as having an intern go on coffee runs, sit in the fashion closet for hours, or similar internship horror stories you have most likely heard from friends—are on the rise because of the bad economy and the need for cheap, or rather free, labor. You know the tasks; you've probably done them.

So how do you know if your potential unpaid internship is illegal? Basically the internship must contribute to your overall career goals in order for it to be legal. For instance, it should be run like a vocational or trade school, training you for future employment. If you're still unsure about a potential internship, be sure to consult with your career services center on campus, which can help you navigate this tricky issue.

FUNDING SUMMER INTERNSHIPS

Kelly Leslie, San Francisco State University

If you're planning to earn credit hours with an internship over the summer, you'll have to pay tuition. Be aware that summer tuition actually costs more than the fall and spring semesters. And this doesn't even include the living and travel costs of completing the internship. Yikes!

If you have to take out a loan to fund your summer internship, consider applying for a partial loan. Partial loans are available through private loan companies at lower amounts than regular loans covering full semesters.

Also, try to only take the minimal amount of credit hours for your internship. If you're able to get by with only taking one credit hour, that's a lot less expensive than having to pay for three!

Last piece of advice on finding that hot internship? Keep your hopes up! Honestly, ever since my senior year of college, every week (if not every day!) I apply to different opportunities. I have a solid résumé and cover letter (which I adapt to each posting) that I am able to send out as soon as I learn of opportunities. The more you put yourself out there, the better your chances. Not applying is the only sure way of not landing that great job or internship.

Insights provided by Pamela O'Leary, University of California-Berkeley

USING SUMMERS WISELY

It's that time of year when all of your exams have finished and this massive ray of sunshine is finding its way through your bedroom window. You reluctantly open your eyes, curl up in the corner of your bed, grab the blanket, and wonder what Mom's made for breakfast as you slowly roll your way out of bed and wander over to the bathroom to brush your teeth. You brush away diligently as you look at the clock hanging on the opposite wall.

What?

Noon.

No way.

You squint again, thinking that maybe your eyes haven't fully opened yet.

Noon.

Seriously? Then you look at yourself in the mirror and think. What am I doing with my life?

WHAT TO DO WITH THE SUMMER

Summertime for a college student can mean one of two things: (1) Sleeping and being a couch bum. This is probably not your best option. As tempting and easy as it is to stay put, let's be honest. You will get bored. You will regret it. And you have so much more that you can do with your time. (2) Getting up off that comfy couch and heading to work. Although you are supposed to be getting an education in the classroom, one of the most valuable educations you can get is through a summer job. In fact, here's some shocking news: your summer job might be the only educational experience you'll need before graduation, as it will be teaching you more about something you will actually be *doing* when you graduate. Where else can you get this hands-on, practical experience?

If you're like most kids at the end of their teenage years and heading into their twenties, you have absolutely no clue what you want to do with your life. So, how does a summer job cure that? And what's the point of having a job if you don't know what job you want?

THE SIMPLE MATTER OF MONEY

Loans don't pay for themselves and neither do those movie tickets or those fancy-schmancy cocktails. There is only so long you can hold on to that cash that your grandparents gave you for Hanukkah or Christmas. Sooner or later, you won't be able to puppy-face your way into some extra money for your bank account and even if you could, do you really want to? One of the rewarding things of having your own money is that it makes you independent. You are your own person and you are one step closer to being a responsible adult. OK, maybe the word "responsible" doesn't make it sound *that* appealing, but trust me, it is. If you are actually going to dive into that world of responsibility, then why not use your summer wisely and get a job that not only makes you money, but also opens up opportunities for your future in a field you actually want to work in.

HAVING SUMMER JOBS IS
KIND OF LIKE DATING

Thanks to this wonderful invention called an internship (or part-time job), you get to essentially date different jobs. You let the man (a.k.a., internship) take you out for a drink or dinner and it's on him; and maybe you realize that perhaps he wasn't what you wanted. No worries; you're only there for a few more weeks. Or maybe you go out on that first date and realize that you don't know enough about him, so you plan for round two—another summer at the same place. Best-case scenario: you realize you really do like him and then not only have you gotten a nice drink or dinner, but you enjoyed it, too, and you are glad you went out and learned something about this guy. This might be the start of a lifelong relationship.

Bottom line: we, as students today, are very lucky. We don't have to just get thrown into any job and stick with it forever like our parents or grandparents did. Thanks to internships and summer jobs, we get a taste of what life is like in the real world, getting a teensy-weensy bit closer to that elusive dream of actually getting paid to do something we love to do. Everybody wants it. Hardly anybody gets it. Fact of life.

YOU'VE DECIDED TO DO
SOMETHING PRODUCTIVE THIS
SUMMER, WHAT NEXT?

So once you've peeled yourself off that couch and made the decision to use that summer wisely…what's next? Where to go?

Finding a summer job starts way before the summer sun shows itself in the sky. Most summer jobs and internships start recruiting for positions as early as the autumn leaves turn slightly orangey-yellow.

So start looking early. It will pay off with a better opportunity in the end—guaranteed.

Career fairs, advisors, professors, alumni, and even friends and family are all great resources for finding summer opportunities—see the section on internships in this chapter for more helpful tips about how to use these resources.

Be persistent. Once you know what job you want, be annoying. Honestly! Just don't call every day, especially when in the job description they ask you not to. Find the place that you want to work at and email them or give them a call. Ask them if they are looking for interns or someone to help out or just ask for some advice about what kind of person they would want or what kind of internships you should take on before you apply for a job there. They might not reply, but if they do, you will have some valuable advice for your future or maybe even a job.

In addition, you can find that famous author or lab specialist you've been dreaming to ask for advice. Contact them. They are only human, and so are you. The worst thing that will happen is they won't answer. Don't be afraid to reach out to people who have your dream job; you never know what could come of it.

If all else fails, ask around. Ask your parents, ask your parents' friends, ask your friends' parents. Ask your professor. *Ask away.* Someone, somewhere must have an opening for the summer, and would certainly love to have an eager college student fill it.

MORE WAYS TO USE YOUR SUMMERS WISELY

Amanda Ferrara, New York University

So you didn't land that hot summer job or internship you were dreaming about. Or maybe it wasn't a good option for you because of scheduling conflicts, cost-prohibitive locations, or other reasons. How can you still put those three months out of school to good use? I've got some tips for you.

- **Get a job related to your field of interest:** Want to become a teacher but can't shadow due to summer schedules? Be a camp counselor. Want to go to medical school but can't find an internship at a hospital? Get a job with the types of people you eventually want to help, like at a daycare (pediatrics) or at a nursing home (geriatrics). Get creative—there are so many opportunities out there that will allow you to gain experience related to your field.

- **Get a "hardworking" job that pays:** As unglamorous as a waitress or a cashier job may sound, there is no better time in your life to get your hands dirty with an "on your feet" kind of job. Not only will it boost your bank account's bottom line, it will give you the ability to say to future employers that you know the value of hard work and customer service.

- **Volunteer:** Volunteering can be an incredibly rewarding and fun experience. In addition to the good you'll feel by giving back, you are gaining experience in the real world.

- **Travel:** There is no better time to travel than when you are young and jobless. Start saving your money now and use your free time to go on some great adventures, from road trips or nearby day trips with friends, to visiting family, to going overseas.

- **Get creative:** For those of you who want to put creative skills to work this summer, consider taking art or foreign language classes. For those aspiring writers, consider launching your own blog.

- **Knock out some credit hours:** Summer courses are known to move at a quicker pace and have longer sessions, but generally, they are smaller and students do quite well in them. This is a perfect way to boost your GPA, lessen your courseload in the following semesters, and enhance your learning by studying something that might not be offered during the school year. If you plan to take a course outside your school, check with an advisor first to make sure your credits will transfer over.

WHAT TO DO ONCE YOU GET THE POSITION

Make sure you get to know the people at your office. Everyone around you can either be someone to learn from or a possible future contact for a job or recommendation. If you make the right impression and show that you are willing to learn, they will want to help you with your career and future.

Go to any of the lunches or dinners they have. Not only will you get a free meal out of it, but you will also gain a better relationship with a boss who you might want to write you a recommendation or offer you another internship or even a full-time job.

Learn as much as you can. Always ask for more work or more responsibility, and do twice as much work as they expect you to do. That way, when you leave at the end of the summer, they will realize just how indispensable you are and that they want you back as soon as you finish college. Even if you don't particularly want to have that job again, chances are that your résumé can use the boost of those new skills you picked up over the summer. Impress your bosses and coworkers. Show them that you are worth a stellar review or even a full-time job.

Last piece of advice for using your summers wisely? Meet up with your good friends—new and old. Let them ground you. Let them be there for you. Have a good time. Live.

Insights provided by Olga Belogolova, Boston University

WHEN TO GO ABROAD

One of the greatest perks you have these days as a college student is the opportunity to study abroad. And why wouldn't you? It almost seems like a requirement that you study abroad at some point during your time in college. What a great requirement! Who wouldn't want to study in some exotic place like Italy, Japan, or even somewhere in Africa?

Still, studying abroad is a big decision, and the key to making this decision is to go when you are *ready*. What do I mean when I say ready? Ready means that you are academically, socially, and financially prepared for this adventure of a lifetime. So here's how you can get prepared.

GETTING ACADEMICALLY READY

Before you study abroad, I highly recommend that you first decide on your major. Some study-abroad applications will even ask you how you will use time abroad to gain credits toward your major. On top of that, several programs are actually targeted to specific majors, making it an added bonus to know your major before heading abroad. Think about it: there's nothing more relevant and fulfilling than going on an archaeological dig in Greece if you're an archeology or anthropology major.

After deciding on a major, try to complete at least one semester of major coursework. This may be difficult for those of you who have been itching to take your first-ever tango class in a bar in Buenos Aires. I completely understand this urge. But a semester of class is really the only way to make sure that you still want to pursue the major. After all, if you decide to change majors, you may need to stick around the good old USA for an extra semester—the one you would have spent abroad—in order to graduate on time.

Which Year Makes the Most Sense?

Deciding when to go abroad is a very personal decision, so I can't say what is right for you. From my experience, sophomore or junior year are more popular years to head to foreign lands, probably because most college students are more settled and ready for the experience of living abroad. Given that most students don't declare their majors until sophomore year, junior year may be the best option to study abroad. Indeed, when I was in Florence, Italy, a large percentage of the students I met abroad were also juniors.

Don't Wait until Your Senior Year

I also feel strongly that you should not hold off on studying abroad until your senior year. The last thing a senior college student needs is to come back from study abroad and have trouble transferring credits and then not be able to graduate on time. When I returned from study abroad, I was surprised when the office told me that it could take up to six months for the grades to come and credits to be transferred. Now, if you're on the five- or six-year plan, this probably doesn't apply to you so much. But for those of you who need to be out in four, I highly recommend that you avoid a senior semester abroad.

Not only can studying abroad put a cramp in your goal to graduate in four years, but your senior year in college is the last opportunity that you get to party and enjoy your best college friends. Most likely, you will all end up with jobs in different cities and states, so it only makes sense to spend your final year with them (especially when senior year gives you a little more time to kick off your shoes, relax,

UCHIC Tip!

Before choosing to study abroad, I highly recommend meeting with your academic advisor and mapping out what credits you still need in order to graduate. *Tell your advisor that you are thinking of studying abroad, and see if it will be possible for you to graduate on time.* Then take that list of necessary classes and look at the possibilities offered to you by study-abroad programs. If you are extremely concerned, make an appointment with the study-abroad office and discuss whether or not studying abroad would stunt your academic progress.

and have fun!). So stick it out and try staying put your senior year.

Going after Graduation

Don't forget that it is always possible to study abroad after graduation. Even better, there is also the opportunity to complete an internship while abroad that would provide you almost the same life-changing experiences as a study-abroad program. I met people abroad from the United States who found internships after graduation. One girl was a design intern for an architect in Florence (an incredible opportunity in a city known for its beautiful architecture) and another one was an intern for a company in Florence that organizes events and trips that are affordable for study-abroad students. Each seemed extremely happy with her decision to work abroad.

You can also go abroad for graduate school. This may be surprising, but there are some well-known foreign graduate schools that can provide equal or better training in your area of expertise. Schools like Sciences Po in Paris or the London School of Economics are top-notch training grounds for budding policy experts or politicians. If not completing your graduate degree abroad, you could get into a program at your school that offers study abroad options.

AM I SOCIALLY READY?

Besides academics, the decision to go abroad should also be based on when you're *socially* ready for the experience. For most people, studying abroad is a step way outside their comfort zone. Even the independence in college doesn't match the freedom of studying abroad. With this freedom also comes an element of responsibility that you've never had to face before: you are far away from your family and friends.

Some people long for that kind of independence, and the fresh new start that a semester or year abroad offers. But it is also important to understand exactly what you are leaving behind: your family, friends, organizations or volunteer activities, and even relationships. Is there a boyfriend? Is a close family member sick? Are you a possible contender for a significant leadership position on campus? Bottom line: don't forget to consider your social life when trying to decide whether to go abroad, or you may end up spending your entire time abroad worrying about what is happening at home. And that would be a waste.

It is important to communicate with the significant people in your life before heading abroad, so everyone knows what the expectations will be. Be prepared for the reality that you will probably not be able to talk every day by phone. If you don't already have one, try setting up a Skype account so that when you are able to communicate, you can see as well as hear each other. Try to set aside time to keep up with friends at home, even if it means sending out mass emails to everyone.

You'll be making a new life for yourself while abroad, and with it comes new challenges and stresses, but also incredible benefits. New friends, different roommates, and new dramas will appear. Prepare yourself for all of these experiences, and you will be certain not to run into any social difficulties during your adventure abroad.

AM I READY FINANCIALLY?

Last, but not least, your financial situation will also influence your decision of when to go abroad. This bit of advice should not surprise you: save up money before going abroad. Depending on the current currency exchange rate, it is entirely possible that everything you buy there will be more expensive than at home. Not a great thing. So if your dream is to be in the United Kingdom or somewhere in Europe, be prepared for a credit crunch. If money is a big concern, consider going somewhere with a better exchange rate. But don't forget that currency rates change often, so make sure that you look it up when figuring out your budget before heading abroad.

Save Some Cash

Saving up money before you head abroad will ensure you have a better experience. Wherever you end up going, you will have many opportunities to travel to other countries and cities that you may never have an opportunity to visit again. The summer before I studied abroad, I saved up a little over $1,000 for travel and souvenirs, and it's no surprise that I spent it all. Most of it went to my gypsy travels to other locales. In the end, I ended up traveling to six different countries! My favorite places that I visited were Dublin, Ireland; Barcelona, Spain; Nice, France; and Geneva, Switzerland. Having some money initially set aside for this extra travel guaranteed that I'd be able to see many places during my semester abroad.

Go for a Few Scholarships or Even Grants

Your study-abroad office should have a list of possible grants and scholarships for your study-abroad programs. Some scholarships are specific to programs or countries and others depend on whether or not you are eligible for financial aid. If you receive financial aid at school, you should be able to get help with study abroad as well. Your office can provide you with the proper forms to fill out for financial aid, but you need to be proactive in tracking down scholarships to fund your travels. With a little effort can come a big payoff. So don't forget to check out all options.

WORKING ABROAD

And don't forget that it is also possible to work abroad. One website, www.workingabroad.org, provides a long list of international internships and work opportunities that are available in many foreign countries. But don't forget to consider the legal restrictions that your host country might have in place. Many countries' work visas limit the hours you are allowed to work to something like twenty hours per week.

But that amount a week could still provide you with enough spending money to really enjoy your experience. I knew someone abroad who didn't speak Italian when she got there, and she walked into a restaurant only knowing the word for work and the owner gave her a job. Moral of this story: if you want a job, even if there are language differences, it is very possible that you can land yourself a sweet and even fulfilling job experience that you'll never forget.

Study abroad is a life-changing experience no matter how many times you've heard it. Step outside of the box and take a chance. Just make sure that you're fully prepared before you take the first step.

Insights provided by Kathryn Lewis, University of North Carolina–Chapel Hill

SPRING BREAK OR BUST!

The last section's focus on study abroad is a perfect segue to the last "college perk"—spring break! When else in life do you have the excuse to travel somewhere exotic for some fun in the sun? But wait. The stereotypical image of spring break is a mixed bag of fun and (sometimes) girls and guys behaving badly. This yearly pastime has been around since 1935 and is still going strong, thanks in part to highly visible media coverage and the many stories you find splashed across the TV throughout the months of March and April.

Sure, you may think it's a good time, but the experts don't exactly agree. In 2002, the American Medical Association actually put out a statement noting, "Spring break is no longer an innocent respite from the rigors of college academics; it's potentially life threatening." So why the hard feelings? Well to begin with, spring break isn't just a fun vacation you take with your friends—it's a huge moneymaking operation that generates more than $1 billion annually (and that's just counting Texas and Florida!). That means there are plenty of businesses out there willing to look the other way if things get out of control. In fact, some college tour companies have come under fire recently for encouraging reckless behavior like binge drinking and excessive promiscuity. It's become such a problem that some towns like Daytona Beach have tried to ban the practice altogether.

While spring break is certainly an important rite of passage for many coeds, putting your safety and health first should always be your top priority. Not everyone may agree, but trust us, the stats don't lie: taking things to an extreme will most likely land you in the hospital emergency room, or worse, cooling your heels in a jail cell.

If you're ready to take on the responsibility of a parents-free trip to an exotic locale, then the first thing you need to do is start researching now. Whether you're looking to kick back and relax or you're even exploring the idea of donating your time to a worthy cause, there's no time like the present to get your facts straight and make an informed decision about your first spring break experience.

TAKE IT FROM A GIRL WHO'S BEEN THERE

I'd never been on vacation with anyone but my family before, so when my sophomore year rolled around, I knew going away for a crazy week with my friends was a rite of passage I just couldn't miss. OK, so I never really saw myself as the typical spring-break girl who danced on tables and hooked up with some random guy I was guaranteed never to see again, but I figured as a college student, going on spring break was something I simply had to do. While Cabo was the hot spot for students at my school, my friends and I (a group of four guys and five girls) decided to hit the Bahamas instead, in an effort to avoid the entire student population.

Although the destination seemed like a no-brainer, determining the details of the trip (especially when trying to plan with such a large group) wasn't exactly a cakewalk. From deciding where to stay to figuring out how to get there, it seemed like everyone had an opinion! We all finally agreed on a nice, all-inclusive four-star hotel (always keep it classy, folks) that allowed us the opportunity to explore both the beach and the local culture.

For me, spring break was not only a time to spend with my besties, but also an opportunity to reconnect with one of our pals who had transferred schools. The Bahamas also served as a great meeting place for a reunion. It was less crowded, the vibe was pretty mellow, and we didn't have to deal with a bunch of drunk jerks hitting on us twenty-four-seven. While most people think spring break has to be all about partying, it can be a great time to rest, recharge, and spend time with the people you love the most.

PLANNING

Waiting until the last minute to plan your trip is definitely a big mistake if you want to get the best deals on hotels and airfare. About 1.5 million college students go away for spring break each year, which means rooms and flights fill up fast if you don't book at least three to four months in advance.

Typically, most college-aged travelers flock to popular spring break hot spots like Florida, Texas, Jamaica, Mexico, and the Bahamas. But don't feel like you have to follow the crowd to have a good time. Keep in mind you can have just as much fun (and score student discounts!) if you head to Europe, or skip the whole warm weather thing altogether and hit the slopes instead (Utah, Idaho, and Colorado are always an option). Cruises are also something to consider.

Just remember, budget is key. If you're looking to save a lot and don't mind staying at a so-so hotel, then sticking to one of the more popular spring break destinations is probably your best bet, since there are quite a few packages to pick and choose from.

Breaking Down Your Budget

Keeping on budget while lounging around on a beach is a lot harder than you think. Sure, hotel and airfare make up a big chunk of your trip expenses, but little things like food, drinks, car rental, cab/bus fare, tips, shopping, tourist excursions, and cover charges for bars and nightclubs can quickly add up. If you don't want to blow a lot of money all at once (or if you want to maximize your return), consider booking your vacation through a national travel agency.

Companies like Liberty Travel offer trips for various price ranges, easy layaway plans, and a trustworthy list of tour operators that circle the globe. While you might be able to snag a better deal with a college travel agency, that doesn't necessarily mean you can trust all the information you're provided with. Again, college travel agencies draw the most business from spring break, so they're eager to book as many people as possible so they can maximize sales. Regular travel agencies get business year-round, so they're less likely to pressure you into a package that doesn't fit your budget.

The amount of money students spend on spring break can differ greatly depending on where you're going and how long you plan to stay. If that amount is more than you had in mind, you might want to consider traveling somewhere stateside that's not typically considered a spring break destination (but still caters to a younger crowd). For instance, Austin, New York, San Francisco, Seattle, or New Orleans are all great vacation options that offer up lots of culture, cool bar scenes, and shopping aplenty. Just make sure you hit travel websites like TripAdvisor.com first before you book anything. They offer hotel reviews from travelers, pictures, ratings, and info on the age range of the average hotel guest.

So What's So Great About an All-Inclusive Hotel?

Should you go with an all-inclusive package? Well, that all depends on what kind of vacation you're looking for. If you don't plan to spend any time at your hotel beyond sleeping and showering, then probably not. But if you're looking for a way to save money and get the most bang for your buck, it's a smart option. Hotel chains like Sandals, Beaches, and RIU Hotels & Resorts offer all-inclusive packages that cover everything from round-trip transportation to and from the airport, meals, drinks, discounts on travel tours, and free activities galore. Bonus: Tipping is generally discouraged at all-inclusive resorts, since gratuities are included in your stay.

Travel Essentials—Don't Leave Home without 'Em!

No matter where you decide to go, there are certain things you can't live without. An updated passport is key if you're planning to cross the border, as is a copy of your passport information (it's generally recommended that you provide this to the nearest U.S. Embassy as soon as you arrive at your destination). Bringing along a copy of your medical records is also a good idea. You should also make sure that you fill all your prescriptions ahead of time, and check the Centers for Disease Control website (wwwnc.cdc.gov/travel) to make sure you don't need any specific shots or immunizations before you head out of the country.

You should also ask if your hotel has an in-house medical staff. If it doesn't, ask hotel staff to provide information about local hospitals or clinics that cater to tourists. If you plan to travel outside the continental United States, purchase an international calling card or plan for your cell phone. While some cell phone providers, like Sprint, automatically update your phone to send and receive international calls without operator assistance, others still rely on the old method and will charge you a ton of money to call home.

PLAYING IT SAFE

OK, you've seen the stories in the media featuring binge drinking and "girls gone wild" during spring break. Since when did having fun become so extreme?

Unfortunately, binge drinking has become the social norm for many college students, and while that in itself is dangerous for a number of reasons, the consequences that can result from bingeing on spring break can be even worse, and sometimes deadly. First, there's the overexposure that videos like Girls Gone Wild bring—something that may seem like harmless fun at the time, but is obviously not so smart when it comes to applying for a job a couple years down the road. And then there are other biggies like getting arrested, raped, contracting an STD, or even worse—a tragedy like the Natalee Holloway case. Most college students think it won't happen to them, but it's happening to someone because the numbers and statistics just keep growing and growing.

Indeed, according to a recent survey conducted by the University of Wisconsin, 75 percent of all college males and 44 percent of all college females were intoxicated daily while on spring break. Spring break is a time to have fun and celebrate, but it should also be a time that you want to cherish. While it may always be five o'clock somewhere, try to keep the margaritas at a minimum and your enjoyment at a maximum.

Hook Up at Your Own Risk!

A recent American Medical Association (AMA) poll showed that 74 percent of college students agreed that spring break trips go hand-in-hand with increased sexual activity. For some people, spring break takes on an "anything goes" approach that includes sloppy bar shenanigans, random hookups, and unprotected sex with strangers. Yes, it's inevitable that you're going to encounter cute guys while on vacation, but that doesn't mean you should do something that you'll later regret. Harmless flirting and a few stolen kisses are fun, but a one-night stand can come with some serious baggage. Be careful and use protection if you're dead set on taking it to the next level. After all, the only crabs you should run into are the ones hanging out on the beach!

The Buddy System Never Goes out of Style

It doesn't matter how cute he is, how close the hotel is to the bar, or how tired (or drunk) you might be feeling—never go anywhere by yourself! Bad things happen when groups get separated—especially when you add alcohol and out-of-control behavior to the mix. Map out a spring break buddy system before you hop a plane to your destination of choice. If you're going with a mixed group, make sure there's a guy for every girl, or team up into groups of twos and threes. The more people together the better. A big crowd not only provides a higher level of safety, it can also work in your favor. (Nothing says spring break sparks like a handy wingman ready and willing to help you make a love connection!)

ALTERNATIVE SPRING BREAK OPTIONS

If a wild week of sun and fun isn't exactly your thing, you might want to consider something a bit more rewarding.

Alternative spring breaks (ASBs) have become increasingly popular, allowing students across the country to give back and help others. Why spend a week partying when you can make an impact in a community here or abroad? Not only does it look great on your résumé, it offers you a unique opportunity few people will ever get the chance to experience.

ASB Options Aplenty

How does building houses in a post-disaster zone like Haiti or teaching English to children in China sound? Of course, you may be thinking, "Hot days and hard labor—why would I want to spend my week off from school doing even more work?" Well, the benefits are nothing but rewarding. Think of all the places you'll get to go, the people you'll meet, and the culture you'll soak in from spending time outside your usual comfort zone. Plus, there are tons of programs, no matter what your interest. From building school libraries on American

Indian reservations here in the States to joining an archaeological dig abroad, ASB excursions offer a "sky's the limit" opportunity you most likely won't encounter traveling to some crowded tourist destination.

Doing Good in Your Own Backyard

If you're not sold on the idea of traveling to some far-flung country, you can always stick close to home and offer your services to one of many student-driven nonprofit organizations here in the States. While Habitat for Humanity is always a good choice, other groups like Live United (www.unitedway.org/our-work) offer programs focusing on education, income, and health care, so there's something for everyone. The University of Nebraska in Lincoln, Lehigh University in Bethlehem, Pennsylvania, and the University of Wisconsin–Madison are just a few schools that offer service trips to desirable destinations without alcohol as the focal point.

Participating in an ASB is both a rewarding *and* enlightening experience. While some people use it as a chance to immerse themselves in their field of choice, others simply enjoy the opportunity it presents to take a step back, learn something new, and help those in need. For more information, search "alternative spring break" online or drop by the student activities or community service office on campus.

Insights provided by Erin Cunningham, The George Washington University

UCHIC ESSENTIALS—
THE COLLEGE PERKS

SEIZE OPPORTUNITIES AND MAKE THE MOST OF THEM

Never again will you have the virtually limitless number of opportunities at your feet that you do in college—including the time and, often, the funding to explore them. Don't let these opportunities slip away—take advantage of them now! Internships, study abroad programs, and other college perks can play a critical role in shaping your future.

TEST-DRIVE YOUR FUTURE CAREER

Internships are the best way to find out if the career you think you want to pursue is actually something you'll enjoy. Plus, they're a great way to learn and practice professional habits and behavior.

USE SPRING BREAK TO DO SOME GOOD

Tempting as a weeklong beach party may be, alternative spring breaks can be incredibly fulfilling. Travel abroad to perform a much-needed social service in a different cultural environment, or stay local to make a difference right in your own backyard. The impact on the community (and on yourself) will be long lasting. We promise, you won't regret it.

Looking for more great advice? Head to UChic.com for even more resources and information—they come highly recommended from our contributors and editors. Be sure to leave your suggestions as well!

"As a nontraditional student, it's common to feel out of place. However, you have to realize college is not about fitting in, it's about standing out! Taking advantage of opportunities your college offers and getting involved is one of the best things you can do. Networking is crucial. Getting involved gives you a sense of college pride and helps you realize you are not alone."

—OCTAVIA O., CALIFORNIA STATE UNIVERSITY, FRESNO

12

FINDING NONTRADITIONAL SUCCESS

ARE YOU A NONTRAD? A mom headed off to college for the first time? Or maybe you took a few years off after high school to volunteer abroad and are now ready to head to college. For many of you, your definition of what makes a college student today is broader than ever before. And you're not alone. While most enrolled college students are still between the ages of 18 and 24, at a few national universities, you'll discover that more than half of their undergraduates are nontraditional students. We all have different paths in life, and college is yet another. So whatever your reasons are for your "nontraditional" path, you've done the right thing. And who knows? What may be considered nontraditional today may become mainstream tomorrow, especially as the cost of college continues to increase encouraging these more creative educational paths. This new chapter is all about celebrating the nontraditional path with a little advice for girls who, like you, have done something amazingly different.

CONSIDERING A NONTRADITIONAL PATH? STAYING TRUE TO YOURSELF IS KEY

WHAT DO YOU PICTURE when you think of a girl in college? Is she in a sorority? Partying every night? Halfheartedly going to class? So, what happens to that girl if she doesn't fit the "norm?"

Well, I am that girl. I'm constantly being told that I work too much, obsess over my homework, and need to take more time to "be normal." But, I found that I'm happiest when I pursue my personal passions. I love staying busy and active. I choose to spend my free time interning and writing because those things will help me accomplish my dreams. Because of this, I don't enjoy going out too much or wasting my time watching Netflix.

However, I wasn't always this confident in my choices. I was originally premed, and although I performed well in the classes, it felt more like a job than anything else. I found that I was running myself down and making myself miserable. After testing the waters with some of my elective classes, I found that writing made me happiest. After switching my major to journalism, I was even happier. For the first time in my college career, I was excited to go to class rather than wanting to crawl back into bed.

If you aren't sure who you are, who you want to be, or what you want to do, then take the time to find out. Explore different types of people, attend various events, and find what gives you purpose. Getting an education is hard; it ultimately tests your time management and patience. However, in the end, it helps you finally understand your true colors.

One great way to do it is through a gap year. What is it? It's typically defined as an academic year taken by a student as a break between secondary school and higher education. In fact, gap years are more common than ever before. There's the select few who take a year off to travel the globe, get a few stamps in their passport, and experience different cultures. There's the college hopefuls who spend a year (or more) making money to put toward tuition. And there's also people who take time off to consider what they want to invest in, whether it's a college education or not.

The number of years can vary—from a few months to decades. Number of years aside, gap years are a viable option for people looking to experience life before they get an education. For you, taking a gap year might be a necessity. You may be forced into it due to unforeseen circumstances or financial issues. But, it's important to realize that gap years are not a step back; they are simply a delay to what's coming next.

WHAT I LEARNED BY TAKING SOME TIME OFF

Amanda Condon, Arkansas Tech University

The gap years between high school and college can be some of the most defining years of your life. When I was eighteen years old, I had a two-year-old daughter. My days consisted of going to work at a department store and caring for a precious baby. I was unsure of who or what I wanted to be, so I decided to take a few years off before I went back to college.

I worked to provide for my children, and this helped me learn more about myself. I learned to have a strong work ethic and how education is vital to moving forward in a career. Food service was not my passion, nor sitting behind a computer in a stuffy office. I wanted more.

The early twenties were some of the best years of my life. I traveled around trying to find my place in the world without limitations. It was then that I learned that the world is a big maze. It has twists and turns that will teach you how to think and respond to it. While it may be challenging, it makes each day worthwhile.

During my midtwenties, I experienced the harsh consequences of domestic violence. Jobs were scarce, bills were unpaid, and I was left to raise three children on my own. Life was not pleasant, which is why I decided to make a change for my future. I enrolled in college and decided to face my fear of failure. If you are going through a similar situation, the best advice I can give you is to seize each moment because you have the authority to control your future. The best thing you can do for yourself is to realize your own power.

Being much older than most of the students on campus was not as bad when I considered how much of an impact I could make in their lives. My ability to connect with others put me in the best position to rise as a leader on campus and later in the community. Academics were easy for me because if I did not know how to complete the assignment, I knew how to find a resource or help to assist me. My years working before college taught me the value of asking questions and finding help when necessary. It's safe to say that my gap years prepared me for college. Gap years are becoming the norm, and I would highly advise any student in a similar situation to take a little bit of time off before enrolling in college. Learning about myself beforehand allowed me to embrace my love of knowledge and education. I am now going to be a better mother and career woman because of it.

Throughout your college journey, you may face criticism from others. What I've learned is that I shouldn't care what anyone else says about me or what they have to say about the path that I'm taking. I'm in college to pursue my dreams of being a writer and not to make anyone else happy. This is my personal choice and no one else's. I get to choose my own actions, and so do you.

I've faced my fair share of judgment. For as long as I can remember, people have been criticizing me for what I do. People have harassed me in public and even over the Internet. Even the tiniest mistakes have provoked people to try and tear me down. People have made fun of me for the craziest things like eating healthy or "working out too much." The truth is that I'm never going to make everyone happy; the most important person to make happy is myself.

So, here's my advice to you: Don't feel like you have to fit the mold of what a college student "should be." Find the person you want to be and don't look back. Do what you love and forget what anyone else has to say about it.

Insights provided by Kristine Fenstermacher, Temple University

HOW TO MAKE
TRANSFERRING A
BREEZE

LET'S BE HONEST: TRANSFERRING is tough. Similar to gap years, it can either be your personal decision or completely out of your control. Making the decision to transfer isn't easy, and the new environment that you will now be a part of will be hard to adjust to.

When you're in high school, you create an image in your head about what you think college is. You expect that your life could be just like what you see in the movies; however, that image is nothing like reality.

Once you've chosen your school of choice and say your good-byes, you head out to what you're told is going to be the best four years of your life. But what if they aren't? What if the school, people, and/or location feels absolutely wrong? For me, I was struggling to afford the school I was attending. Although I did enjoy my time at this particular university, I didn't love it enough to take out monumental loans to stay there.

Choosing to transfer is not an easy decision. It's an all-consuming feeling of self-doubt that plagues you. And then this fear gets far too real when you realize that you're going to have to restart everything. There's a lot to figure out when you transfer: how your new school works, how to make new friends, and how to acclimate yourself to a new area. I went from rural North Carolina to the middle of urban Philadelphia; the location change was a culture shock and required a lot of time for me to get comfortable with my new surroundings.

Some of you may accept the idea of transferring early on—even before you start college. If tuition cost is holding you back from starting college, starting out at a community college is a great option. Community college can provide a foundation that you can later use at the four-year university of your choice. Plus, it's the least expensive route.

WHEN YOU MOVE FROM COMMUNITY COLLEGE TO A FOUR-YEAR UNIVERSITY

Amanda Condon, Arkansas Tech University

As a single mother and sole provider for three young children, paying for college out of pocket was not an option. When I researched colleges in my hometown, I compared the price of tuition among two community colleges and a well-known four-year university. The tuition for fifteen credit hours at the university would cost me approximately $4,000 and the community college would only cost $1,500. After speaking to a financial aid advisor, I learned that the university encouraged students to apply for FAFSA and only offered a handful of institutional scholarships. The community college appealed to me more because they offered a state-funded program that low-income students could use to rent textbooks at no cost to the student, and there was an outstanding amount of scholarships available including transfer scholarships.

I decided to attend the community college first and transfer to a four-year university after I completed my primary studies. This decision would give me two years to prepare for the significant increase in tuition, apply for scholarship opportunities, and ensure my ability to complete my degrees with the least amount of debt possible.

The community college campus was smaller than most department stores, but the opportunities for me to advance were endless. I was able to achieve many academic and merit-based accomplishments that ultimately gave me the competitive edge with scholarships. I selected my four-year university based on my list of needs and began communicating with the admissions counselors at Arkansas Tech University a year before I transferred. I was able to complete the enrollment process slowly, and this is the best way to go about transferring.

I want to complete my degree debt-free and get the highest quality education possible. I'm on the path to earn a master of science degree in emergency management and Homeland Security. My career aspirations are to become the executive director of the Federal Emergency Management Agency otherwise known as FEMA.

The best advice I can give another student who is considering a college transfer would be to find the path of least resistance. Make a list on paper of what you need vs. what you want from your college experience. The purpose of pursuing our education is to reach our dreams of working in our field of passion, and each one of us has different circumstances. Choosing the path of least resistance means making logical decisions about what steps you should take to alleviate unnecessary financial and physical burdens.

When it comes to meeting new people, it's not necessarily as easy this time around because there are no longer hundreds of students in the same position as you. And it's not just about meeting people; it's about finding the right people. It's important to surround yourself with people that make you feel like your best self because there is no reason to have anyone in your life that makes you feel inferior. The environment of college is so different from high school because you are constantly surrounded by your roommates and friends. Whether you're living with your best friends or strangers, it's crucial that you evaluate if it's a positive living environment. Don't put yourself in a toxic environment with negative people.

Getting involved is a great way to meet new people after your transfer. Try out anything that sounds interesting to you—whether it's a sports team, club, internship, or anything in between. It is helpful to have people around your age to talk to about your career aspirations, future plans, and personal interests. Through my job in fashion and editorial internship, I met people who had similar interests as me, which helped me adjust to my new environment.

When you first transfer, you can feel completely out of the loop. The easiest way to make your new school feel like home is to do everything in your power to stick to your guns. Be yourself and everything around you will reflect in the person that you truly are. Don't create an image of what you think college could be. Follow your heart and mind, and everything else will fall into place.

If you're thinking about transferring, I suggest speaking to the financial aid directors on each campus you attend to find out what resources are out there for students. This step opened doors for me to find hidden scholarships that have helped me reach my financial goals. Remember, transferring college is a process and not a race. Take it slow to ensure you meet all your personal needs.

Insights provided by Kristine Fenstermacher, Temple University

MOTHER FIRST, STUDENT SECOND: ADVICE FOR PARENTS HEADED TO COLLEGE

STEREOTYPES ARE BORING, RIGHT? Well, I think so. There are so many students out there who defy the standard and live in a "nontraditional" way.

I found success where it wasn't supposed to be—in my nontraditional life as a single parent. I hit the lowest point of my life during the summer of 2014, as I faced unemployment for what seemed like the fifteenth time. This followed the horrible divorce I went through in 2013, the loss of everything I owned, and the relocation of my children to our hometown. But it was a blessing in disguise.

Have you ever been sick and tired of being sick and tired? In the midst of the chaos, I took what little faith I had left and enrolled into college. I felt like I had nothing to lose, because I had already lost everything except my children. This leap of faith was the first day of the rest of my life.

Enrolling into college was intimidating because I had not seen a classroom in over fifteen years. The biggest challenge I had to overcome was self-doubt and the fear of failing. In my eyes, the only thing I was good at was being a mom. I soon learned that I was actually an incredibly talented woman with a bright future.

I knew how to balance work and children on limited resources. I was resilient and able to bounce back from any disaster that plagued my life.

There is nothing more fulfilling than balancing motherhood, academics, and volunteer service. My life is not always picture perfect, but in time I've learned what works best. The best advice I can give is to focus on what matters the most to you each day. Who cares if your dishes do not get washed every night, or if you have a laundry train that extends the length of your couch? At the end of your educational journey, you will still have dishes and laundry to do. Focus on your destination: network, develop your talents, take time to rest, and participate in new opportunities that could open doors for you in the future.

SIX TIPS FOR COLLEGE MOMS, FROM A MOM

Amanda Condon, Arkansas Tech University

1. CHANGE YOUR PERSPECTIVE

When facing unanticipated obstacles, think of the problem like it is a puzzle. You have all the pieces in front of you. All you have to do is turn them until they fit in the right spot. For instance, it's easy to get distracted by the minor hiccups in college such as not having adequate childcare, but you need to put it in a different light, and realize that it is only a temporary roadblock and that you can overcome it. Consider tapping community programs for parents attending college or contact your student support services department (every campus has one) and share your needs. You would be surprised how quickly you can overcome a challenge when you put forth the effort to do so and enlist others to help you along the way.

2. BUILD YOUR NETWORK

College is the best time to build your professional and personal network. A good rule of thumb is that you need to connect with people that have a variety of talents. Make a trip to your financial aid office, visit your career services center early and often, and get to know the other student support services on campus. Also, the people in these positions are important, so make an effort to make sure they know you. They will be your allies throughout college, and they can tap into their networks if needed to help you succeed. In addition to your campus, search social networks for support. Hashtags, especially on Twitter, are a great way to narrow down the search. For example, type in #collegemom or #nontraditionalstudent to find resources that are tailored to you. Last, reach out to the local workforce center. They often host career development trainings that can link you to more people.

3. DEVELOP YOURSELF

Self-improvement is a journey and not a destination. If you are shy, make a conscious decision to face your fears through exposure therapy. The more times you expose yourself to what scares you the most, the faster you will overcome that challenge. By acknowledging your weaknesses, you can improve yourself and prepare to reenter the workforce as a well-rounded, educated individual.

4. HAVE FAITH IN YOURSELF

It is easy for a mom, especially a single mom, to overlook her talents because she feels like all she is good at doing is running a home and being a mom. However, this is so far from the truth. You are a multitasker, caregiver, financial analyst, organizer, research specialist, problem-solver, collaborator, communicator, and so much more. The most important quality you have is that you are an overcomer. Trust your instincts and have faith in yourself.

5. SHARE YOUR TESTIMONY

Let's be real. Going back to college while balancing kids, classes, clubs, and work is hard work. Don't be afraid to tell the world who you are and where you are going. People love to hear success stories because they are inspiring. Also, scholarship judges look for the applicants that show real passion for completing their degrees. Collaborate with other social media and other blog sites to share what works for you in your life. From my experience, sharing your testimony can transform your life into a never-ending adventure full of love, encouragement, support, and success.

6. DIVE INTO YOUR PASSION

Sometimes we lose ourselves along our way, and that is the perfect time to find out who we are in life. I developed a passion for helping others by trying to help myself. When you find yourself daydreaming about helping people or promoting a cause, lose yourself in it. Think outside the box and find new ways to do what you love. For me, I decided to create a community club, online group, and a website to help other students reach success. The hours I spend on my volunteer work are some of the happiest moments of my life. Each person I talked to on a daily basis became familiar with what service I provided. When you market yourself, people remember who you are and how you made them feel. These lasting impressions continue to promote you in other networks. Those networks can help you achieve your degree—and your dreams!

Balancing kids and college is more simple than it sounds—as long as you learn to tap into your creativity! As president of the student ambassadors one year, I could not miss the Halloween party despite being overwhelmed with classes, volunteer work, and parenthood. I did not have the money to buy a costume, so I looked around my messy house for ideas. This particular month was a busy one packed full of appointments, commitments, meetings, and responsibilities. My desk looked like the desk of Albert Einstein, and that is when I had my "ah-ha" moment. I came up with the cost-efficient, funny, and truly representative costume idea ever—I would become my busy calendar! I grabbed the large calendar off my desk and began filling it with my schedule for that month. In less than thirty minutes, I was on my way to compete with my classmates for best costume—which by the way, I won! As a single parent, college student, and dedicated community outreach coordinator, I have had to learn how to think smarter and not harder. As Albert Einstein stated, "Creativity is intelligence having fun." I try to bring that same perspective to balancing parenthood and my life as college student.

Another great tip that has helped me: allow your children to become a part of the process by giving them a chance to help you along the way. When I volunteer my time in the community or on campus, they are right beside me and that's a great way to make it work. They help me with assignments such as baking a cake model of a cell for my biology class. Each step of the way they are the first to know when I achieve something great or when I bomb a test. Treat your children as your personal assistants and reward them for their sacrifice and contribution to your life. The bonding experience between you and your kids will change your outlook on life. Most importantly, don't let fear stop you from reaching your dreams. It isn't easy, but nothing worth having in life ever is.

UCHIC ESSENTIALS—
FINDING NONTRADITIONAL SUCCESS

PUT YOU FIRST

When it comes to taking a nontraditional path, make YOU the priority. It's easier said than done, but you'll be better for it. Being selfish isn't always a bad thing—especially when it comes to your education. Take the path that makes the most sense to you, whether that entails transferring, gap years or another nontraditional route. At the end of the day, it's your life and you need to live it in a way that's truest to you.

BE KIND TO YOURSELF

Treat yourself like you would treat your best friend. This stage of life isn't easy but it's more manageable if you're more forgiving for your own missteps. Don't be too hard on yourself when you're struggling to make friends at a new school or having a tough time balancing school and internships. Always remember that life is a big learning experience and you'll get where you're meant to be in no time.

NEVER BE AFRAID TO TAKE A CHANCE!

When an opportunity arises, jump on it. Don't let your personal fears hold you back from going after what you want—especially when it comes to your educational path. You always end up right where you need to be!

Looking for more great advice? Head to UChic.com for even more resources and information—they come highly recommended from our contributors and editors. Be sure to leave your suggestions as well!

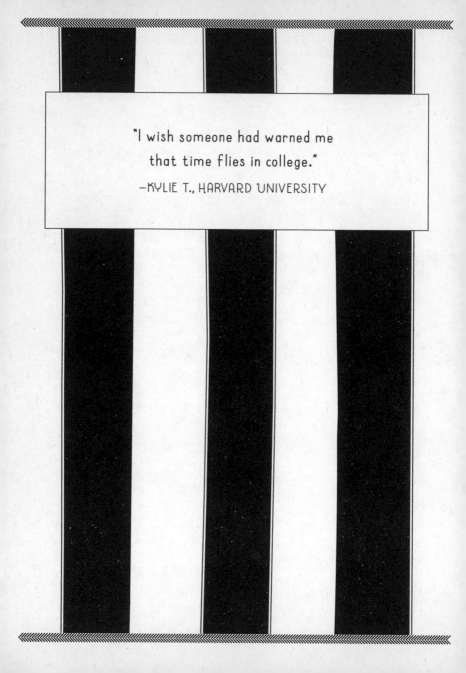

"I wish someone had warned me
that time flies in college."
—KYLIE T., HARVARD UNIVERSITY

13

WHAT'S NEXT?

SENIOR YEAR IS NEARING, and you're starting to wonder, "What's next?" Great question. Maybe you're considering grad school. Or is heading to the real world the best next step? And some of you may have no clue. No worries—although we can't promise to help you figure it all out, we definitely have some great advice. So sit back, relax, and enjoy our last chapter and your time in college because the future is looking great no matter what you decide next!

GRAD SCHOOL OR CAREER? HOW TO DECIDE

Should I go to graduate school? I'm not sure I want to. Should I get work experience first? What if I never go back to school? What if I get a graduate degree and then change my mind about my chosen field? Can I afford it? I'm tired of school; maybe I'll wait—is that OK?

These questions plagued me incessantly in the months before college graduation. And I know I was not alone. Experts say that graduating from undergrad is one of the hardest times in one's life. It involves massive transitions and major decisions, including whether to go straight to grad school or join the workforce.

If you already know that you need an MA or a PhD to get your dream job, and you are certain that's what you want to do, then go for it! Do whatever it takes to get there. But if you're like me and think you should go to grad school but still have many unsettled questions, take your time, do your research, talk to your mentors and advisors, and then decide. You should not feel rushed or stressed at any point. The best decisions in life are usually made on your own terms. Here's how I made mine.

I went to California State–Los Angeles for my undergrad. I got a BA in history and a minor in women's and gender studies. I am in love with history, and if I could marry school, I would. I love class. I love reading. I love learning more than almost anything. Now, don't stop reading because I'm a nerdy bookworm and you're not. I'm just trying to set up the background. My plan was to be a professor—Dr. Monica Taylor, professor of U.S. women's and social history. At some point I began to wonder if that was what I really wanted. What if I went to the trouble to get an MA and a PhD, and then changed my mind? I was also scared that if I took some years off from school to decide, I would never go back. Both were very scary options.

ASSESS YOUR INTERESTS, SKILLS, AND GOALS

So, with all this stress, how did I move forward? First, I decided that it was OK for me not to know or have a plan. I used to dread people asking me what I wanted to be in the future because I hated saying, "I don't know" or "Maybe a professor, most likely." Once I got past worrying so much what other people thought, I felt more at ease to make the decision that was right for me.

Next, I took an inventory of myself. It may surprise you, but this doesn't take as long as you would think. I sat down and made a list of what I'm good at. What are my skills and my natural talents? For me, they are academia, reading, teaching, and helping people. Next, I thought about what my passions were. After writing down social justice, education, history, and women's issues, I realized that my list of talents and passions made a pretty strong argument for going forward in my dream of being a professor. And I did. Currently, I am a graduate student at California State–Los Angeles, working on my MA in history.

Now, I am still not completely sold on being a professor. But taking the time to figure out my real passions has put me in a place where I know that whatever I eventually do will require some sort of graduate degree. You can do the same thing. What are you good at? What are you passionate about? What direction does that pull you in? Start with these questions, and you are putting yourself one step closer to making the right decision.

OTHER POINTS TO CONSIDER

If you're still feeling unsure, see if you agree with any of the following statements. If you do, then getting started on your career instead of going straight to grad school might be the best choice for you.

- **I don't know what I want to do with my life:** Every girl struggles with uncertainty in her senior year, but if you truly have no idea what you want to do, it's best to try out different careers before committing to several expensive years of school that you may not even like. One friend of mine got a degree in library science, and then took paralegal courses—neither of which has been very crucial to his current position as a marketer. He still doesn't know what he wants to do with his life, and with so much school to pay off, he lives with his parents. A few years testing out library and legal careers would have saved him the costly decision.

- **I am up to my ears in debt:** So why add more? If you can get a full ride to grad school with a stipend, that helps—but they only go out to a select few. Grad school costs a lot of money, and can be way more intense than undergrad. You may find it difficult to hold a job while in school. Best to go to work and pay down your debt for a few years until it's manageable. Your employer may even help defray the cost of grad school with a tuition assistance program.

- **I don't necessarily need the degree:** In journalism, the number of degrees you've obtained doesn't entitle you to a higher salary—rather, it's the quality of your writing, and the reputation of the places you've been published. This holds true for several other professions. Ask other people in your field if they think a master's is crucial to getting your foot in the door, and if they say no, test the waters by applying for a few jobs.

- **Frankly, I'm really burned out after undergrad:** One argument for going straight to grad school is that you maintain the habits and pace of student life. But by the end of senior year, just the thought of more school may be too exhausting to bear. If you're burned out but think that grad school may be in your future, take a year off to travel, work, and learn for your own sake. Recharge your mental and physical energy. Figure out who you are outside of school. You'll be a far more well-rounded and polished candidate with a year or two of grown-up work under your belt, and you'll probably have a much better sense of whether an advanced degree is something you really need in order to achieve your goals for your future.

WHY I CHOSE MY CAREER OVER GRAD SCHOOL

Maura Judkis, The George Washington University

I've got bills to pay. A year out of school, I've realized that bills are what separate the grown-ups from the not-quite-there-yets. The sooner you have to pay them, the quicker you grow up. That's one of the reasons that I went straight into the workforce after graduating from The George

Washington University, rather than piling on more student loans for another degree.

As a journalism student living in Washington, DC, I'd already worked for several publications to help pay my way through school. A master's in journalism wasn't something I really needed to get a job, and after sixteen years of education—well, I was tired. Tired of papers and research and required reading, when all I wanted to do was just get out there, write, and learn on my own terms.

I spent three difficult months interviewing for every journalism job I could find, but I stuck it out, and eventually I got a job that was a perfect fit for me.

Working is a welcome break from the classroom environment. It feels fantastic to come home from work and have my evenings to myself, rather than worrying about studying for a test or writing a paper. I feel challenged by my job, but without the pressure-cooker environment of exams and grades, my stress level has halved. I read books on my own timeline. The only thing I've envied my straight-to-grad-school friends for is the enhanced opportunities they have to meet new people, which can be harder when you've left the melting-pot environment of college. That and the leisurely winter, spring, and summer breaks, of course.

I'm not sure when I'll go back to school, or even what I'll go back for. I do know, however, that bills will play a factor in that decision. I hope to finish paying for my first degree soon, and then I'll be looking for someone else—an

employer or a scholarship fund—to pay for the next one.
It could be in two years or ten. I'll know when I'm ready.

I hate to break it to you: it's going to be a little scary no matter what you decide, grad school or not. There is always that little concern that you're not making the right decision, but that's life.

We can't predict the future, but we can make an informed decision. And remember, you're not alone; every graduating college student faces these challenging questions. But relax a little; take time to think and talk about it. You don't have to have everything perfectly planned out; the goal is to just figure out what is best for you.

Insights provided by Monica Taylor, California State University–Los Angeles and Maura Judkis, The George Washington University

THE INS AND OUTS OF NETWORKING

You probably have heard it many times before: networking can be the key to landing your dream internship or job. In today's work world, networking is the name of the game—even in college. It's incredibly important to your success and advancement in the workforce.

As a college student, you have tremendous access to resources and many different kinds of networking opportunities such as professors, campus lectures, career fairs, internships, student organizations, social media, etc. Before you know it, graduation will be here, so you need to take advantage of these opportunities now! Simply put, networking is about connecting with people, knowing how to talk to them, and later utilizing those connections.

WHERE TO START

Networking can take place in person and (even more so these days) online. And networking can be done with anyone around you at any time, not just in professional settings. You can network with your roommates, people who live in your residence hall, classmates, coworkers, friends of friends, professors, supervisors, members of clubs you are in, etc. I feel that I gained significant networking skills through recruitment for my sorority, for instance. If you are at a lecture on a topic you are very interested in, approach the speakers afterward and introduce yourself. Try to even get their email addresses for future questions—they could end up being a mentor. Also, it's important to build relationships with your professors and teaching assistants, as they, too, can help connect you with potential employers. So don't be shy. Visit them during their office hours so they can get to know you. These relationships are crucial to getting a good letter of recommendation when you apply to all those exciting internships.

NETWORKING: PLAN YOUR ATTACK

Before you begin heading out to networking events, try making a list of your priorities. This will help focus your efforts. Ask yourself:

1. What organizations or events are related to your interests, but you have not yet pursued?
2. What dreams do you have that you've always wanted to make a reality?
3. What are your strongest skills that you can share with others?
4. What skills would you like to improve, and who could help you develop them?

5. How can you take more initiative in networking (maybe
    going to an event by yourself, checking out a new group,
    asking a friend to introduce you to someone, etc.)?

PRACTICE MAKES PERFECT

Like anything in life, networking may be awkward at first, but
know that your skills will grow with practice. If you are attending
a networking event, first and foremost, have confidence and enjoy
yourself. Don't think of it as "I am networking." This will make you
nervous. Approach the event as if it's a new opportunity to meet new
people. Most of all, don't doubt yourself; you are awesome, so act like
it—*smile*! Have welcoming body language—make eye contact, don't
fold your arms, and give a pleasant greeting with a firm handshake.
Bottom line: be your confident self.

When networking, you need to take initiative. Sitting in a corner
alone or clinging to your friends won't expand your horizons. Go
ahead, approach others, and introduce yourself. A great icebreaker can
be something as simple as "Oh I like your bag…where did you get it?"

Have a purpose to your networking—a concrete goal. For example,
let's say you are interested in summer internship opportunities; this
narrows the conversation and makes it less awkward. Ask open-ended
questions rather than questions that evoke a simple yes/no response.
Also, recognize that networking is just as much about how you can
help someone as it is about how they can help you. Without even
knowing it, you have something of value to them. Keep talking; you'll
never know what you'll discover. It's like the idea of "to have a friend,
be a friend."

And really try to build rapport. People love to talk about themselves. Let the other person talk, and listen intently to what they have to say (show this with positive body language). When the conversation ends, repeat their name when you leave: "It was great meeting you, Maria." People like to hear their name and will be impressed you remembered it.

FINDING INSPIRATION IN VIRTUAL MENTORS

Alethia Russell, Auburn University

Finding someone whose work inspires you—an online mentor—can change the way you think, act, and live both on- and offline. Two years ago I decided to transition my hair from chemicals into its natural state. Bloggers like Nikki Walton, from Curly Nikki, were my inspiration, because she helped me understand a deeper meaning to having natural hair. After following her hair and life therapy blog for a month, I had a sense of what I wanted from my process to make it more than just an aesthetically pleasing experience. I also look to Nikki Walton because her writing inspires me. I have always wanted that inspirational voice in my writing, and it takes practice to get there.

UTILIZING YOUR CONNECTIONS

Make up some business cards so the people you meet can contact you later. This is probably the most important thing you should do in advance of any major networking events, and they don't have to be anything fancy. Your name, contact info, major area of study, expected graduation date, and school should appear on the card. Do you have an online résumé? Put the link on your card too! You can get business cards made for free (plus shipping and handling) at www.VistaPrint .com or www.MOO.com.

You'll also want to be collecting other people's business cards, or at least writing down their name and some form of contact information to get in touch with them later. After you make a connection, write down some details about the person on the back of their card or wherever you record their contact info so you can remember details about them later.

HOW TO BUILD YOUR DIGITAL NETWORK

Sarah Dougherty, University of Alabama–Tuscaloosa

So you tweet, Instagram, and share the latest viral articles on your Facebook wall. Your high school friends all "like," "share," and "retweet" them...but what about the network beyond your existing personal circle? How do you network with fellow students, mentors, brands, and potential employers? And how can you make yourself stand out and be memorable?

The secret is that *you should be treating your digital network like you treat your personal network*—staying in touch, staying current, and being consistent. Here are some tips on how you can convey a strong personal brand and build your digital network.

- **Be genuine:** Don't retweet something because everyone else is, and don't tweet simply for the most "likes"— being popular online with your hometown homies and being relevant, timely, and interesting to peers and professionals in your industry are two very different things. Share content in a variety of ways. On Twitter, share things, retweet things, add your own insights, and reply to others. On Instagram, don't be the girl with a million selfies. Mix up your posts. Be yourself, but convey yourself in a good light.

- **Know your audiences:** It is important to have a genuine understanding of your followers. If you take 13 Buzzfeed quizzes within a span of 4 minutes, and share every result and quiz link to Twitter, your professional mentors (and even friends) may become a little impatient with your part of their feeds. Know what you believe in, enjoy, and find interesting, and pair it in a way to complement your digital network.

- **Know your brand:** Know what makes you a valuable member of your audience's network, and know what sets you apart from everyone else in that network. For example, if your personal brand is about helping high school and college girls stay up-to-date with the latest fashion trends, then writing a personal blog, posting amazing photos on Instagram, or even writing for a brand like UChic are great ways to get your name out there and build on your brand. Your audience will follow you and get their friends hooked too! Also, be consistent. It will really throw your followers off if they follow you as "CollegeGirl1" on Pinterest, @college_girl_xo on Twitter, and @collegegirllll1 on Instagram. By being @CollegeGirl1 on every network, you will be easy to find and easy to tag.

- **Use hashtags:** Events, shows, chats, and campaigns often come with an assigned hashtag for you to tweet, Instagram, or even Facebook about. Use it! Maybe you like to live tweet *The Bachelor* and then blog about it later; use that hashtag and join the conversation!

- **Participate in Twitter chats:** Twitter chats are awesome ways to find people with similar interests who are willing to share advice and perspective; one hour of tweeting can not only gain you followers, but you can also learn a ton.

- **Network in real life:** Attend conferences and other networking events where you can meet people you can later network with online. Follow keynote speakers and other contacts on social media. Typically, they'll follow you back, and some of their followers will see that they attended the same event you did, and follow you. Each follow sparks a chain reaction!

- **Follow the golden rule of the Internet:** "Engage with others the way you'd want to be engaged with." Be careful not to get involved in a Twitter fight or heated discussion in Facebook comments. If you're respectfully engaging with others, your followers will respect you and stay in your network.

Having a unique and engaging social media presence

is a 24/7 balancing act. Be yourself, maintain your personal brand, and enjoy it!

The most important piece of advice? The great connections you just made do not go anywhere unless you follow up, and the sooner the better. Ideally within a day, send them a quick email. Remind them who you are and where you met. Thank them for taking the time to talk with you. End with an action item of how to build your connection with them, such as getting coffee together.

Sample follow-up email:

Hi Maria,

It was great meeting you at the UC–Berkeley environmental career fair. Thanks for talking with me about summer opportunities with the National Park Service. I am very interested in learning more about your career as a research scientist. Please let me know if you are available for coffee sometime next week.

Thank you,
Sunitha

If you don't necessarily want to meet with your new contact soon to get advice or discuss a certain issue, then don't feel that you are obligated to do so. You could start by adding them on LinkedIn (best for professional contacts) or Facebook (best for peers).

USING LINKEDIN TO FIND A JOB

Rachael Smith, Radford University

Have you tried LinkedIn yet? If not, you should. The goal of this social networking platform is to use the people you know to network and connect with the people you don't know for internship and job-hunting purposes. In fact, some employers have quit looking for applicants through traditional means and do their recruiting primarily through social media sites instead.

On creating your profile: make sure your profile is updated with the latest from your résumé, and that your portfolio and personal websites are up to date and professional.

Once you declare a major, join LinkedIn groups revolving around it. You may have to wait to be "accepted in" by an administrator, but some are open to anyone. You will also want to join your academic program's LinkedIn group, if they have created one, to keep up with any important announcements related to on-campus recruitment and networking opportunities you may want to participate in. For the other LinkedIn bells and whistles, if you have work or internship experience, ask your former employer or mentor to submit a recommendation for you through LinkedIn. This way, potential employers can see your work ethic without even having to ask. You can also upload your résumé to your profile, which you should do if you're on the hunt for an internship and/or job. HR professionals are better able to get a good assessment of your potential for an open position if this is in place. You also cut out extra work that they would otherwise have to do.

In terms of building out your network, send invitations to only folks that you personally know. If you send too many LinkedIn requests to people you don't know (and especially to those who you haven't asked someone for an introduction to connect with), people may report you, forcing LinkedIn to block you from sending future requests...even to folks you know. Don't be that person.

After meeting professionals at a networking event, it is completely appropriate to immediately add them to your network and send a note reminding them of your acquaintance with a note like, "It was great meeting and talking with you today at the seminar!" LinkedIn also has a "Jobs" board where you can find and apply to open job and internship positions nationwide.

LinkedIn is a great resource, so take some time to familiarize yourself with what it has to offer. And remember: it's not Facebook. So don't post about the crazy things you did with your friends last night!

INFORMATIONAL INTERVIEWS

Believe it or not, you requested an informational interview with Maria and you got one! Richard Nelson Bolles, author of the career guide *What Color Is Your Parachute?*, describes the informational interview process as "trying on jobs to see if they fit you."

Informational interviews are a first step to introduce yourself to an organization you'd like to work for in the near future, so be prepared to make a strong first impression. Everyone loves to meet with students, so don't be afraid to try to contact people you have never met before. For instance, you can call an organization and ask for someone by job title or search through professional associations. Assure them that the purpose of your inquiry is to learn more about the employer and occupation rather than to hassle them for an actual job. Informational interviews are separate from your applying for a job, so don't make this the time you ask them for a job.

DID YOU KNOW?

Studies estimate that 1 out of every 200–1,500 résumés results in a job offer. However, *1 out of every 12 informational interviews results in a job offer.* Truly, informational interviews are a great tool in landing your dream job!

Since you requested this interview, you will be the one asking the questions. Research the organization and the person you are going to meet, and make a list of questions you plan on asking. Dress appropriately, bring copies of your résumé, and be prepared to take notes. Listen intently to the person to fully take advantage of the knowledge they are sharing. At the end, kindly ask if they can give you referrals of other people in the industry that would be willing to meet with you. Make sure you send the person you met a thank-you note shortly after the interview.

The more people you meet, the more chances you have of making successful connections. Since you're investing in yourself and reading this book, you are already on your way to being a networking queen. Go out there, show the world how amazing you are, and meet tons of amazing new friends and colleagues! That's what college is all about.

Insights provided by Pamela O'Leary, University of California–Berkeley

MOVING IN WITH THE PARENTS: HOW TO MAKE IT WORK

Between the rising cost of living and the increasing amount of debt students accrue, moving back home after graduation is an increasingly popular money-saving stop on the way to your own place. How can you make living with the parents work?

R-E-S-P-E-C-T

The foundation of making life with the parental unit work is respect. You're not in high school anymore; you are an adult now with a college degree. When you return home, sit down with your parents so they can put all their rules and expectations for you on the table, and together you can come to an agreement about what is reasonable. Then show them how much you've matured in college by respecting their rules and their home.

Respect means cleaning up after yourself, being nice to your parents, and…honoring boundaries. Living at home shouldn't mean you put a halt on socializing and dating, but your parents probably wouldn't appreciate late-night callers. Move the party to his place if the occasion arises.

PAY THEM BACK

Sure, the point of moving back home post-graduation is to save cash, but you can show your gratitude to your family in many ways. Offer to run errands for your parents. Go grocery shopping for your mom. Make dinner once a week. Babysit your younger siblings. Clean the house. By taking you back in, your parents are doing you a big favor; you need to show them your appreciation.

CONTINUE TO LIVE YOUR OWN LIFE

Just because you're stuck with your parents doesn't mean you should go into a self-imposed social exile! Make an effort to meet up with friends, get into the city if you're close by, and make new acquaintances if all your buds have flown the coop. Sequestering yourself at home will drive you crazy. You'll be much happier, healthier, and more motivated if you continue to have a social life.

INVOLVING PARENTS IN YOUR JOB SEARCH

Pamela O'Leary, University of California–Berkeley

Do ask your parents to supply you with their network of contacts, if they have connections to your field of interest. It's fine to say you're "so-and-so's" daughter when sending an email expressing interest in an internship, but NOT OK to do so when it's a job. Talk to your parents' friends, see who they know, and feel free to ask for an introduction, if they can put you in contact with a higher-up at the company of your choice. Then it's up to you to take it from there.

Under NO circumstances should your parents have any involvement in you finding your first job, beyond providing you with a contact, driving you to an interview, or footing the bill for a new outfit. Not only does it undermine your ability to project a confident and mature persona, it also suggests you're not really ready to be a professional candidate. Why should a company trust you with a million-dollar budget or a huge campaign for a client if you constantly have to run to mommy or daddy every time you need help with something? If you want to be taken seriously, sideline the helicopter parenting ASAP.

YOU'RE NOT ON VACATION

Don't get too comfortable: this should be a temporary arrangement. Living rent-free with your mom and pop is not an excuse to sit on the couch all day watching soaps. You should get into a productive routine: continue job-hunting, work a part-time or full-time job, and help out around the house. The more you put off making money and saving money, the longer you'll be forced to stay with the folks. No one likes a thirty-year-old living in her parents' basement.

Insights provided by Alexandra Straka, University of Missouri

SAY BYE-BYE TO GRADUATION ANXIETY

Does the thought of graduation bring a rapid heartbeat or even sweaty palms? Or maybe it makes you a little nauseous? You might be suffering from a case of grad anxiety. Guess what? It's completely normal. In fact, there are millions of college seniors across the United States facing the same pangs of anxiety that you're feeling at this very moment. Leaving friends who have become your life for four years, trying to find a job or a new place to live, or even adjusting to a move back home with your parents again can be super stressful. The trick is to not allow the stress to take over and make you feel hopeless. This section is all about how you can relax and enjoy your final year even when the future is still a question mark.

RELAX A LITTLE!

First, take a deep breath. In between preparing for the big move, a new job, or even simply the unknown, take time to *relax*. Whether it be exercise, television, writing, or just enjoying times with your friends, take advantage of any time that you have for yourself. The stress has been coming on fast and hard for me recently; I've taken all of the nervous energy and channeled it into exercise. Every time I start to feel overwhelmed with all of the work I have to do, I hop on the treadmill and work off those nerves.

Go Brunching!

One of my favorite things to do during college was grab brunch with my girlfriends on the weekends at the school cafeteria. We would all roll out of bed, throw on our sweats, and meet at the café for a long, relaxing meal. There were never any time limits, nothing was rushed, and we could just sit there and gossip for as long as we wanted. You certainly won't ever get your college days back, so you might as well take advantage of the time you have left.

Pamper Yourself

No matter how hectic your schedule may be or how much the stress is building, be sure to give yourself a little TLC once in a while. Consider going for a massage or having a spa day with your friends. It will be a great way to temporarily escape the stress. And who doesn't love a spa day? If you're like most college students and are low on cash, try something a little less expensive like a manicure or pedicure. And if you really have no cash, try creating a spa day of your own with your friends! I did this a few times with my girls. We'd paint each other's nails, try on new shades of makeup, and occasionally dye each other's hair. After all of your hard work, be sure to treat yourself to something nice; you deserve it!

ENJOY THE MOMENT

The most important factor in coping with your graduation anxiety is to focus on the *now* and really *enjoy* the end of your time at school.

Make the most out of every aspect of college and save the worrying for tomorrow.

Take Time to Document the Memories

I'm a huge fan of photographs. There is no better way to bring back a great memory than to look through old pictures of some of your favorite experiences. I suggest bringing your camera absolutely everywhere. I know we're all fans of taking pictures at the bar or at a party, but I mean literally everywhere. Are you having a movie night at a friend's apartment? Bring your camera! You'll find that it's those low-key nights that end up producing the most memorable moments. And then you can have a scrapbooking party at some point with all your friends to create something that will remind you of the fun you had for the rest of your life.

Get Out and Explore

Take a look around at your campus and the area that you are living in and really explore. It wasn't until the end of my senior year of undergrad that I realized how many great activities were being thrown at me, and for free.

Go Out!

You're never going to have as much free time as you do in college. Take advantage of your schedule and go out once in a while. I'm not saying party like an animal, but just take time to enjoy yourself. Go out for martinis with your girls, or check out that frat party down the street. Some of my best college memories came from a night out with the girls. There was a bar down the street from

CCSU—Elmers. Tuesday nights were "Bar Bingo" nights. We'd all walk down to the bar, play bingo, hang out, etc. It was so simple, but always so much fun.

Take a Class for Fun

After three years of sitting through several classes that were unrelated to your major, try taking something that really interests you even if it has nothing to do with what you're studying! As an English and journalism major, I took a *ton* of writing courses but was interested in psychology. During senior year, I took a great psych class the second semester that was really interesting. These amazing educational opportunities are right at your fingertips, so get out there and don't be afraid to try something new.

THE FUTURE IS UNKNOWN. SO WHAT?

Most of you have spent a good portion of your life planning for what comes next. However, when college graduation approaches, sometimes it is not always clear what the best next step will be. Although this realization can be a major stress, it really shouldn't be. After all the hard work that you've put in over the years, you owe yourself a break. Take some time. Travel. Live in a different city. No matter what, it's worth your time because every new experience is an opportunity for growth.

As graduation gets close, it's really important to cherish the friendships that you've built and appreciate everything your school has given you over the last four years. If you've made your best effort to prepare for the future, then there is really no need to worry too much about what's ahead after graduation. Prepare what you can, give yourself some time to relax, and truly enjoy the life that you have built for yourself as a college student. Your anxiety is certain to melt away.

Insights provided by Katie Reynolds, Central Connecticut State University

UCHIC ESSENTIALS— *WHAT'S NEXT?*

DON'T FORGET YOUR GOALS

A proven method for making your dreams come true is to self-actualize. What does that mean? Dream it, write it down, and go back to your goals over and over. The more you envision where you want to be, the more likely you are to make it happen. And if your goals change, that's completely OK. That's the point of having goals in the first place—to always be in tune with what you really want and then not be afraid to change course if necessary.

NEVER STOP NETWORKING

Networking is a critical activity for landing your first job after college, but you shouldn't stop there. Keep in touch with professors and alumni, attend industry events, and continue to reach out to new people who can help you develop your skills. Careers, especially today, often take unexpected paths, and you never know how a networking contact could lead to an exciting new adventure.

SLOW DOWN A BIT

As you near graduation, don't be in such a rush. Take time to relax and really make the most of your time in school. You'll have the rest of your life to work, but you won't be with your college friends forever. Brunch with your girlfriends. Visit those museums that you've always wanted to see. Now is the time to really build bonds that will last a lifetime.

Looking for more great advice? Head to UChic.com for even more resources and information—they come highly recommended from our contributors and editors. Be sure to leave your suggestions as well!

ACKNOWLEDGMENTS

This book is the product of a lot of hard work, support, and passion from a group of people whom I love dearly. Thanks must first go to my agent, Loretta Barrett, who sadly passed away this past year and is dearly missed. Without Loretta, this book and the work UChic is doing to help provide life-changing opportunities for young women could never have happened. A big hat tip to Michelle Lecuyer, my Sourcebooks editor, for her hard work in helping me turn the inspiration behind UChic.com into a fifth edition(!) of this book. Thanks to the team at UChic.com and our fantastic group of college writers. I also want to thank my parents, Jim and Nancy, and my grandfather Bill for their endless support. Thanks to my lifelong partner and soul mate, Matt. You—and our beautiful daughter Georgia—are my greatest joys.

CONTRIBUTORS

Olga Belogolova, Boston University

Ana Berkovich, Missouri State University

Janine Camara, University of North Carolina–Greensboro

Miryam Chico, Kean University

Nisha Chittal, University of Illinois

Amanda Condon, Arkansas Tech University

Johannah Cornblatt, Harvard University

Amanda Cross, University of Central Arkansas

Jessica Cruel, University of North Carolina–Chapel Hill

Erin Cunningham, The George Washington University

Allison Davis, Barnard College

Sarah Dougherty, University of Alabama–Tuscaloosa

Emma Ehlers, University of Arkansas

Kristine Fenstermacher, Temple University

Amanda Ferrara, New York University

Susan Fiorentino, Manhattan College

Ikee Gardner, Duke University

Solange Gorleku, University of South Florida St. Petersburg

Madeline Greene, Minnesota State University

Donyel L. Griffin, Kean University

Melanie Harris, Virginia Tech

Harmony Haveman, Pacific Lutheran University

Laura Iglehart, Georgetown University

Sanah Jivani, University of Texas–San Antonio

Aja Johnson, University of Maryland–College Park

Anna Jonas, Dalhousie University

Katie Jones, Missouri State University

Lativia Jones Bolarinwa, University of North Carolina–Chapel Hill

Maura Judkis, The George Washington University

Emily Kaplan, University of California–Davis

Kelly Leslie, San Francisco State University

Kathryn Lewis, University of North Carolina–Chapel Hill

Emma Martin, Ithaca College

Victoria Mazzella, Rutgers University

Rebecca E. Mill, Sweet Briar College

Krista Naposki, Elon University

Megan O'Connell, University of Wisconsin–Platteville

Pamela O'Leary, University of California–Berkeley

Briana Peppers, Spelman College

Anna Prestek, University of Washington–Seattle

Victoria Reitano, Quinnipiac University

Katie Reynolds, Central Connecticut State University

Claudia Romkey, Queen's University

Alexa Rozell, Georgetown University

Jennifer Rubino, Kean University

Alethia Russell, Auburn University

Amanda Sandlin, Rider University

Rachael Smith, Radford University

Jillian E. Sorgini, Hofstra University

Alexandra Straka, University of Missouri

Erica Strauss, Kent State University

Alisa Sutton, Temple University

Monica Taylor, California State University–Los Angeles

Kylie Thompson, Harvard University

Ashley Tripp, University of Alabama

Alyssa Vande Leest, University of Wisconsin

Raneisha Williams, Ripon College

Ashley Yenick, Merrimack College

INDEX

ABOUT THE AUTHOR

Christie Garton is an award-winning social entrepreneur and founder of the 1,000 Dreams Fund, a scholarship fund that provides young women, both college-bound and in college, with up to $1,000 in funding to help fulfill their professional dreams.

© Jenny Wheat, 2014

Christie has made it her life's mission to open as many doors as possible for young women through the 1,000 Dreams Fund. From her own experience, Christie realized the importance of extra-curricular experiences in fulfilling both her own dream as well as those of other young women. Many cannot pursue the experiences they seek in realizing their dreams, due to lack of funding and the crippling burden of student loan debt.

A longtime supporter of young women's professional and creative growth, Christie is also the creator of UChic.com, an online magazine which became the bestselling college guidebook for girls—*UChic* (Sourcebooks). With more than 100,000 copies of *UChic* sold, the book is now in its fifth edition. She has penned six books on various facets of the college experience and millennial generation, including the award-winning *Marketing to Millennials: Reach the Largest and Most Influential Generation of Consumers Ever* (New York: AMACOM, 2013).

A millennial marketing and college life expert, Christie has appeared on the NBC's *Today* and *The Better Show*, a nationally syndicated lifestyle TV program. Christie is also a contributing writer on young women's issues for the *Wall Street Journal, The Huffington Post, U.S.News & World Report*, and *Seventeen*. During her tenure as *USA Today*'s social good columnist and blogger, Christie covered how Americans are making an impact in both their backyards and abroad.

A graduate of the University of Kansas with a double degree in Business Administration and French, Christie also holds a JD from the University of Pennsylvania School of Law. While in college, Christie was chosen as a one of twenty "best and brightest" college students by *USA Today* and was a finalist for the *Glamour* "Top 10 College Women" award.

To learn more and Christie's efforts to empower young women through scholarships, visit www.1000DreamsFund.org.

ABOUT UCHIC

The UChic book series and product line was created by Christie Garton, founder of www.UChic.com—the #1 online resource for college women—to help young women succeed in school and life.

 UChic: The College Girl's Guide to Everything: Dealing with dorms, classes, grades, sororities, social media, study abroad, dating, staying healthy, staying safe, and making the most out of the best four years of your life
A fully updated guide for women to the entire college experience, from the day the acceptance letter arrives to graduation.
978-1-4926-4599-3 | $14.99

 UChic's Getting a Grip on Your Freshman Year: The College Girl's First Year Action Plan
A companion workbook focused on helping you take action during your freshman year to have a successful college transition.
978-1-4022-4398-1 | $19.99

 UChic's Diploma Diaries: The Chic Grad's Guide to Work, Love, and Everything in Between
An essential guide for college grads to creating a fabulous life in the real world, with stories, tips, and tricks from other young professionals like them.
978-1-4022-8061-0 | $14.99